MAN-MONKEYS

By the same author:

What's the Play and Where's the Stage?
A Theatrical Family of the Regency Era

MAN-MONKEYS

Alan Stockwell

Copyright © Alan Stockwell 2017

All Rights Reserved

The right of Alan Stockwell to be identified
as the author of this work has been asserted
by him in accordance with the
Copyright, Designs and Patents Act 1988

ISBN 978-0-9565013-7-0

Published by VESPER HAWK PUBLISHING
WWW.VESPERHAWK.COM

CONTENTS

TIME CHART
FOREWORD
PREFACE

Chapter One	LA PEROUSE	1
Chapter Two	THE PARSLOE FAMILY	7
Chapter Three	MAZURIER	17
Chapter Four	E J PARSLOE	25
Chapter Five	C T PARSLOE	41
Chapter Six	GEORGE WIELAND	44
Chapter Seven	MONSIEUR GOUFFE	64
Chapter Eight	EDWARD KLISCHNIGG	92
Chapter Nine	HERVIO NANO	98
Chapter Ten	FREDERICK MARTINI	112
Chapter Eleven	HARVEY TEASDALE	120
Chapter Twelve	MUSIC HALL MAN-MONKEYS	130
Chapter Thirteen	MR PONGO: ENTER THE GORILLA	143
Chapter Fourteen	MAN-MONKEYS IN PANTOMIME	157
Chapter Fifteen	20th CENTURY MAN-MONKEYS	183
Chapter Sixteen	CINEMA MAN-MONKEYS	192
APPENDIX	PEOPLE MENTIONED IN THE TEXT	203
	GLOSSARY	206
NOTES		209
BIBLIOGRAPHY		214
INDEX		215
ILLUSTRATIONS		220

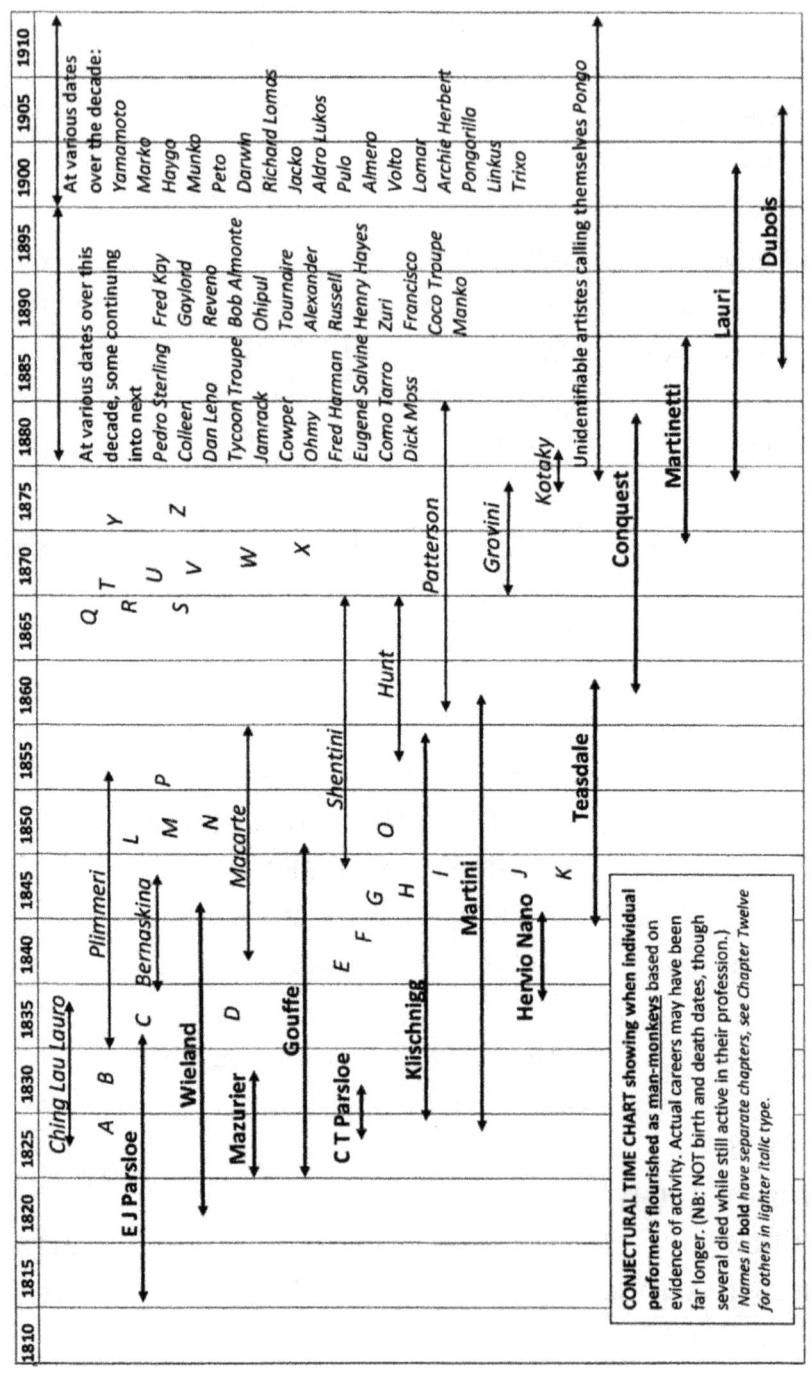

PREFACE

MANY YEARS AGO, sometime in the 1970's, I took my small son to a family travelling circus. One of the acts was heralded with the announcement that the gorilla had escaped from the zoo. A man in a hairy gorilla costume entered and clambered up a vertical rope, performing one or two simple tricks before descending to roam around the sparse audience. The children squealed and the adults laughed indulgently as the gorilla snatched a boy's cap and put it on its head, stole some popcorn, and other jollities. The gorilla then grabbed a lady's handbag and retreated to the ring where it started pulling out the contents which included a bra, whereupon the lady from the audience entered the ring to retrieve her bag, belabouring the animal with her umbrella.

Regaining her bag, the lady turned to resume her seat, not realising that the gorilla was right behind her. The punch came when the gorilla pulled off her skirt and she ran off, screaming, in her ludicrous red bloomers, followed by the gorilla.

I did not know at the time that this simple routine was the last knockings of a theatrical phenomenon that had started two hundred years ago. I do now.

Shylock: *It was my turquoise; I had it of Leah when I was a bachelor: I would not have given it for a wilderness of monkeys.*
　　　　　　　　　　The Merchant of Venice Act III Sc 1

INTRODUCTION

IT CAN NEVER BE KNOWN who the first man was to don a replica monkey suit and caper about for the entertainment of the public. In retrospect, it seems such an obvious idea that perhaps it was adopted by a Shakespearean clown or an acrobatic busker in some medieval market place. We are told by Joseph Grimaldi, the great Regency clown, that he made his stage debut at the age of two when, dressed as a monkey, he was led on a chain by his father. Part of the routine was to swing the monkey around on the end of its chain and at one performance the chain broke allowing the infant Grimaldi to fly out into the audience where providently he landed in the lap of a well-upholstered gentleman in the front row. Children dressed as monkeys were hardly likely to have been a very recent novelty even then.

Since Grimaldi's time a multitude of contortionists and acrobats have earned their living by impersonating, to a greater or lesser degree, various simians, and the heyday of the music hall stage was replete with them.

However, the history of the stage monkey as a character in drama is better attested and many an actor has found it expedient to eschew his ambitions to play Hamlet and don an ape outfit. Plays with a monkey, ape or chimpanzee character almost became a sub-division of the legitimate stage over two hundred years ago, heralding a public interest that led to *King Kong* and *The Planet of the Apes* in modern times.

Whether they purported to be an ape, a chimpanzee or a gorilla, it was all the same to both impersonator and audience, the genre embraced them all. Meet the man-monkeys . . .

The infant JOE GRIMALDI garbed as a monkey flies out into the audience.

Chapter One
LA PEROUSE

JEAN FRANÇOIS DE GALAUP, Comte de La Pérouse was a French navigator who, greatly admiring the English Captain Cook, undertook to follow his predecessor's work in mapping and discovering new lands. He set off in 1785 firstly visiting Hawaii – where Cook had been killed by the inhabitants – then sailed on to Alaska, thence to California where he inspected the Spanish settlements and missions, being the first non-Spaniard to visit since Sir Francis Drake in 1579. Sailing on, he reached Manila and landed on the coast of Korea. He touched on Japan and Russia where in September 1787 he received a letter from his government ordering him to investigate the British settlement in New South Wales. On the way, 12 of his men were killed and 20 wounded on Samoa, but the expedition made a safe landing in Botany Bay in January 1788.

LA PÉROUSE

Staying six weeks in Australia, he sent despatches home indicating he expected to be back in France by June 1789. This was the last that was heard of La Pérouse, he seemingly vanished from the face of the earth. Search parties were sent forth but no traces of his men or ships were found. The lack of evidence did not deter speculation at the end of the 18th century on the fate of La Pérouse.

One particular item of conjecture was in the form of a play by Kotzebue. August von Kotzebue was a German lawyer and diplomat in St Petersburg, who fathered 18 children and wrote over 200 plays. Although not as highly regarded as his contemporaries Goethe and Schiller, his works were far more popular. As there were no copyright regulations in those days, these plays were mercilessly plundered by French and English hack dramatists, and their versions often proved to be hits in London. His *Das Kind der Liebe* became *Lover's Vows*, and his *Menschenhass und Reue* became *The Stranger*, two of the most popular plays of the Regency era.

Kotzebue's play *La Perouse* of 1797 posited that La Perouse was the only survivor of a shipwreck and Crusoe-like had fetched up on a desert island where he encountered a beautiful native woman called Malvina who, after she had saved him from danger, became his wife and they produced a child. His real wife Adelaide and son, who had set out to search for him, discovered him eight years later thus throwing La Perouse into a quandary as to which of the two women he should reject. After much grief and heartache, his domestic situation is resolved by the unlikely expedient of deciding to stay on the island – because of the current revolution in France – with the two women living in one hut, and La Perouse in another as a sort of brother of them both!

The play was translated into English by Benjamin Thompson, while another version was written by Anne Plumptre. Neither of these was ever acted but a third adaptation of the story was made by John Fawcett, an actor at Covent Garden theatre, where it was first presented on 28 February 1801 as A New Grand Historic Pantomime Drama in Two Parts called *La Perouse; or The Desolate Island*. Fawcett made a much stronger, but just as improbable, work which became an instant hit, having some 35 showings during the season.

As before, La Perouse is the sole survivor on an island but there are hostile natives from a neighbouring island. The native girl who falls in love with the navigator is called Umba and has a suitor called Kanko. She is less than pleasant. Most importantly, an original character is introduced – a chimpanzee! The first night review described the plot:

Perouse makes his escape from a wreck on the shore of a luxuriant but desolate country. Here he meets a chimpanzee with whom he becomes familiar and friendly. Shortly after, a canoe full of savages comes on shore, and Umba, the mistress of their chief, falls in love with Perouse. A battle ensues, in which the savages defeated by Perouse fly to their native island, leaving Umba behind. A French ship arrives, and sends its boat on shore with Madame Perouse and her infant son in search of her husband. A meeting takes place between them; but their joy is destroyed by the return of the savages with fresh forces, thirsting for revenge. The savages are interrupted by the hindrance of the chimpanzee, and finally defeated by the arrival of the crew from the French ship.[1]

The Chimpanzee was played by Master Menage, thus we cannot

The Theatre Royal, Covent Garden, where La Perouse *had its premiere on 28 February 1801. This theatre was destroyed by fire seven years later. An occupational hazard of the times!*

gainsay that he was the first straight actor to play a simian as a character in a play. The tremendous success of this afterpiece kept it in the repertory through four seasons until shelved in February 1804, by which time Menage had played the part well in excess of 100 times.

After his role in *La Perouse*, Menage never played an animal again but remained in the Covent Garden company for years growing into adulthood as a notable pantomimist and player of modest roles of little importance. He disappears from Covent Garden playbills some 18 years later, probably never realising he was the pioneer of a whole new genre.

On 30 September 1808, Covent Garden theatre was totally destroyed by fire. As a result the company moved to the Haymarket theatre while its home was being rebuilt. At the temporary venue *La Perouse* was revived for the first time in five years. It had a run of some weeks until 4 May 1809. The cast for this revival included Jack Bologna Jr as Perouse, Joe Grimaldi as Kanko and Miss Adams as Umba. Frustratingly, the press advertisements do not name the actor of the Chimpanzee, neither have I as yet located a playbill for the production. There were several youths in the Covent Garden company who could have taken over the role from Menage, but it was probably Master Morelli who was to play the Chimpanzee when the company returned to their new theatre.

Plays that proved popular in London were taken up by provincial theatres as they were promptly published and available for all to buy. *La Perouse* became an instant hit and productions were mounted throughout the land from 1802 onwards, the play taking its place in the standard repertoire. A performance at Preston in Lancashire was the last ever for actor James Bannerman, as he died after receiving a wound in the thigh during the performance when struck by the wadding from an overcharged musket.[2]

Press advertisements rarely give the names of actors except popular favourites and on benefit nights, so one has to rely entirely on playbills to ascertain who played the Chimpanzee. I have found only a handful of playbills for *La Perouse*, which being an afterpiece was not heavily publicised, and the part was played by either a regular member of the company or a youth drafted in for the job – often the son of one of the players; at this juncture there was no specialist man-monkey.

Remarkably, I have found only one example of any monkey role played by a female when the Chimpanzee was portrayed by Miss Andrews at Liverpool in 1809. When repeated in 1810, Master Howell had replaced Miss Andrews. She remains the only Miss among the many Masters and Misters in this book which covers 200 years, until the Hollywood actresses blossomed forth in *The Planet of the Apes*. It seems extraordinary when most modern contortionists are women.

In August 1811, it was reported in the newspapers that an English ship had found 12 seamen thought to be the wretched survivors of Perouse's crew, on a desert island of the South Seas, where his ship was wrecked. They were now back in Paris and would be able to give an account of the fate of their companions.[3]

This news may have given an extra fillip to *La Perouse*, again revived at Covent Garden. Like its rival theatre in Drury Lane, the Garden classified its actors by type – tragedy, comedy or pantomime. A few star actors like Charles Kemble and Robert Elliston were versatile enough to accommodate both tragic and comic roles, but usually players worked within their genre. Actors lower down the pecking order were utility players who could be used in any bit-parts and walk-ons. Obviously the pantomime performers were very few compared to the other two categories but they were used in those too as required. *La Perouse* is described as a Grand Historic Pantomime Drama so the cast came from the pantomime section of the company. Joe Grimaldi was the most famous clown of the Regency pantomime but he played other roles too, he was not always a clown. In *La Perouse* at Covent Garden,

Grimaldi was cast as Kanko the Suitor to Umba, and his Harlequin partner Bologna Jr was Perouse. The Chimpanzee was played by Master Morelli.

It is hard for us to imagine what that kind of show must have been like. The play was performed chiefly in mime, with songs and music a major feature. This is a verse from one of the lyrics from *La Perouse*, it's hardly Stephen Sondheim or Tim Rice, but tastes change:

UMBA'S SONG

But oh! poor Umba sometimes sigh;
For sighs of love be hard to smother;
White man, for whom me gladly die,
 In this country love another!
Of wife at home he often speak;
 It almost break my heart to hear him:
But, as the tear steal down my cheek,
Me try to smile, and sing to cheer him.
 With tira la, my true love!
 Sing tira la.

A play boosted in London naturally encouraged the provinces to follow suit so *La Perouse* was again to the fore in many venues. An interesting sidelight is the unknown Edmund Kean, languishing in obscurity as leading man on the Dorset circuit, had devised a ballet afterpiece called *The Savages* based on *La Perouse*. Kean, considered a first-class Harlequin and mime, was playing in his own version on the night an emissary from Drury Lane came to see him act Octavian in *The Mountaineers* at Dorchester. Whisking him off to London, Kean became an overnight sensation and a major star within weeks.

At Covent Garden the same cast was retained throughout several seasons with Master Morelli playing the Chimp until achieving adult status when he appears to have left the company at the end of the 1815/16 season. Thereafter, I found a trace of him on the York circuit from 1821 to 1823, but his roles were not large, being on the level of Second Gravedigger in *Hamlet*.

Leeds was one venue on the York circuit, and the city holds an excellent collection of playbills including several that advertise *La Perouse*. In 1811, the Chimpanzee was played by Mr Cope, in 1821 and 1822 by Mr Doré the resident dancer and choreographer while Mr Morelli who had played the role many times in London was merely Taski, one of the lesser natives. However, when repeated in 1823, Morelli was promoted to the part and one wonders why he was not used before. He was clearly successful as later the same month he played the ape role in *Philip Quarl* another early man-monkey play. Further Leeds productions had Master Jackson in 1826, Mr Muir in 1833, and it was still being performed in 1853 when the Chimp was Mr Lamb.

Morelli, himself, in later life became a noted Pantaloon, scene painter, and agent, dying at an advanced age in 1882.

For years *La Perouse* was in the repertoire of many theatres throughout the land – the latest glimpse I have found was at Liverpool in February 1864 when the Chimpanzee was played by Fred Leopold.

Chapter Two
THE PARSLOE FAMILY OF COVENT GARDEN

INEVITABLY CHILD PERFORMERS soon grew into adults but that was of no concern of the theatre managements because there were lots more children available, with their parents eager for them to work. The theatres of Drury Lane and Covent Garden were large enterprises each with a staff of some 700 persons, of which going on for a 100 were actual stage performers. Apart from the players and musicians, as everything was created in house, there were scenery constructors, costume makers, backstage staff to work the performances, gas men for lighting, front of house staff and so on. Actors and actresses were no less fecund than other married couples, and with no reliable means of contraception everybody had large broods of children to feed and clothe. A utility player at the bottom of the pecking order was unlikely to be on more than a £1 a week, so if he could get one of his children on to the payroll, even for a few shillings, it would be a great boost to the family wages.

Joe Grimaldi's father was the Dancing Master at Sadler's Wells and through his influence he got young Joe a very respectable 15/- a week, but when Grimaldi Senior died, the nine-year-old had his wage slashed to the more conventional 3/- and it remained at that sum for three years.

At Covent Garden there was a generous supply of youngsters ready and eager to work, and from the 1812/1813 season the names of the Parsloe brothers and sister were often scattered among the lesser lights on the playbills. I have not been able to confidently place the father of these children and what his position was at the theatre. There was a puppet showman called Parsloe at Southwark Fair in 1752 who presented 'a moving skeleton, which dances a jig upon the stage, and in the middle of his dance falls all to pieces, bone from bone, joint from joint, all parts of his body separate from one another; and in the twinkling of an eye up in his proper proportion, and dances as in the beginning.'[1] This was an early presentation of the trick marionette known as the Dissecting Skeleton still popular today. The

7

puppeteer may have been an ancestor of the Mr Parsloe in Sarah Baker's Canterbury company in 1791, and again in February 1794 when he acted as Clown to a family of tumblers and tightrope walkers. This man could well be the Edward Parsloe who married Sophia Kerby at St Mary Lambeth on 9 November 1795.

The couple produced five children:
>   Sophia born 21 August 1796
>   James born 18 October 1798
>   Edmund John born 16 August 1801
>   Charles Thomas born 16 July 1804
>   Ann Eleanor born 27 January 1807

The first four were all humble members of the Covent Garden company as was Mrs Parsloe who appeared in choruses and ensembles, however Edward Parsloe, himself never advertised in any position, may well have occupied some backstage function. He may have been a posture-master which was the current term for a person we today call a contortionist. This surmise is based on the fact that at least two of his sons were trained in that occupation from an early age.

The playbill for the new pantomime opening at the Aquatic Theatre in April 1810 called *The Astrologer; or Harlequin and Old Moore's Almanack* included 'Protean Transformations by the Masters Parsloe'. This venue was actually the long-established and familiar Sadler's Wells theatre that had some years before added a large water tank which enabled spectacles such as sea battles and the like. For a few seasons it was renamed to promote this new feature before reverting to its former name.

Sadler's Wells theatre during the course of an aquatic play in 1810.

THE PARSLOE FAMILY

Apart from the water, otherwise it was business as usual with the pantomimes starring Grimaldi as its main attraction. Grimaldi had two contracts for many years – Sadler's Wells in summer and Covent Garden in winter. Grimaldi also played dramatic mime parts as well as Clown. The afterpiece during the Parsloes' appearance was a revival of *The Wild Man* with Mr Hartland in the leading role. When this play had first been presented at the theatre, Grimaldi himself had played the Wild Man and gained plaudits for his depiction in mime of how the power of music calmed the savage mind, with the Wild Man exhibiting the passing of his various passions as the flute player varied his measure. This little scena lived on independently as a feature of many a benefit programme billed as *The Power of Music.*

The concepts of the wild man and the noble savage were both greatly to the fore in Regency times and, as will be seen, the ideas of the feral man, the educated ape and the 'missing link' were often too blurred against all common sense.

When the programme at the Aquatic Theatre changed in August to a new comic pantomime called *Bang Up; or Harlequin Prime*, the Masters Parsloe continued with their 'Protean Transformations'.

MASTER PARSLOE'S *Wonderful Protean Transformations as Exhibited at Sadler's Wells*

It is not clear which or how many Masters Parsloe were involved at the Wells, but in light of their future careers it would certainly be Edmund John aged nine, and Charles Thomas aged six, but whether elder brother James made up a trio is impossible to say as the only extant illustration depicts a single Master Parsloe whom I suspect is the future E J Parsloe.

After this burst of activity, the Parsloe boys next surface at Covent Garden, appearing on playbills often alongside Master Morelli. In an after-piece called *At Home*, the Two Masters Frisk were played by Masters Morelli and Parsloe. *Aladdin* had Morelli and both Parsloe boys. Sophia, Edmund and Charles were used constantly over the years, growing up there, season by season until adulthood. It was long and tiring work for youngsters as an evening's programme comprised a main play and an afterpiece. It was not unusual to have *Hamlet* followed by a pantomime. Doors opened at 5.30 and the show started at 6.30. The final curtain aimed to be about 11 o'clock but was often later than that. No performing child ever had the luxury of an early night.

La Perouse, being an afterpiece, may not have started until 9.30 or 10 o'clock, and pantomimes were always played as an afterpiece even when they were the main Christmas and New Year attraction.

Our present 21st century pantomime is but a shadowy remnant of a 300-year history. The typically English Pantomime is descended from the Italian *commedia del* Arte and the characters Harlequin, Columbine, Pantaloon and Clown are anglicized versions of Italian originals. The first recognised English pantomime was *The Magician; or Harlequin a Director* in 1721, the actual word pantomime coming from the Greek *pantomimos* – panto meaning all, mimos meaning imitator. Pantomimos – imitator of all.

The year 1800 saw the debut of Joseph Grimaldi in the role of Clown. He was twenty years old and had been on the stage since the age of two. In 1806, Joe had a huge success with *Harlequin and Mother Goose; or the Golden Egg*. Although Clown now became the main man, the titles still referred to Harlequin. The first two decades of the 19th century were a golden age for pantomime, and Grimaldi was the king.

Pantomimes were short in length, about an hour to 1½ hours, the last item in the evening's programme. The first part of the pantomime comprised the story part, with songs and rhyming couplets in three or four scenes. At a certain point in the story a character known as a 'benevolent agent' appeared – this would be a fairy or a god who then transformed

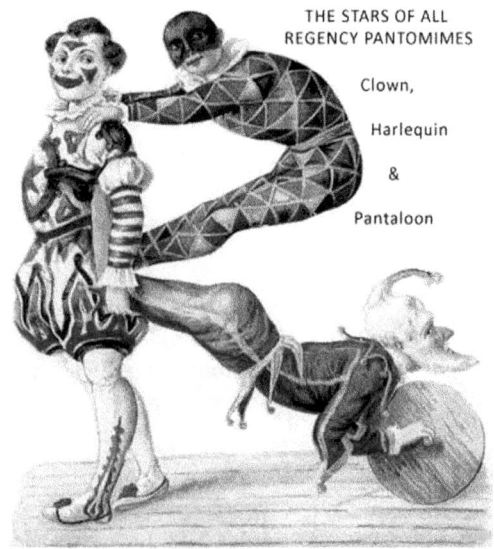

THE STARS OF ALL REGENCY PANTOMIMES

Clown,

Harlequin

&

Pantaloon

the characters in the story to the personnel of what came to be called the Harlequinade which would then run for ten or so scenes.

The Harlequinade relied on trick scenery and acrobatic chases with the performers diving through flaps in the scenery to be caught in canvas slings held by stagehands at the back. It was physically exhausting and downright dangerous. A Harlequin called Paul Redigé leapt through a scene flap and, because of the absence of the stagehands with their sling, hit an iron staple on the stage floor and was killed instantly. The artistes relied on these same men to propel them with pulleys up through trapdoors in the stage, shooting them high in the air.

Invariably the Parsloes could be found in Covent Garden's annual pantomime which always starred Joe Grimaldi, James Barnes and Tom Ellar as Clown, Pantaloon and Harlequin. In *Harlequin and Fortunato*, the pantomime for 1815/16, Madame Parsloe played a Lady from Brighton, and Grimaldi's son J S Grimaldi made his debut at the age of thirteen.

During the same season there was a major overhaul of the cast in *La Perouse* with only Bologna and Mrs Watts amongst the principals remaining. Kanko was now played by Mr Norman, Sophia Parsloe was Perouse's son Theodore and Master E J Parsloe was the new Chimpanzee.

During the 1817/18 season Master E J Parsloe gave his Chimpanzee in *La Perouse* at the Royal Coburg theatre. The difference in Parsloe's interpretation compared to that of all the other previous actors in the various productions over the years is that he was a posture-master and was able to contort his body into all kinds of twists and turns as he copied antics of a real ape. His future career was to specialise in contortionism.

By 1820 E J had reached adulthood and subsequently his parts were many and varied – but rarely very important ones – mostly in plays that are now long forgotten. E J's forte was not in drama, he was of the pantomime unit where his skill as a contortionist could be seen to advantage.

E J's younger brother Charles Thomas reached adulthood in 1823. His child parts had been very similar to those of his brother, indeed he often took them over as E J grew up. Again, his grown-up roles were little more than walk-ons, but in 1825 Mr C T Parsloe played a Sailor in *Jocko, the Brazilian Monkey* which is particularly interesting to our theme as this was the play which ignited the whole man-monkey furore when the French dancer Mazurier visited for a short season, inspiring a whole host of copies.

Sophia Parsloe made a career for herself as a dancer and Columbine, appearing all over the provinces, often with the Ridgway Brothers. She was a young lady who did not hide her modesty and was often taken to task for her skimpy stage dresses, and excessive acrobatic movements that were not considered ladylike.

> Miss Parsloe as Columbine was certainly lively and vivacious, but wanted delicacy in climbing on to Harlequin's back. Similarly, her action of whirling around on one leg with the other stretched out to its full extent while clad in an exceptionally scanty dress might be judiciously dispensed with.[2]

James Parsloe, the eldest brother, was the prompter at Covent Garden and in 1824 when Barnes the Pantaloon was suddenly indisposed just as the pantomime was ready to start, James volunteered to step in. Never having played such a role previously, he donned the costume and set to, by all accounts making a decent fist of it. Unfortunately, when a later scene involved Harlequin, Clown and Pantaloon in a great bustle, instead of dodging a blow from Harlequin's sword, James received it in his right eye. He was carried offstage unobserved by the audience, but a clamour arose when Barnes's special scenes were not performed and the audience started shouting for the absent Barnes and the non-appearance of Pantaloon. Grimaldi was obliged to step forward and explain there had been a serious accident. Immediate medical aid was sought but the eye had been struck out and James was in a high fever for some days. Eventually he was able to resume his position as prompter, albeit with a single eye.

Having left Covent Garden, E J Parsloe went to the Royal Amphitheatre, better known as Astley's. There were three theatres south of the river commonly called the transpontine houses – the Surrey, Astley's and Coburg. The last of these is still thriving, now famously known as the Old Vic. These were large venues that attracted the lower orders housed in the immediate vicinity of the rapidly growing city. Astley's had a circus ring as well as the stage, the plays presented being referred to as hippodramas as horses always featured, even in such plays as *Macbeth*.

E J adopted the guise of a 'Chinese Buffoon' which is interesting as his nephew Charles Thomas Parsloe Jr went on to make an entire career of some repute in America with a similar character.

THE PARSLOE FAMILY

> After which will be performed (26th time) a New Grand Hiſtoric Pantomime Drama in Two Parts, called
>
> # PEROUSE;
> ## Or, The DESOLATE ISLAND
> With entire New Muſic, Scenery, Machinery, Dreſſes, and Decorations
> ### EUROPEANS
> Perouſe (the Navigator) by Mr. H. JOHNSTON,
> Theodore (the Son of Perouſe) by Miſs JENKINSON,
> Congé (Servant to Madame Perouſe) Mr. KING
> And Madame Perouſe by Mrs. H. JOHNSTON
>
> ------
>
> Chimpanzee (an Animal of the Deſolate Iſland) Maſter MENAGE.
> *Natives of a Neighbouring Iſland.*
> Kanko (Suitor to Umba) Mr. FARLEY,
> Negaſki (Umba's Father) Mr. DELPINI,
> And   Umba by Mrs. MILLS

MASTER MENAGE

Covent Garden

Detail of playbill 1801

> To which will be added the Grand Hiſtoric Pantomime Drama called
>
> # LA PEROUSE;
> ## Or, The DESOLATE ISLAND
> The Action &c of the Ballet under the direction of MR. FARLEY.
> ### EUROPEANS
> Perouſe (the Navigator) by Mr. BOLOGNA, Jun.
> Theodore (ſon of Perouſe) Miſs Worgman, Congé, Mr. Heath
> Madame Perouſe by Mrs. PINCOTT
>
> ------
>
> Chimpanzee (an Animal of the Deſolate Iſland) Maſter MORELLI.
> *Natives of a Neighbouring Iſland.*
> Kanko (Suitor to Umba) Mr. GRIMALDI,
> Negaſki (Umba's Father) Mr. King, Potepataw Mr. Norman, Tetafemar Mr. Cardoza
> Potoomora, Mr. Yarnold,   Tangaboo, Mr. Sarjant
> Umba by Mrs. PARKER

MASTER MORELLI

Covent Garden

Detail of playbill 1811

> The whole to conclude with the Popular and Favourite Pantomime of
>
> # LA PEROUSE;
> ## Or, The Desolate Island
> ### EUROPEANS
> Perouſe (the Navigator) by Mr. BOLOGNA, Jun.
> Theodore (ſon of Perouſe) Miſs Parsloe, Congé, Mr. Heath
> Madame Perouſe by Mrs. WATTS.
>
> ------
>
> Chimpanzee (an Animal of the Deſolate Iſland) by Maſter E. PARSLOE
> *Natives of a Neighbouring Iſland.*
> Kanko (Suitor to Umba) Mr. NORMAN,
> Negaſki (Umba's Father) Mr. King,
> Potepataw Mr White,   Tetafemar Mr W. Chapman
> Potoomora, Mr. Sutton,   Tangaboo, Mr. Sarjant
> Umba by Mrs. PARKER

MASTER PARSLOE

Covent Garden

Detail of playbill 1816

> We should do injustice to Mr. Parsloe, who made his first appearance at the Amphitheatre in the character of a Chinese Buffoon, as the Manager chooses to style the Clown, if we did not say that his exertions were much and deservedly applauded. We have seen one man of more flexible limbs than he possesses, and only one, and that is the celebrated Mr LeMasurier of the Theatre Port Saint Martin, of Paris, who is at present, and has been for some time, the astonishment and delight of the Parisians.[3]

This comment is probably the first mention in the English press of Mazurier, but others were to soon follow – most struggling with the man's name:

> All Paris is mad to witness the exhibition, at the Theatre Port Saint Martin, of the actor Mazurier, in the part of the Monkey of Brazil, *Jocko*, which draws crowds to this theatre. He took great pains to study his part, as for days together he used to visit the collection of monkies in the King's menagerie to become a proficient in the art !!

Astley's – officially called The Royal Amphitheatre – combined stage and ring and was the delight of Londoners for over a hundred years.

THE PARSLOE FAMILY

E J continued at Astley's receiving good reports and popular acclaim:

> A Ballet, under the quaint title of *Punch Swallowed by a Whale*, afforded Mr Parsloe an opportunity of exhibiting some of his extraordinary and skilful displays in the art of posturing, in which we deem him to be altogether unequalled.[5]

E J returned to Covent Garden for the pantomime. He does not appear to have been one of the English actors or managers who attempted to cash in on the reputation of Mazurier in spite of his being hailed as England's finest equivalent.

In August, the Covent Garden management announced that it had contracted M Mazurier 'the famous French Punch. Masurier's powers are wonderful; we understand that, in the *Vampire* particularly, his acting is astonishing.'[6] It was erroneously rumoured that the prodigious Frenchman had agreed to £50 per night as his salary.

Unfortunately, Mazurier was not free until November but, starting in June, apes began arriving in the London theatres, all trying to steal a march on the great originator. It seemed as though every minor theatre in London was eager to have its own man-monkey. Managements turned to their costume departments to make ape suits, and asked their resident clowns to wear them, even the rival major theatre turning to the old favourite *La Perouse*:

Sadler's Wells: *Jocko; or The Ape of Brazil* (J S Grimaldi)
Royalty: *Jocko; or the Ourang Outang of Brazil* (Mr T Hill)
Tottenham: *Jocko; or The Ape of Brazil* (Mr Warren)
Astley's: *Death of General Jocko* (Mr Ducrow)
Surrey: *Jocko, the Ourang Outang of Brazil* (Mons Simon)
Drury Lane: *La Perouse* with Master Wieland

The theatre world could laugh at itself, and a spoof on the opening night of the season at the Adelphi had various actors applying for jobs, one arriving dressed as a man-monkey. All these man-monkeys gave rise to a squib:

> *Hide your diminished head, I pray,*
> *Ye Thespians of the present day;*
> *Heroes of buskin and of sock-oh!*
> *Monkeys are more than men — for see*
> *The town is mad as mad can be,*
> *And follows Chimpanzee and Jocko!*[7]

So did Mazurier turn out an anti-climax after finding that he had been largely upstaged when he eventually arrived in London?

MAN-MONKEY AND BOY IN THEATRICAL COSTUME 1822

The earliest picture that I have yet discovered of a man-monkey in his performing outfit. It is anonymous in both artist and subject, also it is not clear how accurate the dating may be, but if correct it pre-dates the Mazurier craze of 1825. It may well not be theatrical at all but a market-place busker.

Chapter Three
MAZURIER

CHARLES-FRANÇOIS MAZURIER was born at Lyon in 1798. Commencing his career as a comic and grotesque dancer in 1819 at Bordeaux, he returned to his home town in the following year where he played to rapidly-growing success. He made his debut in Paris early in 1823 with the ballet company at the Théâtre de la Porte-Saint-Martin. Within weeks he was the star of the show, and choreographers were obliged to ensure there was a suitable comedy role for Mazurier in every ballet they created.

CHARLES-FRANÇOIS MAZURIER

The first ballet especially devised for the new star was *The Shipwreck of Policinello; or Neapolitan Revels*. Pulcinella was one of the lesser characters in the Italian *commedia del arte* who for some reason achieved his fame in puppet form as the French turned him into a marionette (a puppet on strings), called Polichinelle, and the English version Punchinello was compressed by name and stature into a glove puppet called simply Punch. For his role, Mazurier copied the puppet with an enormous hump and distended belly in his costume which cannot have made his dancing and postures any easier.

When Mazurier appeared as Jocko the Brazilian Ape on 16 March 1825, all Paris went mad and his fame rapidly spread. Extravagant stories told of his preparations for the part. Attiring himself in his ape costume he entered the monkey cage at the Jardin des Plantes, where the animals disdained to acknowledge him. Eventually a veteran ape snatched an apple from Mazurier's hand with a look that proved he was regarded as a brother. The artiste delightedly cried "Enfin je suis singe!" and having being sorely tested considered he was fit to become an ape on the stage.

The French have always preferred their performers to be a little

outré, and certain stars have attracted worship just this side of idolatry. Parisian fashion houses, always on the lookout for the next 'big thing', often turned to the theatre. When the English actor T P Cooke played the monster (in mime) in the first-ever dramatisation of *Frankenstein* he played 80 consecutive performances in Paris, setting the ladies' hearts a-flutter, with many wishing they could take him home with them. The green colour Cooke painted himself became the fashionable shade for gloves called *vert de monstre*. When an English Shakespeare company appeared in Paris, the attractive leading lady Harriet Smithson made a great hit with Ophelia's mad scene in *Hamlet* resulting in the admiration of the men – she was eventually captured by Berlioz – and the fashion for women to wear a headdress, called *à la folle*, which comprised a black veil with wisps of straw woven into the hair.

So it is not surprising that the home-grown Mazurier became *the* fashion of 1825, packing the theatre nightly with his simian capers:

> The Parisians continue to be attracted in crowds to the theatre of the Porte St Martin, to witness the performance of Mazurier, in *Jocko*. Every thing in Paris is still *a la Jocko*. The favourite colour for ladies' dresses (a red brown) is called *Le Dernier Soupir de Jocko*; and the hats, without brims, are also called *a la Jocko*.[1]

No doubt today the dedicated followers of fashion would be cladding themselves in fur body suits.

The ballet version, which was based on the novella *Jocko* by Charles de Pougens, was written by Jules Joseph Gabriel de Lurieu and Claude Louis Marie de Rochefort-Luçay. It was taken up by other continental companies either as the original with choreography devised by Blache, or versions by other hands. Jules Perrot (*Sapajou*), Taglioni (*Lanina ou le Singe Brésilien*) and Petipa (with Laurençon in the lead role) all came up with their own versions.[2]

When Robert Elliston approached Mazurier with an offer to bring Jocko to Drury Lane, the dancer demanded £40 a night. This was beyond contemplation as the manager had recently agreed with Covent Garden that neither house would pay more than £20 a week for any player no matter how eminent. That cartel agreement was soon breached and eventually Charles Kemble the popular actor-manager of Covent Garden agreed to pay £25 a night for the star which, if he worked every night during the week, would bring him £150. As this news was given out by the press, comments were unfavourable to the Frenchman:

MAZURIER

> *One hundred and fifty pounds per week* to a fellow who plays Punch! Who will have the presumption to say we are not an *'enlightened people'*? In this respect, the education system has already done wonders; we dare say that in twenty or thirty years more, it will be a thing of common occurrence to hear of £500 a night being given to *Punch* and *Judy*.[3]

Mazurier's salary at Covent Garden astonished the French as it was considerably larger than that paid to Talma the greatest French actor of the time. Mazurier opened his limited season on 31 October with his earlier success as the marionette Polichinelle.

On the whole the press was underwhelmed:

> Last night, Masurier, the celebrated French Punch, made his appearance. All that can be said in praise is, that he is a sort of man-Punch, and that his squeak, contortions, and attitudes, are as like the original as they can be made by any human being. He is a very fit personage for the Christmas Holiday.[4]

This best of all *Punchs*, as he is called, does not appear so very extraordinary a person as we were given to expect. His body, most assuredly, is very flexible, and he walks upon a pair of very high stilts, and puts his head into a variety of very odd places, and jumps in at the window by the assistance of a rope, and does a great many other very strange vagaries – but he is, nevertheless, not half so amusing as our wooden friend in the box, with his little dog, his check curtain, and his brazen trumpet; nor do we think he will be ever half so popular.[5]

MAZURIER as Polichinelle

The audience too was not over impressed and there were some signs of disapprobation. Many thought that the proprietors had disgraced their stage and failed to uphold the dignity of the profession by paying 'this foreign mountebank' £25 a night. As the *London Magazine* sarcastically remarked, no doubt soon the principal tragedian will be singing a comic song, with his leading lady throwing a somersault over the head of her leading man to the accompaniment of a violin!

Mazurier played this same piece for seven nights until 7 November. On the following night he gave his famous Jocko. The play

> **Theatre Royal, Covent-Garden.**
> This present WEDNESDAY, Nov. 9, 1825,
> Will be acted the Opera of
> ## Rob Roy Macgregor
> Sir Frederick Vernon by Mr. EGERTON,
> Rashleigh Osbaldistone, Mr POWER, Francis Osbaldistone, Mr. DURUSET
> Owen, Mr. BLANCHARD, Capt. Thornton, Mr. CONNOR,
> Rob Roy Macgregor Campbell, Mr. WARDE,
> MajorGalbraith Mr J. ISAACS, Dougal, Mr RAYNER, Macstuart Mr MEARS
> Allan, Mr. HENRY, Baillie Nicol Jarvie, Mr. W. FARREN,
> Saunders Wylie, Mr. CLAREMONT, Andrew, Mr. BARNES,
> Diana Vernon, Miss PATON,
> Martha, Miss J. SCOTT, Mattie Mrs WILSON, Jane Macalpine Mrs HUDSON
> Hostess Miss APPLETON, Helen Macgregor, Mrs FAUCIT.
> After which will 2d time a Melo-Drama, in two acts, called
> ## JOCKO,
> THE
> ## BRAZILIAN MONKEY.
> IN WHICH
> **MONSIEUR MAZURIER,**
> will make his 9th appearance in England.
> The OVERTURE and Incidental MUSICK selected and arranged from the Works of BISHOP and PICCINI,
> by Mr. WATSON. The MUSICK of the Ballet composed by Signor V. CASTELLI.
> The Scenery painted by Mess. GRIEVE.
> The Dresses by Mr Palmer and Miss Egan. The Machinery by Mr. E. Saul and Mess. Bradwell.
> Fernandez de Ribera (a Portuguese Settler) Mr. CONNOR,
> Pedro (Bailiff of his Rice Grounds) Mr. MEADOWS,
> Dominique (Pedro's son) Mr. KEELEY,
> Juan (Fernandez' son, a child of seven years) Miss GREENER,
> Brazilian Planter, Mr. EVANS,
> Sailors, Mess. HENRY and C. PARSLOE,
> Jocko, (a Brazilian Monkey) Monsieur MAZURIER,
> Brazilian Planters, Mess. Ashton, Guichard, Ley, Miller, May, Robinson, Shegog, I. S. & C. Tett, Tinney,
> In act I.
> An entirely **NEW BALLET,**
> Composed by Signor VENAFRA,
> who, assisted by Mrs. VEDY, will dance a celebrated
> **BOLERO.**
> A PAS de TROIS by Mrs. Bedford, Miss Romer, Miss Thomasin.
> Dancers in the Ballet.
> Mrs. Bedford, Misses Kendall, Griffiths, Hebbard, Romer, Thomasin,
> Mesdames Bates, Bineki, Marsano, Shotter, Thorpe, Vials,
> Mess. Austin, Collett, A. Cooper, Grant, Heath, O'Bryan, Sutton.
> Donna Inez (wife of Fernandez) Miss GARDNER,
> Cara (a Mulatto Girl, beloved by Dominique) Miss J. SCOTT,
> Brazilian Girls, Negroes, &c. Mesdames Appleton, Brown, Gifford, Grimaldi, Smith Wilson,
> **JOCKO, The Brazilian Monkey.**
> will be repeated every Evening.
> Tomorrow, The BEGGARS' OPERA.
> Captain Macheath, - - - MADAME VESTRIS,
> Peachum, Mr. BLANCHARD, Lockit, Mr BARTLEY, Mat o'th' Mint Mr. J. ISAACS, Filch Mr MEADOWS

is very similar to *La Perouse* and *Robinson Crusoe* in the *mise-en-scène* and the story is a simple one.

The hero Fernandez is a Portuguese planter living on the coast of Brazil. He saves the life of Jocko, an orang-utan that is threatened by a snake. The animal is suitably grateful and a bond develops between the two with Fernandez teaching his protégé various tricks. The settlers in the village are not amused by Jocko's antics but he evades all attempts at capture. A ship is wrecked by a storm driving it on to rocks, and the crew and passengers struggle ashore. Among the passengers are the planter's wife and small son.

Later when all have left the beach, Jocko sees a little boy struggling in the sea and rescues him. At first the boy is frightened of the animal but when Jocko performs some tricks and stunts to make the child laugh they become friends. Jocko then saves the boy from being bitten by a snake, and in gratitude the little lad hugs his saviour. At that moment, villagers appear and, thinking the boy is being molested, shoot Jocko who expires at the feet of Fernandez who has arrived. He then realises the boy is his son who has been saved, but only at the expense of the death of his animal companion.

This was the Mazurier the London public was waiting to see, Policinello had meant little. Were the English going to follow the French in their adulation, or had the several home-grown imitators dulled the appetite with their various premature versions?

> The house is apt to expect more from M Mazurier than perhaps any man who tumbles upon two legs can well perform. Making allowance for the effect of this difficulty, in justice to several apes who have been breaking their collar-bones at the minor theatres, we cannot declare M Mazurier very decidedly their superior. What he does is very good, and a great deal of it very ingenious; but there be monkeys bred out of Paris – we saw a M Gouffe at the Circus, whose claims run the foreign gentleman very hard. . . . Mazurier plays in an admirable dress . . . and an ape who might be thought to have been brought up in a university . . . but has not so much strength in his tumbling and climbing as poor ragged M Gouffe has; and, as regards the acting – if Mr Grimaldi were but shut up in Exeter 'Change for six weeks, we should be inclined to back him to make faces or crack nuts against the universe.[6]

Some newspapers and citizens were clearly not going to accept that Mazurier was in any way superior to English performers, and were not going to give themselves up to the charm and talent of the French visitor. They considered him a mere posture-master – nothing more than a particularly supple acrobat who pretended to be an ape. They did not appreciate that the man was from a ballet company and, while not a *danseur noble* but a comic and grotesque, was a mime actor and not just a capering circus act. In France, the work was a pantomime-ballet, at Covent Garden it was billed as a melo-drama. No doubt the ballet dancer and the posture-master trained by similar callisthenics but their purpose was different. The dancer strived for artistic perfection, the posture-master for the bodily impossible. Fortunately many realised that they were seeing a form of genius:

> We apprehend that few who saw him for the first time last night will hesitate to join in the general acknowledgment of the surprise, interest, and admiration, excited by his performance. In the first place, the imitation of the appearance, movements, and habits of the animal is so complete as to create as perfect an illusion as can be supposed upon the stage. Having accomplished this, the actor, (for a most able actor he is) by a hundred good natured and playful tricks, appeals to those of our natural feelings, which are always so actively alive to the indications of sagacity and benevolence in the inferior animals. And so powerfully is this done, that when the faithful creature is shot in the act of saving the child from the pursuit of a serpent, the interest is absolutely painful. We know that M. Mazurier could afford no higher proof than this of the excellence of his acting; but we think the drama would end better without the death of poor Jocko.[7]

The public flocked, whether they appreciated the finer points or not. The houses were packed and when Mazurier, to vary his performances and show additional skill, performed a Chinese dance the applause was so rapturous and overwhelming that the audience clamoured for his return to do an encore. Eventually, as the demands became so outrageous that a riot appeared imminent, Mr Farley the acting manager had to step forward to give M Mazurier's apologies. It was some time before the poor chap could get enough silence to make himself heard, and when the explanation was that M Mazurier begged to be excused as he had now to perform the arduous role of Jocko, the audience cheered and permitted the show to continue. One wonders if they were able to read the playbill which set out the night's entertainment!

The public was far more indulgent than the professional critics and, while not going to the extremes of Mazurier's French admirers, turned out in great numbers to see the great man and were largely enthusiastic, but chiefly for Jocko rather than the other attractions. There may always be a small coterie of disgruntled or disappointed patrons, but in Regency times displeasure was always to be openly expressed and audiences regularly vocally complained about many things – when a replacement actor was substituted for the advertised one; if a play they disliked was announced for a repetition; some objection to a player's private life; and most famously when the seat prices were increased in 1809 and the rioting went on for 67 nights.

Though the English won the Battle of Waterloo and defeated Napoleon, that was a mere ten years previously, and many English people still resented the French as enemies on principle, no matter how talented. Paying good money to boo a French ballet dancer was far safer than fighting another war.

The critics largely dismissed the play itself as feeble and merely a showpiece for the star, one stating the theatre would have been wiser to revive *La Perouse*, which had now been in the standard repertory for 25 years, as a stronger vehicle for Mazurier. Also being ballet based proved a handicap, Covent Garden having no ballet company, and the supporting actors were inadequate. Some critics found Jocko himself too far-fetched to be credible and highlighted rather dubious antics such as the ape being able to tell the time, and the occasion when a net is set to catch Jocko, and he turns the tables trapping the setters in their own net.

On the whole, Mazurier won the naysayers round in spite of the ones who claimed M Gouffé at the Surrey was better. The Surrey Theatre was south of the river and classed as a minor theatre that was licensed only for burlettas, pantomimes and other musical offerings. Prices were cheaper than the major theatres, and it attracted a lower class of audience mainly interested in having a good time. Though, as M Gouffé also claimed to be French, he could hardly be promoted on the grounds that the home-grown performers were as good as, if not better, than invading foreigners. Basically, the main hostility arose not against Mazurier himself, who was almost universally praised for the actorly quality of his performance and the truth of his monkey impersonation of the real animal, but against Covent Garden. The two patent theatres were regarded as national theatres that were supposed to uphold the legitimate drama, and it was a disgrace to soil the hallowed boards with jumped-up fairground performers. These severe critics would have much disappointment coming to them in future years as the distinction between major and minor theatres became more and more blurred, with horses and wild animals, acrobats and rope walkers becoming just as common at Drury Lane and Covent Garden as in the minor theatres.

Jocko, the Brazilian Monkey had 13 performances from 8 November to 23 November, followed by a further single performance of *Shipwreck of Policinello; or Neapolitan Revels* on 25 November. Mazurier gave his *A Pas Chinois* dance during *Aladdin* on 23 and 28 November, 6 and 15 December. *The Deserter of Naples* a Ballet of

Action in which Mazurier played Simpkin received three showings on 6, 10 and 14 December. *Jocko, the Brazilian Monkey* had its 14th and final performance on 13 December. His 27 nights work must have netted Mazurier a gross of £675 plus a benefit of an unknown amount probably adding at least another £200.

Mazurier, in London only 46 nights in total, then returned to Paris. The impression he made in that short time lasted for 150 years as several star-turn man-monkeys arose, and scores of lesser acrobats made a living in the circus and variety side of show business as performing apes. Many of these were often held up against Mazurier for comparison.

The man himself resumed his career in the ballet troupe at the Théâtre de la Porte-Saint-Martin where a new choreographer Corelli had supplanted Blache. Another immediate hit was a pantomime transposed from Molière's comedy *Monsieur de Pourceaugnac* which made Mazurier the talk of Paris again and achieved 36 performances. This was followed by *Gulliver* a knock-about vehicle for the comic dancer, and *La Neige* a ballet based on the comic opera of Auber. This follow-on from Jocko also set a kind of precedent too, as many of the most successful man-monkeys relinquished the role after having made a tremendous success in it.[8]

Charles-Francois Mazurier died in Paris on 4 February 1828 following a chest illness. He was only twenty-nine, and is buried at Père Lachaise.

The Death of Jocko

Chapter Four
E J PARSLOE

MAZURIER, HAVING LEFT England just before the start of the pantomime season, would not have witnessed the blossoming of his imitators in the London theatres. The Olympic theatre had *Harlequin & Golden Eyes* in which 'The Young German' gave some excellent imitations of Mazurier. The young German was presumably an early reference to the as yet unknown Klischnigg. At the Surrey there was no pantomime but a new Melo-dramatic Extravaganza, in two Acts, called *Crom-a-boo; or the Ape and the Infant,* the part of the Ape performed by Monsieur Gouffé. Gouffé, who had been at the Surrey since June of 1825, 'proved himself a most accomplished imitator of the link between the human and the brute creation.'

At Covent Garden, the regular pantomime team had been diminished as Grimaldi had been forced to retire two years previously at the early age of forty-four when he found his legs would no longer support him, and he had persuaded the management to take his son known as J S Grimaldi to replace him as Clown. The younger Grimaldi had been in the Sadler's Wells and Covent Garden companies since his debut at the age of thirteen when he played a character called Clowny-Chip. He was now twenty-three.

In the 1825/26 pantomime *Harlequin and the Magic Rose* with J S Grimaldi as Clown, the *Evening Mail* reported: – 'his improvement bids fair to revive the excellent qualities of old Joey, and to excel Monsieur Mazurier'. Everybody wanted J S to be a 'chip off the old block' but 'Mr Grimaldi did all he could do, but could not always secure approbation. Mr Parsloe becomes a feature in the Lover: he is a very active posture-master and jumper.'[1] E J Parsloe had returned to Covent Garden to play Turlebrock a Sprite after his stint as clown at Astley's:

> Unfortunately the only really interesting part of the Pantomime is the opening of this story, or rather the sprites and scenery by which it is aided. One sprite, (Mr E Parsloe) afterwards Dandy Lover, astonished by dancing and twisting about à la Mazurier, and rivalling, in many points, the great French original. It is said

> to be his first appearance on this stage; he evinced extraordinary agility of limb, and one might imagine absence of bone! As the Dandy, however, he did not sustain his ascendancy.[2]

Why anybody should think it was the man's first appearance at Covent Garden, having grown up there constantly from 1813 to 1824 and hardly worked anywhere else, is hard to imagine. However, two of the cast have now been compared to Mazurier and the comparison goes on:

> a Mr E Parsloe, as one of the fiends, and subsequently a Dandy Lover, exhibits an elasticity of limb which may vie with that of Mazurier himself. He does the most difficult things in the world.[3]

> An addition of some importance to the stock of agility possessed by the posture-masters of the Theatre has been made by the engagement of a Mr E Parsloe. He made some incomprehensible displays. The dimness of the light and the darkness of his dress, added to the strange effect of some of his contortions, so that they actually seemed to be things impossible to one having the bones and sinews of a man.[4]

Not all the comparisons were totally praiseworthy as one critic remarked 'The new Mock Lover, Mr Parsloe, distorts himself almost as ingeniously as Mr Mazurier did, but, in revenge, becomes very nearly as tiresome.'[5]

It is fairly obvious from these extracts that E J Parsloe had made an immediate impression and – it seems from the use of the expression 'a Mr Parsloe' – indicates that he was thought a newcomer. Also his younger brother C T Parsloe had actually been playing a sailor in the supporting cast to Mazurier's Jocko at every performance. It only shows how the names of those at the bottom of the pecking order are meaningless to the average audience, as they still are today. Whether E J's other brother James the one-eyed prompter helped him to this job back in the company cannot be known.

What is known is the rather tepid response at the first night's conclusion. J S Grimaldi stepped forward to announce its repetition, amidst strong symptoms of disapprobation, partially mingled with applause. It was too long and too dull and, unless alterations were made, it was expected that the run would be cut short.[6] It does not appear to have achieved more than 34 performances and closed on 13 February.

As father Grimaldi was the most admired and beloved of all clowns, whom the critics regarded as an exemplar, and used as a yardstick ever since he came to star status with *Mother Goose* in 1806, it follows that as a suitable replacement, J S Grimaldi was required to be very good indeed. Unfortunately, he was no more than competent. Parsloe had been a boost to the regular Harlequinade trio and was highly regarded by his new, or rather renewed, paymasters. He was re-engaged for the following year's pantomime.

But E J had immediate commitments, playing some provincial dates prior to leaving later in the year with a team of English pantomimists for Paris where they had been engaged by the Théâtre de la Porte-Saint-Martin to follow the highly successful *Le Monstre et la Magicien* starring T P Cooke. The troupe was led by Ellar, Barnes, E J Parsloe, and Paulo the Drury Lane clown to present *Scaramouch* – a pantomime in the English fashion with elaborate sets and highly diverting acrobatics. 'First the English make us shudder now they are to make us laugh English style' said an amiable critic. Although French performers of all kinds had been welcomed in England for many years and amply rewarded – often excessively so – traffic in the opposite direction had been minimal. Only four years previously the first English theatre company since Shakespeare's time had appeared at this same theatre to be howled off the stage by vitriolic Frenchmen still angry at their defeat at Waterloo.[7]

During rehearsals, a mistimed trapdoor caused an injury to E J's leg, resulting in a delay in opening, but the first night was well received with Parsloe succeeding in the main role. Mazurier was among the French performers, and one wonders if he may have been the catalyst to the idea of importing an English pantomime. It is pleasant to imagine the two young performers – Parsloe was twenty-five, Mazurier twenty-seven – enjoying each other's company at work and having fun in their leisure time. There was surely some mutual influence and, if early death had not intervened, a future working relationship might have developed.

The visiting troupe made little impression except for Parsloe who, adapting his style by playing up the English elements, caught the French fancy achieving 'un success complet'; high praise indeed, especially considering the abuse the previous English Shakespearean actors had suffered. However, there was some dissention pointing out that while the Englishman was able and vigorous, he did not have the sublime artistry of their beloved Mazurier. Parsloe appeared almost every night for a month before returning home.

As well as the upturn in his professional fortunes, Parsloe having married Dorothy Ellen Dickenson in March 1824 at Nottingham, went on to father three children in 1827, 1829 and 1830.

Ever since John Rich had devised the first English pantomime, Harlequin had been the leading man, hence the cumbersome titles always incorporating his name. The status quo was overturned with the rise of Grimaldi who was so exceptional a performer that in his pantomimes Clown became the principal figure. This started a trend for all Harlequinades to place emphasis on the clown, and it had now become accepted that in pantomimes a good clown was the most important ingredient.

The 1826/27 pantomime at Covent Garden employed the established team of J S Grimaldi as Clown, Ellar as Harlequin, Barnes as Pantaloon and Miss Romer as Columbine. But now Parsloe's popularity was such that he too must be included in a leading role. The pantomime was *Harlequin and Mother Shipton; or Riquet with the Tuft* in which Parsloe played Mother Shipton's cat in the opening and Pierrot after the transformation.

> The performance of young Parsloe as Mother Shipton's Cat, is most excellent, and by no means inferior to the celebrated Jocko; his antics, his attitudes, and his nimbleness are true to nature; and his activity, when changed to Pierrot (a kind of Scaramouch), is truly astonishing.[8]

When the pantomime opened, one critic opined that it augured to be the biggest success since the legendary *Mother Goose* that brought Grimaldi to stardom. It was certainly not that, but it did reasonably well, running into late February with occasional performances to the end of the season.

On 16 April came the first night of 'A New Melo-dramatic Romantic Spectacle in Two Acts, founded on the Fanciful Popular Adventures of *Peter Wilkins; or The Flying Indians*'. It seems a strange idea to dramatize this very odd book by Robert Paltock. One can only assume it was having a vogue 75 years after it was first published. The novel is inevitably compared to its predecessors *Robinson Crusoe* and *Gulliver's Travels* as it features a shipwrecked sailor who discovers a gawry or naked flying woman on his island and marries her. A critic has written 'The description of Nosmnbdsgrutt, the country of the flying people, is a dull imitation of Swift and much else in the book is tedious.'

However, the dramatization was not so and proved to be extremely popular. It must have been a complex play to stage as it is full of flying women (the Gawries) and flying men (the Glums). E J Parsloe was cast as The Wild Man or Nondescript:

> He here twists around and up trees, along branches, across the stage, and athwart apparently inaccessible places with all the agility and nature of a wild animal. The action was as surprising as it was natural.[9]

> ... a nondescript or wild man, excellently played by E J Parsloe, is introduced. Nothing can surpass the agility and dexterity which he displays throughout the piece. He climbs the lofty trees, and vaults over the stage like a genuine savage, and he springs across chasms with a freedom of limb worthy of the character he assumes.[10]

However, one critic went on to point out that after Parsloe's first scene, all his subsequent appearances were copies of the same thing, and that the enthusiastic applause and reception that he received gradually waned as the play progressed. It is obvious from this that the public regarded these wild men and monkey antics as speciality turns rather than characters in a play.

Nobody would dream of criticizing Edmund Kean, or indeed

E J PARSLOE in the role of the Wild Man or Nondescript in Peter Wilkins

Kenneth Branagh, for being just the same throughout the play as Richard III or Macbeth. Just as much as those, Parsloe's Wild Man was a character throughout the play. He was a feral man rather than an ape, but the description of him swinging among trees was probably very akin the performance Parsloe gave as the Chimpanzee in *La Perouse* and *Jocko* with a very similar body suit and the addition of a monkey mask.

The play ran until the end of the season, the final performance on 25 June 1827 being the 50th. In Covent Garden's summer recess, Parsloe performed his Wild Man in a production of *Peter Wilkins; or The Flying Indians* at Birmingham which he directed. He also played Simpkin in *The Deserter*, one of the pieces that Mazurier had featured, and other items from his growing repertory. For his last night, which was his benefit, he really flogged himself by doing Clown in a scene from *Mother Goose* featuring the famous *pas de deux*, followed by 'his unrivalled Gymnastic Exercises, Corpuscular Transfigurations and Eccentric Metamorphoses'. He then held his body in a horizontal position with 168 lbs weight upon his back, and supported himself on one hand with 56 lbs weight upon his loins. After all that he had a break while the resident company gave a comic piece called *Too Late for Dinner*, and he clambered into his Punch suit for *Punch's Transformations* in which he performed a solo dance as Punch, as Mother Shipton's Cat he gave a 'celebrated scene from the pantomime *Mother Shipton*' and *Jocko* with 'a number of surprising feats'. Then came, for the last time, *Peter Wilkins* in its entirety. It is to be hoped he had 'a bumper' for his benefit with all that work!

Parsloe spent all July at Birmingham, then progressing to Peterborough for three days where he was advertised as 'Mons Parsloe, the extraordinary Posture Master and Clown, of the Theatre Royal, Covent Garden', with Howell, the Harlequin from Drury Lane, as his partner presenting 'Pantomimical Entertainments'.[11]

The duo then moved on to Huntingdon for four nights where they opened with *Don Juan; or the Libertine Destroyed* in which Howell was the eponymous lead supported by Parsloe as Scaramouch. They went on to do the Cat Scene from *Mother Shipton* coupled with *La Perouse* for their third night, and presumably pulled out all the stops again for their joint benefit on the final night.

While E J was in the provinces a report of an evening at Vauxhall Gardens said:

> The Prince of horse-riders—a singular performer, named in the bills as Ching Lauro Lauro, obtained much notice and applause by several astonishing positions and attitudes, doubling and twisting his body in various directions. We confess, with the

exception of young Parsloe of Covent Garden Theatre, the performance stands unequalled.[12]

The young newcomer, who only a few months ago was being hailed as a challenge to Mazurier, was now the lodestar to be emulated.

The new season at Covent Garden opened on 1 October with *Julius Caesar* and *Peter Wilkins*. It must always be kept in mind that Parsloe was regarded as a pantomimist and, no matter how successful the plays in which he appeared, they were always afterpieces just like the pantomimes. In those days when children were taken to the pantomime they had to sit through a long evening of drama or tragedy first. For many years it was customary at Covent Garden to precede the opening night of the pantomime with *George Barnwell; or the London Merchant* in which a young apprentice is enamoured of a prostitute who persuades him to a life of sin culminating in the murder of his employer. Whether they thought this sordid tale of an innocent lad seduced by a prostitute into committing murder was a moral lesson for the young, I do not know. The idea of festive fun was obviously very different in those days.

Peter Wilkins had a good number of performances and was then rested when it was time to launch the 1827/28 pantomime *Harlequin and Number Nip of the Giant Mountain*. There was a marked change

---

After which (*for the 36th time*) a NEW COMIC GRAND PANTOMIME called

Harlequin and Number Nip

Number Nip, of the Giant Mountain, Mr E. J. PARSLOE,
Nangpo-Rattibo, a Chinese Prince (afterwards Harlequin) Mr ELLAR
Pap-Pee, the old Nurse, (afterwards Clown) Mr J. S. GRIMALDI
Emperor Japano-Longo-Heado, (Pantaloon) Mr T. BLANCHARD,
Molewort, Miss HENRY,   Herald, Mr MEARS,
Mine-Frow-Dumple-Doddy-Squatzer-Down-Kin-Fromp, Mr Heath,
Mason in the Tunnel, Mr J. ISAACS,   Madam La Blonde, Mrs Wilson,
The Princess Brinhilda of Japano, (Columbine) Miss EGAN.

---

in the panto team – Ellar and J S Grimaldi were still Harlequin and Clown, but Tom Blanchard replaced the aging Barnes and Miss Egan came in as a new Columbine. Parsloe was Number Nip, 'a Gnome possessing the Power of assuming all Forms and Characters'. It was obvious that the whole production was built around the talents of

Parsloe.

> Mr. Parsloe's wonderful flexibility of body was displayed to great advantage. It really seemed as if he had no bone; and his monkey would have raised a sigh in the bosom of Mazurier had he witnessed it.[13]
>
> His changes into an old woman – a Thames waterman – an ostrich – a peacock – a monkey, and many others, were extremely well executed, and drew forth repeated testimonies of applause. In the last of these changes he escaped from the Zoological Gardens in Regent's Park, and making his way into the streets, delighted the youthful part of the audience by his destruction of the finery of a milliner's and the frail contents of a china shop.[14]
>
> The street scene in which Mr. Parsloe appears as a monkey, is still better; and the conclusion very laughable – his throwing himself down the chimney.[15]

The pantomime had reached its 40th performance by 13 February. Though Parsloe had several changes of character in the piece, the monkey was again tops with the public.

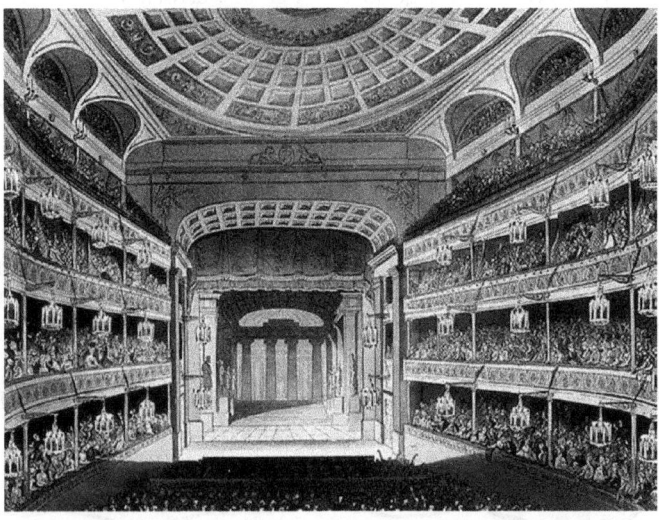

The Covent Garden theatre of 1810 where E J Parsloe grew up and became one of its biggest panto stars.

Elliston, who had taken on the Surrey after losing control of Drury Lane, engaged E J Parsloe to play in *Jack Robinson and his Monkey* which had its premiere on 14 July 1828 and was nothing more than a melodramatic rehash combination of *La Perouse* and *Jocko* with a shipwrecked sailor befriending a mischievous monkey. The crew of a passing ship mutiny and, tying the captain to the mast, make off in a boat. One loyal member saves the captain, but his wife and child are presumed lost as the ship is wrecked and loyal hand, captain, his wife and their infant son are all cast into the waves. Of course the baby is saved by Mushapug the monkey, and the parents separately struggle ashore both believing they have each lost spouse and child. The plot is embroidered with the mutineers also gaining the shore and given the hospitality of Robinson's crude hut, but run riot with his meagre stores. Good triumphs and the curtain falls on the victors preparing to sail back to England in the captured boat.

Parsloe was able to take the job because it was in the summer recess at Covent Garden, and when the run ended at the Surrey he departed again to Birmingham where Tom Blanchard had also been booked. On this occasion his main presentations were *Polichinelle Vampire* – presumably a rip-off from Mazurier – and *Jack Robinson and his Monkey*. On his benefit night he gave his 'unrivalled gymnastic exercises', his 'celebrated ladder dance' and danced a hornpipe on his head.

The 1828/29 Covent Garden season saw revivals of both *Number Nip* and *Peter Wilkins* before the new pantomime was launched. This had the snappy title of *Harlequin and Little Red Riding Hood; or the Wizard and the Wolf*. Needless to say Parsloe was the Wolf. After the transformation he became a variegated nondescript rival to Harlequin. The regular team did their usual tricks but these were neither as many as usual nor as good. 'We lament to say that the agility, which we confess young Grimaldi possesses, is but a sorry makeshift for the drollery we were wont to see in his father.'[16] Parsloe was still regarded with favour:

> It seemed as if his limbs were in reality pulled about with string and wire instead of their motion being regulated by the agency of muscles and sinews. He threw his arms and legs around as though they did not belong to him, and equalled Mazurier himself in the pliability of his members, as he certainly exceeded that renowned posture-maker in strength.[17]

But some critics were perceptive enough to see the chief difference between Mazurier and Parsloe:

> Mr Parsloe displays some feats of extraordinary activity. His skill in postures is nearly equal to that of the late Mazurier; but he is

deficient in that intelligent humour and whimsicality of which the French mime had so large a portion, and which, in some instances, elevated his distortions to the rank of real acting.[18]

The run ended on 18 February after only 38 performances.

Parsloe's work seemed to have fallen into the pattern of Covent Garden October to June, and the Surrey from July to September. In 1829, T P Cooke had his phenomenal star-making season as William in *Black Eyed Susan* which ran and ran. Parsloe was in the nightly afterpiece, playing his entire repertory turn and turn about – often not a whole work but scenes such as *Dame Trot's Cat*. He came up with a new piece called *The Protean Footman* in which he played a theatrical factotum called Nimble. One of the various characters was Clown and one press report opined he sustained the part so well 'that we do not hesitate to pronounce him the best Clown that has played his antics upon the stage since the days of Grimaldi.' First Mazurier now Grimaldi – this was heady stuff.[19]

In September, Parsloe moved to the Pavilion Theatre in Whitechapel Road where he gave his Mushapug in *Jack Robinson*. For his benefit he was joined by his colleague Tom Blanchard who performed his favourite *Don Juan; or the Libertine* supported by Parsloe as Scaramouch.

Theatrical gossip indicated that J S Grimaldi had resigned from Covent Garden and gone to Drury Lane tempted by an offer of £8 a week. Pantomime performers were not as highly rewarded as actors, and far below opera singers. Joe Grimaldi, at the height of his fame, earned £10 a week at the Garden and £12 at Sadler's Wells while actors of lesser standing earned more. Leading tragedians at Covent Garden earned twice as much, top comedians around £16. Opera singers were regularly paid in excess of £20 a night. Barnes the old Pantaloon was on £4 a week. Another disadvantage pantomimists suffered was the fact they were not allowed membership of the Theatrical Fund which enabled active performers to pay a small weekly amount to qualify for a modest pension in old age penury.

Presumably J S Grimaldi must have been on lower money than £8 to make the move, and as it was rumoured that E J Parsloe was being considered for Clown in his place, he in his turn must have been on lower money still. For all the comparisons to Mazurier, E J was nowhere near the £20 a night league.

Covent Garden was very hierarchical compared to theatre today. There were three greenrooms – one for performers whose salaries were above £10 a week, another for those between £5 and £10, and a third for those under £5 a week. Pantomimists with few exceptions were in the lowest category.

When the Covent Garden 1829/30 season opened, E J Parsloe was straight away hurled back into *Peter Wilkins* and on the launch of the new pantomime *Harlequin and Cock Robin; or Vulcan and Venus*, Ellar and Miss Egan were back again as Harlequin and Columbine, Pantaloon was now Mr F Sutton, and Clown was Paulo. Again Parsloe had to be given a specially written character, this time called Whirligig.

In opposition at Drury Lane was *Jack in the Box; or Harlequin and the Princess of the Hidden Island* with J S Grimaldi as Clown, Barnes as Pantaloon, Howell as Harlequin and 'Mynheer Von Kleshnig' as Mushapug the Monkey.

It looked as though it would be a battle royal for the best business. Paulo the new clown was the son of the Paul Ridigé who met his death via an absent stage-hand. He was favourably received though not blessed with much humour, and over-endowed with vulgarity. He was advised to avoid talking as the more he spoke the more obvious the vulgarity appeared. As the show progressed on the first night, it became apparent that Parsloe was not going to be much in evidence, and a clamour was started up demanding his appearance. Bartley the stage manager had to take to the stage to apologise for his absence. Parsloe was missing for no slight reason. In fact he had been severely injured at rehearsals and it was likely to be some time before he recovered sufficiently to appear.

Accidents were usually described as 'severe' because there was no immediate way of knowing how bad any damage was, but fortunately it often proved to be not as serious as first feared with the stricken performer back within a few days. In this case, whatever the injury may have been, it was truly a serious matter as it put Parsloe out of business for months. A widely circulated news item in June 1830 said:

> E J Parsloe, the clever pantomime actor, of Covent Garden Theatre, who it will be remembered during the rehearsal of the last pantomime at that theatre, met with an accident which nearly cost him his life, is now rapidly recovering his strength, and it is hoped will shortly be able to resume his performances; in which, having no rival, he can have no substitute.[20]

When the 1830/31 pantomimes opened there had been a major shake-up in personnel and Parsloe, absent for the major part of the year, was now at Drury Lane playing Second Clown to Southby. It was becoming a fashion to double-up on the basic characters of the Harlequinade, for truly pantomime was running out of steam, and managements were beefing them up with unrolling panoramic scenery and other innovations to attract the public. Whether Parsloe had been lured to Drury Lane by more money, or had been dropped by Covent Garden as a result of his long invalidity is impossible to say but

> There were two Clowns, but number will not always satisfactorily fill the place of talent, and on this occasion it was glaringly deficient.[21]

> Southby makes a tolerably good clown, but Parsloe is a mere posture-master, sufficiently active, possessing not a single grain of comic humour.[22]

On 22 February, a command performance was given for the king and queen of *The School for Scandal* followed by the pantomime. The final night was on 8 March 1831.

We have not followed the other members of the Parsloe family as, apart from E J's brother Charles Thomas (whose career is covered separately in the next chapter) they are not directly concerned with the man-monkey business. However, an incident concerning James Parsloe, the one-eyed prompter, provides a Dickensian look at the times. With other theatrical members he was attending the funeral of Mrs Sarah Siddons and, as he peered into the grave, he felt a tug at his pocket – his handkerchief had gone. Peering around, he saw a constable with two boys in custody. These lads, called Whooley and Arthur were well-known to the police, and the constable pulled James's handkerchief from Arthur's trousers. It transpired Whooley had taken the article and passed it to Arthur to conceal. James then took a handsome silver snuff box from the same pocket and remarked he had good reason to congratulate himself that this had not gone also. Whooley's defence was 'Wery likely, indeed, that I should pick that 'ere gemman's pocket of a bit of a handkerchief, and leave a silver snuff box behind!' Our next encounter with James will be over a far more serious matter.

E J Parsloe and Howell took themselves off to the Norwich circuit in June where they performed for several nights each at Norwich and Ipswich with *The Dumb Savoyard and his Monkey, Punch the Director; or Magic and Murder, Harlequin and the Three Wishes; or The Fairy and the Puddings*. Then Parsloe, returning to take up his summer residence at the Surrey, appeared in another new play especially devised to show off his talents. There is little about this play:

> A "melodramatic extravaganza," called *The Odd Volume; or There's Spirit in Punch*, was produced on Monday evening; it is no more than a vehicle for the tricks of Mr Parsloe, in the character of Signor Punchinello, and, so far, it may be allowed to pass, although we must say that we have seen much more amusing performances by his great namesake in the streets.

This was obviously Parsloe's attempt to copy Mazurier's Polichinelle, and was no more successful with the English public.

Parsloe's next venture was at the City Theatre, a new minor theatre that had started life as a chapel, then a temperance hall, became a theatre on a subscription basis in 1829, then with an amateur company before settling as the New City Theatre. In the list of London theatres it was well down the pecking order. The venue was a comedown for one who had spent several seasons in the Covent Garden pantomime and attracted a huge following of admirers. He opened in October with a new starring vehicle by the prolific playwright William Thomas Moncrieff called *The Monkey That Has Seen the World* but it had to be shelved after several performances because of the star's indisposition. Whether this was a passing illness or a recurrence of symptoms from his recent serious injury is not related.

On top of his injuries and illness, Parsloe's wife died leaving him with three small children. It is not certain exactly when this melancholy event occurred but she may well have died giving birth to their daughter who was baptised on 23 July 1830.

At this point mists gather over the next gambit of E J Parsloe. William Blanchard an actor who had spent 30 years in the Covent Garden company was offered a lucrative engagement at the Bowery Theatre in New York by his son-in-law. It was decided that a genuine English pantomime would be a novelty as one had never been seen at that time in New York, therefore the party included Parsloe as Clown, John Gay as Harlequin, Miss Johnston the Garden's latest Columbine, and the Pantaloon by a distant Blanchard relation called Sonas.

Whether Parsloe felt he was played out in England, or whether the offer was too good to turn down, or whether his brother Charles Thomas, who had already ventured out to the States, influenced him is impossible to say. In any event, Parsloe left his three small children behind in the care of brother James and sailed out to the New World.

Reports say that on the journey out there Parsloe fell down the companionway steps, injuring his spine. If so, this was not good for a recently ill posture-master and clown. The pantomime to be presented was *Harlequin and Mother Goose*, the show that brought fame to

Grimaldi in 1806. This had been popular ever since, but it must have relied on Grimaldi's genius because it always seemed to fall flat when performed by other clowns. One advantage in choosing this piece is that its simplicity and charm could be economically staged with a minimum of elaborate stagecraft. This stemmed from the fact that when Grimaldi first played it, nothing had even been written six weeks before the opening night, so the usual production values were lacking. Even today, *Mother Goose* is regarded as an economical production compared to *Cinderella* and, to balance the books, is often staged at a theatre the year following that most expensive of pantomimes.

On the Bowery first night the pantomime was a major flop. The American audience just did not 'get it' and the poor clown was acutely depressed by his troubles and failure. At this point stories differ as to what actually happened. They cannot all be correct, indeed probably none of them are strictly true but, alas, the result is the same.

o   He was taken ill on the first night and removed to his hotel where two weeks later he died of consumption.[23]

o   On the voyage out poor E J Parsloe, who as clown was mainstay of the piece, hurt himself severely by falling down the companion-way. Despite his weakness he did his best on the opening night at the Bowery, towards the end of February 1832 to rouse the customary mirth; but the audience was small on account of the extremely rough weather, and ill-attuned to levity. Three nights passed with equal discouragement and on the fourth the unfortunate clown, broken down by illness and mental anxiety, actually burst into tears in the middle of the performance, and was obliged to retire. Early on the following day, 8 March, poor E J Parsloe expired at his lodgings with a prayer on the lips for the wife and children he had left behind him in London.[24]

o   The rumour of the death of Mr Parsloe has happily been contradicted by a letter from friends in New York who say that severe illness prevented him from appearing more than one night.[25]

o   A letter was received from New York stating that Parsloe, while playing the Wild Man in *Peter Wilkins,* at one of the theatres there, was precipitated on to the stage in consequence of some failure in the machinery, and killed on the spot.[26]

It has not proved possible to confirm which, if any, of these stories is true but what is beyond doubt is that Edmund John Parsloe was dead on 8 March 1832 in New York. Having been compared to Mazurier all his professional life, like the Frenchman, Parsloe died far too young being only thirty-one years old.

As we have seen, Parsloe's wife had died some months previously, thus his tiny children were now orphans. It appears that one of the three must also have died because when James Parsloe, the one-eyed prompter brother of the late posture-master, appealed for the organising of a benefit only two orphans were mentioned. For any worker of those times to lose his position whether through illness, accident or other blameless cause, the results could be instantly calamitous.

E J Parsloe's swift descent from stardom was initially caused by a serious accident while rehearsing a pantomime, and as 'no play no pay' was the rule of day (and for a 100 years after) he had no income until he could perform again. It also appears that he was no longer wanted at Covent Garden, and obtained work at the rival Drury Lane where as Clown he proved to be devoid of humour. Not surprising as his lovely young wife had just died, and he was probably still struggling with bodily infirmity. His work at the Surrey also ended with the death of Elliston who had been his employer there. One by one, the doors of the principal theatres in London were closing on him. Then when he attempted an original play at the New City theatre, illness struck again. The offer of an American engagement must have seemed a welcome lifeline, especially as his brother was already out there. Perhaps he could start again in a new country, after all he was only thirty-one years old, but ill-luck followed him to the New World.

Brother James, who had suffered his own misfortunes which left him with the meagre salary of the prompter, was left to support his own wife and family, his aged parents and now the infant orphans of his ill-starred brother. An appeal for relief was started with a benefit night at the Surrey which raised £200. Also an anonymous donor sent a £50 note via the 2d post. However, the main concern was that pantomime artistes had no benevolent fund, and as a result one was started, with James active in the organisation. He himself was granted an annual benefit but no doubt his life continued as an endless struggle until he died in 1847 'after a lengthened period of mental disturbance and bodily suffering'.[27]

The Parsloe family do appear to have been blighted with ill-luck all along the line. We must now look at the remaining brother Charles Thomas Parsloe – who was also a man-monkey – to see how he fared in this difficult and arduous profession.

The Bowery Theatre in New York where E J Parsloe gave his final performance, dying there in 1832 at the age of 31.

Chapter Five
C T PARSLOE

CHARLES THOMAS PARSLOE, the younger brother of E J, was born in 1804. As children they performed together as contortionists, and professionally developed to manhood via annual seasons at Covent Garden. C T was last seen in the walk-on role of a Sailor supporting Mazurier during the latter's short visit to the Garden.

Having left Covent Garden, C T made his living as a dancer and man-monkey in the provinces. In January 1827, he was engaged in the resident company at Sheffield under the management of De Camp. For some reason he was dismissed without notice and took his complaint to the local magistrates on the grounds that he was entitled to a month's notice and was claiming £5 in lieu, which would indicate his weekly salary was £1.5.0 (25/-). He lost the case and as a result took the theatre himself for a benefit night. The entertainment commenced with *Parsloe's Flight* which would be C T dressed as the Monkey sliding from the back of the gallery to the back of the stage via a rope. This was followed by *King Henry IV* with Mr Carter and Mrs Lee supported by amateurs. Having treated the audience to a comic clog hornpipe, Parsloe then performed as the Monkey again in several feats of strength and agility with the big finish of running round the front of the boxes and gallery.

Later in the year C T could be found at Cheltenham, and then in October back at Sheffield where the manager was now Samuel Butler the 6ft 4in tragedian with the big voice.

In October 1828, C T was at the Minor Theatre in Manchester playing Mushapug in *Jack Robinson and his Monkey* and other roles including Clown in pantomime. In January 1829, he had graduated to the Theatre Royal, Edinburgh with his Mushapug, and Man Friday in *Robinson Crusoe*. His last night was on the 15th when he took his benefit.

C T probably played several towns in Scotland as in March he was in Aberdeen where he was billed somewhat misleadingly on two accounts: it was brother E J who was the artiste at Covent Garden, and the play *Jack Robinson* was premiered by E J at the Surrey Theatre as explained in the previous chapter. It is a moot point whether this was the management under the notion they had captured E J, were deliberately pretending so, or whether C T was fond of giving that impression.

> Mr Ryder, is happy to announce his engagement with the Wonderful Phenomenon
> **C T PARSLOE**
> Whose representations of Monkeys and Nondescripts actually astonished the Metropolis, in the Theatre Royal Covent Garden, where his acting was crowned with unparalleled success for a succession of nights. He will have the honour of appearing in Aberdeen Tomorrow Evening, in a New Piece written expressly for him called
> *JACK ROBINSON AND HIS MONKEY*
> Mushapug (the Monkey) - Mr C T Parsloe
> The popular Pantomime of PEROUSE is in active preparation – Chimpanzee by Mr Parsloe

In January 1830, C T was at the New Adelphi Theatre, a small minor venue in Dublin, which had recently opened under new management with *Robinson Crusoe*, C T appearing as Man Friday ('as originally performed by him at the Theatre Royal, Covent Garden'). This must have been another stretching of the truth, unless at some time he went on for an indisposed J S Grimaldi whose part it was. He went on to play Pantaloon in *Harlequin and Mother Malkin.*

In April, C T was at the Liver Theatre, Liverpool playing the Chimpanzee in *La Perouse*. Here he was honestly billed simply as 'from the Theatre Royal, Covent Garden'. This may have been his farewell to England because Liverpool was the port from which the ships sailed to America, and it was in that country he made his future.

His debut on the American stage was on 1 October 1830 at the Park Theatre, New York as the Nondescript in *Peter Wilkins*, later giving his Man Friday, then his Mushapug in *Jack Robinson and his Monkey*. C T took this play on the road, playing Philadelphia among other towns. He returned to the Park for the 1832/33 season where he added a black-face role, also appearing as the Cat in *Dame Trot's Cat*. The latter did not go down too well as the *New York Times* pointed out he was too tall for a monkey, and ridiculous as a cat. Returning to the monkey he appeared in a new afterpiece called *The Cabin Boy and His Monkey*.

One night a Mr Greene was watching C T Parsloe performing his monkey antics and was puzzled as to why he kept abruptly disappearing into the wings and reappearing shortly afterwards. Intrigued by these antics Greene made his way backstage to find a man in the wings with a pot of paint and a brush. Parsloe's dyed brown stockinet costume made contoured to his body was old and worn and kept splitting under the artiste's exertions revealing his white flesh, so whenever he gaped he dashed to the wings to have his white bits rapidly covered with brown paint.[1]

C T must have been aware of his brother E J's arrival in New York and his subsequent death, but nowhere does there seem to be a connection made between the two men. In a study of C T Parsloe Jr, who became more famous than his father, the author regrets he could not find an illustration of the Wild Man in *Peter Wilkins* as played by C T and supplies the one of E J Parsloe whom he describes as 'no relation as far as I know'![2]

C T Parsloe did not have the monkey business to himself in America as other posture-masters had also made the journey from Europe. These included Gabriel Ravel of the Ravel family of acrobats:

> The fame of poor Mazurier (who now lies quietly in the cemetery of Pere la Chaise, in Paris where a handsome monument has been erected to his memory by the actors of the Port St. Martin Theatre) is likely to be eclipsed by a new man-monkey, named Ravel, at Bordeaux. It is said, in his postures and tricks, to set all the rules of anatomy at defiance.[3]

With advancing age and so much competition around, C T left the monkey business to others while he carried on acting and dancing. He also married, started a family, and gradually became a manager and theatrical agent.

C T Parsloe's son, Charles Thomas Jr, born in New York in 1836, followed in his father's footsteps as comic dancer, with character sketches and mime. He first played a monkey role at Purdy's National Theatre in *Pongo, or the Mischievous Ape* in 1857. However, his forte was elsewhere and he developed a comic character – the Chinese Coolie which made him more famous than ever was his father.

Chapter Six
GEORGE WIELAND

IT IS DOUBTFUL THAT George Wieland was a trained posture-master, rather an excessively flexible dancer in the style of Mazurier. He was born circa 1811 – making him ten years younger than E J Parsloe – but he had a very similar childhood as he too took to the stage at an early age. Earliest glimpses show him in the company at the Royal Coburg theatre at the age of ten taking various dancing roles.

The Royal Coburg Theatre, where Wieland spent his early years.

The theatre is still going strong as the famous Old Vic.

George made his pantomime debut in 1817 appearing in a trick bottle brought on by the Clown. From this he jumped out on to the stage, dressed as a sailor-boy, danced a hornpipe, and accompanied himself on the violin. A press advertisement dated 7 October 1822 states: 'In the course of the evening Master Wieland will, in the character of the Monkey in *Philip Quarl*, Dance with Miss C Bennett *The Minuet de la Cour*.' This would pre-suppose that he had previously appeared in the play itself. *Philip Quarl; or The English Hermit* is an 1803 play by Charles Dibdin based on Peter Longueville's Robinson Crusoe-like novel of 1727, and an early addition to the limited range of monkey plays, following close on the heels of *La Perouse*. Dibdin churned out plays almost weekly on any topic that took his fancy, and specialised in his own versions of plays produced elsewhere.

Wieland, who was a protégé of William Barrymore, an author and

producer of pantomimes, joined the Drury Lane company as dancer and pantomimist when Mr & Mrs Barrymore were taken on by Elliston at the Lane. From the autumn of 1823 he was regularly employed there season after season well into his manhood in a similar manner to the Parsloe boys at Covent Garden. Clearly catching the public's attention from his debut, he even started getting mentioned in reviews as this one from *Zoaster; or The Spirit of the Star*:

> that wonderfully clever and sprightly pantomimist, little Master Wieland, showed himself capable of doing much more than he here had scope for. The elastic precision with which he springs from a distance upon a little trap, just big enough to let him through, vanishes like a spirit indeed instantly through the boards was one of the neatest exhibitions we ever saw of the kind.[1]

When Mazurier's Covent Garden season captured all the public and press attention in November 1825, Drury Lane's riposte was to bring out a new production of *La Perouse* which ran until time for the Christmas pantomime. Having done the monkey in *Philip Quarl*, Wieland was the natural choice for the similar role.

> To conclude with the Melo Drama of
> **De La Perouse**
> Perouse, (the Navigator) Mr NOBLE,
> Theodore, (Son of Perouse) Miss LANE,
> Conge, Mr T. BLANCHARD,
> Madame Perouse, Miss SMITHSON,
> Chimpanxee, an Animal of the Island, Master WIELAND
> NATIVES OF A NEIGHBOURING ISLAND
> Kanko, Mr O. SMITH,   Negaske, Mr HOWELL,
> Potepataw, Mr Yarnold,   Tetasemar, Mr Webster,
> Umba, Mrs NOBLE

La Perouse *was brought out to combat the season of Mazurier at the rival Covent Garden. The Chimpanzee role was played by 15 year-old Master Wieland. Playbill November 1825 (detail).*

The press was kind to the boy, by now an established performer:

> Chimpanzee, an animal of the island, was supported by a Master Wieland, who performed his monkey tricks with a good deal of humour, and no small share of activity.[2]

> Recently it has become so much the fashion for men to ape monkies, that Drury Lane, we presume in self-defence, the other theatres having already set them the example, in procuring clever men-monkies. Upon this occasion Master Wieland was the

monkey, and fell very little short of the now celebrated Mons Gouffe.³

Mazurier's short visit to London inspired a number of new man-monkeys but it was already apparent that Gouffé was capturing all the attention and plaudits as he had been working nightly at the Surrey since June for five months prior to Mazurier's visit.

Wieland now disappears from concrete record over the next two years, but presumably he was beavering away in a range of small supporting roles. Then arrived the first night of *The Dumb Savoyard and his Monkey* on Easter Monday, 7 April 1828. This was a new work by C Pelham Thompson who had been commissioned to write two new monkey plays – *Jack Robinson and his Monkey* and *The Dumb Savoyard and his Monkey* – these he had given to Barrymore to place. Thompson then went off to Paris – probably to steal a few more plots for future use. On his return he found *The Dumb Savoyard* playing to success at Drury Lane with Master Wieland as the Monkey, and Mrs Barrymore in the breeches role of Pepino the Savoyard. Thompson's other play was also doing excellent business at the Surrey Theatre with E J Parsloe performing as Mushapug the monkey. At this juncture, E J Parsloe and the much younger George Wieland were contemporary man-monkey rivals.

Expecting to reap a decent return, Thompson found that Stephen Price the American manager of Drury Lane had bought one play for £50, and Robert Elliston had paid £54 for the other. Unfortunately, Barrymore had passed them off as his own work and refused to pay a penny to the true author. The wrangling between the authors and subsequent legal decisions need not concern us here, but it is plain that there was money to be made in new monkey plays and concomitant work for actors and posture-masters specialising in that field.

At Drury Lane the play was a great success with the outstanding features being the panoramic scene of a trip down the Rhine, and Wieland.

> Master Wieland was Marmazette, and with a little more industry he will become a dangerous rival to Mr Parsloe. His antics, and action were in general admirable.⁴

> The principal, and doubtless the most amusing actor of the piece is the monkey (Master Wieland), who capers and climbs with "surprising agility", and executes his mischievous tricks with a degree of skill and intelligence which would do honour to a more rational creature.⁵

On Tuesday 15 April, when climbing up the side scene, Wieland fell to the stage. The height was 12 to 14 feet and he landed on his side and head. Moaning loudly, he was carried off and the curtain dropped. Browne, one of the principal actors, came out and said he would return to inform the audience as soon as the nature of the accident could be ascertained. The audience waited, no doubt chattering anxiously, for a quarter of an hour before Browne reappeared with the news that Master Wieland was seriously hurt, but the piece would proceed as well as possible. The audience assumed that Wieland had been taken for medical assistance and, not being familiar with the piece, some kind of substitute actor would be provided.

However, when the curtain rose, Wieland was discovered sitting in a chair, whereupon the audience as one demanded, with proper feeling, that the boy should be removed to seek immediate medical attention. At this Wieland was helped off the stage in an obvious state of great suffering. The panoramic scenery was displayed – this being a great feature of the piece, a painted scene some hundreds of feet long which unrolled across the stage to simulate a journey down the Rhine. Then the curtain fell again and Browne appeared once more to say Wieland had been taken home, and was in the care of a surgeon who had said his hurt was dangerous.

The Duke of Sussex who was at the show and witnessed the accident, made particular enquiries after the boy, and sent several times in the days after to learn of his progress. The news was that Wieland had suffered several severe contusions of the head and shoulders, and fractured two ribs, but was considered to be out of danger.

He was so much out of danger that on the last night of the season, 28 June, which was Grimaldi's farewell performance, Wieland performed a comic *pas-de-deux* with Master Chikini.

After the season closed Wieland, together with Mr and Mrs Barrymore and the panoramic Rhine, went to Edinburgh in July to present *The Dumb Savoyard and his Monkey* there. Whether Wieland had performed the piece since his accident is not clear, but on the first night at Edinburgh in the first scene he fell again. It sounds as though it happened exactly as at Drury Lane – Wieland intending to suspend himself from the top of a scenery piece some 12 feet above the stage, hanging by his feet upside down, lost his grip and fell to the stage head first. Again he was hastily carried off, apparently insensible, and Dr Thatcher who was in the audience hastened backstage to offer assistance.

After some minutes, Mr Murray the manager came forward to ask the indulgence of the audience, explaining that the boy was not seriously hurt but somewhat shaken and there would be a few minutes pause before the play was resumed.

After 20 minutes wait, Master Wieland re-appeared and the play recommenced and he went through his business apparently as normal, though nobody but he would have known if he curtailed anything in his routine. Obviously a sombre gloom descended on the rest of the evening with the audience looking on in trepidation at every clamber or leap by the monkey, but no further calamity occurred.

Master Wieland appeared as usual on the second night, but when the third night audience was assembled, Mr Murray had to go onstage and explain that though Master Wieland had performed after his accident, and again last night, the effort was too exhausting, and today he was unable to rise from his bed. It was thought after a night's rest he would be able to continue with his engagement. This proved to be true and he completed his contract.

In October, Wieland was back at Drury Lane for the 1828/29 season when more performances of *The Dumb Savoyard and his Monkey* featured in the repertory plus a varied assortment of roles making use of Wieland's special talents.

During the summer break, *The Dumb Savoyard and his Monkey* with Mrs Barrymore, Wieland – both specially featured – and the panorama played at the Royal Pavilion Theatre.

To conclude with DURING THE WEEK
The Splendid Melo-Drama, written by Mr W Barrymore, and produced under his immediate direction, called The

Dumb Savoyard & his Monkey.

Giovanni, Count Maldichini, (a State prisoner) MR. HARRISON.
Barcorolo, (Ferryman at Ober Wesel) MR. GOLDSMITH.
Vatchvell, (Jailor to the Fortress of Speilemberg) MR. SAKER.
Pepino, (the Dumb Savoyard) MRS. W. BARRYMORE.
Marmazette, (his Monkey) MASTER WIELAND.
Zingari Chiefs, Mr. Maynard & Mr. Cressall. Zingari Tribe, Messrs Jackson, Chapino, Smith &c
Officers of the Imperial Guard, Messrs Wilson, Jones, Jenkins &c.
Celestina, Countess Maldichini, MRS. MAKEEN.
Alexis, (her infant Child) Miss NORMAN.   Teresa, (Hostess of the Black Eagle) Mrs. CLIFFORD

When Drury Lane was closed, Barrymore took 'his' play (he was still claiming authorship) to the minor London theatres and provinces with his wife and young protégé as guest stars. Royal Pavilion Theatre, playbill week com 23 August 1830. (Detail)

Wieland, without the Barrymores but partnered by the Harlequin Howell, also appeared at the Cheltenham Theatre, and suffered a serious accident running a metal spike up one of his feet. In those days many theatres had a row of spikes between the pit and the orchestra to prevent angry people mounting the stage.

In the course of his leaping and bounding Wieland had managed to land with one foot on one of these spikes. A pantomimist could be a dangerous profession by its very nature, but the poor lad seems to have been particularly accident prone.

The Drury Lane management realising that Master Wieland had grown up – he was now eighteen – billed him as an adult from the 1829/30 season. The pantomime was *Jack in the Box; or Harlequin and the Princess of the Hidden Island* in which Mr Wieland played three small roles including a Siamese Twin with Chikini who had also come of age. Considering the pantomime was staged by the customary Drury Lane producer Barrymore – George's mentor – the ape Mushapug, rather bizarrely, was played by 'Mynherr Von Kleshnig' which cannot have pleased George very much. Why was the resident man-monkey not given the role?

According to Klischnigg, he first donned a monkey costume when asked to take over from a sick colleague at Drury Lane. Therefore the answer seems to be that Wieland, whilst able to play the small roles allotted to him, for some reason was not in a fit state to appear as Mushapug. Perhaps the accident at Cheltenham was still taking its toll?

In the 1830/31 pantomime *Davy Jones; or Harlequin and Mother Carey's Chickens*, for the first (and only?) time, Wieland and E J Parsloe appeared in the same pantomime, neither of them playing monkeys.

On 7 June 1831, at the Surrey Theatre, George performed the Chimpanzee in the First Act of *La Perouse* for the benefit of Mr Blewitt.

On 25 June 1831, George Wieland married Charlotte Lidbury Poole. He was twenty years old, she was two years older.

Also in June, it was announced that 'the industrious Thompson of Drury Lane' was to take a group of actors to the continent to cash in on Miss Smithson's success in Paris. 'Young Wieland goes as Mazurier Anglaise and Joe Grimaldi Redivivus.' I cannot find any evidence that this visit actually took place. If it did, it would seem that Thompson was in danger of over-selling George as the English equivalent of Mazurier as well as a reincarnation of the sainted Grimaldi. In actual fact, by this time Miss Smithson's triumphs in Paris were wearing very thin indeed, and headgear *à la folle* long out of fashion.

Around this time, George Wieland actually went to America – with Mr & Mrs Barrymore – where in August 1831 they were playing *The Dumb Savoyard* at the Park Theatre in New York. Wieland scratched and jabbered after the most approved fashion of stage monkeys. Their visit seems to have been highly successful as they were away for over a year. Presumably, George being newly married, his wife went with him. Although the Barrymores stayed on, with William staging a pantomime in Philadelphia, George returned for the 1832/33 season at Drury Lane, where he had been promoted to Clown for the pantomime *Harlequin Traveller: or the World Upside Down*. It appears that he was rather less than first-class in the important role, being merely 'the most promising that we have seen for a considerable time.'[6]

Rather oddly, the Harlequin Howell, who was also producing in lieu of the absent Barrymore, had engaged a newcomer called Green 'whose feats, as a posture-master, transcended anything of the kind we ever saw.' This must have been a bit of a slap in the face for our George who had hitherto captured a monopoly of comic grotesques at Drury Lane.

> Mr Wieland, after having been Master Wieland for a sufficient length of time, has at length risen to the dignity of Clown, and a very tolerable one he is; he is active and attentive to his business and if he have not humour, it is not his fault, for nobody tries harder to display it. He is too apt to vociferate and discourse – for he ought to say nothing.[7]

George changed allegiance for the 1833/34 pantomime and went to Covent Garden to appear in *Old Mother Hubbard and her Dog; or Harlequin and Tales of the Nursery*. Wieland was Old Mother Hubbard in the opening but with little to do, and strangely did not have a part at all in the Harlequinade after the transformation.

J S Grimaldi, no longer Clown at Covent Garden, had moved to Drury Lane – the rumour being he was sacked from the Garden – where he managed one pantomime before his name disappeared from their playbills too. Having lost his place at Sadler's Wells as well as the two major theatres, J S sank lower through drink and indiscipline until getting work even at the minor theatres became difficult. He succumbed to debtors' prison and had to be rescued with a £40 payment from his long-retired father whose meagre savings were just about keeping himself from penury. His soft-hearted father never stopped trying to assist his son into work – he would propose freely giving a manager a manuscript of all his best mechanical jokes and tricks, assisting him in how to make and stage them, providing there was a job for his son in the show. There rarely was, because Grimaldi Jr had become unemployable. His luck seemed to have changed in November 1832 when he was engaged at the Queen's Theatre at £4 a week, with an engagement as Clown at the Coburg to follow at Christmas. All hope ended when he died on 11 December, a month after his thirtieth birthday.

Wieland was back at Drury Lane for the Easter production *Anster Fair, or Michael Scott the Wizard* when he played Cheops an Egyptian mummy.[8]

In June, his wife Charlotte gave birth to a daughter they named Charlotte Elizabeth. Whether the mother died in childbirth or from an unrelated matter is not known, but the poor woman died not long afterwards at the age of twenty-five. George was thus left to care for a tiny baby who must have complicated his life, especially when taking work in the provinces.

Wieland was constantly working with engagements seamlessly following one another at both the major theatres. Drury Lane, instead of a pantomime, presented a New Grand Chivalric Entertainment *King Arthur and the Knights of the Round Table* with Wieland as Ulfo a Goblin Dwarf 'a demon with a good notion of character, and a vast deal of Grotesque agility'.[9]

> The most surprising feats are executed by Mr Wieland as Ulfo, the goblin dwarf, with an ease and precision which render posturing – in unskilful hands a repellant exhibition – absolutely attractive. But the talent of this pantomimist, in which he is superior even to the celebrated Mazurier, is not confined to mere muscular exertion. His ballet of action is strictly dramatic, and merited the liberal applause bestowed upon him, and his antics formed no inconsiderable portion of the amusement afforded by this gorgeous exhibition of chivalry.[10]

With E J Parsloe dead, plus critics hailing him as superior to the sainted deceased Mazurier, Wieland was now the pre-eminent purveyor of grotesques.

Early in February when George returned to his home near Regent Square after playing the Goblin in *King Arthur*, his housekeeper told him his daughter Charlotte had been very disturbed during the evening. Of course, George was now a widower. The woman had lifted the baby on three occasions and lulled her to sleep placing her back in her bed. George thought nothing much of this, settling to his supper when he heard a loud scream from Charlotte. Running to the bedroom, he lifted his child from the bed and discovered blood around her feet. Handing her to the housekeeper, who had also rushed up, George pulled back the sheets and discovered a huge rat. With great presence of mind he threw the bedclothes back to cover and trap the vermin which he was then able to destroy. The rat measured 16 inches and Charlotte's feet were both bitten. Dr Ramadge attended and expressed astonishment at the girl's escape, but pronounced her to be out of danger.

George was at Sadler's Wells in July, once again with *The Dumb Savoyard and his Monkey* complete with panoramic scenery of the Rhine journey. He also gave his Punch:

> The great lion of the night, however, was "the Wieland", whose personation of the *Polichinel Vampire* is an astonishing performance, and was never surpassed, if ever equalled by Mazurier himself. The house was crowded in every part.[11]

In September George was at the Gravesend Theatre giving his Marmazette and Punch. The last night of the season was for George's benefit when he gave *The Monkey Lover*, in which 'Wieland stands unrivalled in his personation of the monkey tribe.'[12] Wieland was now a star and, in spite of all his goblins and grotesques, still played monkey roles, in many cases being hailed as superior to Mazurier.

On 11 November 1835 George Wieland (widower) married Sarah Bradley (spinster). He was now twenty-four, his new wife a year older.

Back at Drury Lane for the 1835/36 panto *Whittington and His Cat; or Harlequin Lord Mayor of London* George was not the cat – that was played by a dog! Once again he was lavishly praised for his role of a monkey and again considered superior to the late Mazurier.

> Wieland has a monkey scene, which is rather lengthy, but which has not been excelled even by the renowned Mazurier. Wieland must have studied Landseer, or have been a constant frequenter of the Jardin des Plantes in Paris, or of the Zoological Gardens, to have acquired such an accurate imitation of the monkey tribe. The Regent's Park chimpanzee would have been in ecstasies had he been a witness to the scene at the toilette, where the monkey dresses himself as a female, after a model in a dress-maker's show-room. It was laughable in the extreme to hear the monkey playing on the violin the popular airs of the day, with occasional passages and *tours de force*, after the style of Paganini.[13]

In December 1836, came a new ballet starring Wieland called *The*

Devil on Two Sticks based on the 1707 novel *Le Diable Boiteux* of Alain-René Le Sage which, in those days, was a well-known story to most people. The ballet too proved very popular, with Wieland cast as Asmodeus, a grotesque magic imp who hobbled on crutches and flew through the air. Wieland brought the merry devil Asmodeus to life; constantly astonishing and making the audience laugh at the same time.[14]

At the end of the season Wieland presented a novel walking stick made to his own design to Willmot the prompter at Drury Lane. Made of American hickory, the top was contrived to hold an inkbottle, pen, penknife and pencil case, while the ferrule unscrewed to disclose a holder for paper, rubber and wafers. It was inscribed 'From the Devil to his friend John Willmot 1837'[15]

After the Drury Lane season closed, George went to Astley's where he performed a routine called *The Musical Monkey* that would indicate he was playing his violin again as well as re-donning his monkey skin. After a spell in *Punch's Budget; or the Metropolitan Vampire,* followed by *Punch's Vagaries*, his next monkey offering *The Shipwrecked Mariner; or Philip Quarl and his Domestic Ape* was a return to his earliest days as he had played Philip Quarl's ape 15 years previously.

A return to Drury Lane for the 1837/38 season saw Wieland reprising *The Devil on Two Sticks* before the debut of a new ballet *The Daughter of the Danube* in which Wieland's performance, playing yet another imp, was judged a masterpiece of comic humour and wonderful agility. 'We never saw anything of the sort, so good.'[16] The piece was inordinately popular with Wieland receiving heaps of plaudits – 'really a man of genius in his way.'[17]

George was also a father again as his second wife gave birth to George Bradley Wieland on 8 November 1837.

The 1837/38 pantomime was *Harlequin Magic Lantern; or the Witch of the Dropping Well* with Wieland as Jack O'Lantern. For the rest of the season Wieland was occupied ringing the changes on *The Devil on Two Sticks, The Daughter of the Danube* and *The Dumb Savoyard*. In many cases only one act would be performed. It seemed as though Drury Lane must use Wieland but had not enough new material to keep him occupied. When Wieland was not a simian variation, he was some sort of imp, devil or other grotesque; otherwise he imitated Mazurier by adopting the guise of Punchinello.

In the summer break, Wieland went to the English Opera House where he gave his Chimpanzee in *La Perouse*. This, the precursor of the monkey craze, was now over 35 years old but still a stand-by for man-monkeys desperately short of drama repertoire. When booked for a week at a provincial theatre, especially in a small town, it was necessary for the artiste to offer a change of programme for each of his appearances, and not all man-monkeys were versatile enough to play Punch in other routines, and display Gymnastic Exercises, Corpuscular Transfigurations or Eccentric Metamorphoses. Neither were all man-monkeys posture-masters i.e. contortionists, most were acrobats, or simply athletic actors.

Wieland played yet another devil role in *The Devil's Opera*:

The Devil (Wieland) ... does fly away with her, no doubt on the wings of love, and the scene closes upon the happy pair locked in each other's arms, the Devil burning with an intense flume from the fireworks. His whole performance is replete with humour, and the activity, grace, and agility he displays, render it both astonishing and unique.[18]

GEORGE WIELAND in
The Devil's Opera

On 9 September 1838, there was a farewell benefit for Barnes the old Pantaloon organised by George and James Parsloe the prompter at Covent Garden, both being committee men of the Theatrical Fund. Since having to appeal for himself when left with his brother's children to care for, Parsloe had busied himself in trying to have pantomime artists included in the fund. Whilst these artistes were quite willing to contribute in the same way as the actors, they were prohibited on professional grounds: 'because pantomimists have to undergo so much fatigue, and to encounter so much danger in their profession that they are sooner likely to become chargeable to the fund.'

James Barnes, formerly Grimaldi's Pantaloon, had been renowned

– a scene between the two 'being the acme of pantomime drollery'. He was now in dire poverty. Through age and infirmity he was no longer able to work and, as during his active career he was poorly paid, he had no savings to fall back on. His old colleague the Harlequin Tom Ellar was his closest friend, who on many occasions helped him out with small loans that both knew would never be repaid. It was George Wieland who found out the destitute Barnes, and set the wheels in motion to relieve the poor old chap's desperate condition.

Barnes was not able to perform at his own benefit, but the support he received from the active pantomimists of London and the fond memories of how the man used to be, engendered a good turn-out. He was led on by Wieland and Ellar who seated him centre stage in a chair while the current pantomimists in turn appeared in character and mimed their farewells.

JAMES BARNES in his heyday as Pantaloon to Grimaldi

The benefit was far too late. Barnes infirmity was principally caused by chronic starvation, the three days prior to the benefit he had not eaten, and was reduced to one calico shirt. He was too proud to beg, though there were always people willing to stand him drink. After the benefit, Ellar had him moved into a comfortable room and stayed with him, as Barnes would not let him out of his sight. With his recent bounty, Barnes ordered a new suit and a pair of crutches, but he was never to use them as he died only a month after his farewell benefit. The frail old man was actually only fifty years old.

The first new attraction in the 1838/39 season at Drury Lane was a ballet called *The Spirit of the Air* in which Wieland played the North Wind. His comic purpose was to keep intruders from his mistress and resorted to blowing them up with air, puffing them away, and freezing them with his icy breath. As usual Wieland's 'jumpings, caperings, and curvetings were exceedingly grotesque and truly comic.'[19]

Between eleven and twelve o'clock on 22 November, Messrs Gilbert and Wieland were enacting aerial spirits suspended by wires high above the stage when the wires snapped and they hurtled 20 feet to the stage below. Both were immediately carried off into the greenroom, apparently insensible with blood gushing from nose and mouth.

Gilbert, who hit the ground first, suffered internal bruising but remarkably no broken bones. Wieland, who landed on top of him, received a broken finger, two dislocated ribs, and severe bruising to arm and shoulder. Gilbert was soon able to walk about, but Wieland's ribs overlapped each other and, once restored to their correct alignment, he had to lie in a recumbent and quiescent position to give them time to heal.

In fact the indomitable dancers were considered well enough to return to work within a fortnight, appearing in the same play on 4 December. Gilbert, who was more hurt than at first thought, recovered via copious hot baths and the application of leeches, whereas Wieland, by being bound up and immobile plus 'the administration of the necessary internal and external remedies' was considered by his doctors to be fit enough to proceed. It was considered extremely fortunate that both men had been bled before leaving the theatre on the night of the accident. In those days bloodletting was considered an essential panacea for every disease and injury.

On the night the ballet resumed, the typically eclectic programme comprised Rossini's Grand Opera *William Tell*, followed by the American lion trainer Van Amburgh 'The Brute Tamer of Pompeii', ending with the ballet *Spirit of the Air*. Both the injured men were warmly greeted on their re-appearances, and the ballet went off with great *éclat* with the conclusion of the first act – where the accident had happened – omitted.

The 1838/39 pantomime was *Harlequin and Jack Frost* with Howell as Harlequin, Wieland as Clown. The critics proclaimed it as the first time Wieland had essayed Clown, which revealed a lot of short memories as he had taken the role six years previously, albeit not very successfully. This time the critics enthused about his playing:

> Wieland appeared for the first time as Clown. He is the best we have seen since the days of old Joey Grimaldi, and frequently reminded us of our old favourite.[20]
>
> ... the exquisite foolery of Wieland, who has made a decided hit

> in his newly-assumed character of Clown, and promises to restore the pantomimic days of *Mother Goose*.[21]

> Mr Wieland for the first time, appeared as Clown; and certainly, since the days of the elder Grimaldi, we have never seen his clownship so humorously supported. Wieland is not an imitator; he has a style of his own; he is indescribably ludicrous, but he does not excite your laughter by the old trick of face-making or of posture deformity. He incites you to laughter without distorting his features or twisting his limbs into unnatural positions. His success was complete.[22]

Incredibly, Wieland was now being hailed not merely as superior to Mazurier, but the best clown since the almost legendary Grimaldi.

Though one spectator was so alarmed in one scene where Clown is caught up in the revolving sails of a windmill, he wrote to a 'notes and queries' column to ask how old was Mr Wieland and does he whizz round the windmill in person? The reply said Mr W was at least thirty years of age, and it was a dummy figure that whizzes round.

The query may seem naive to us today, but not many people in those days realised that the members of the pantomime team of a theatre were often used as stunt men doubling for actors in straight plays where 'derring-do' was needed. Tom Ellar the well-known Harlequin raised this point when complaining that he and his cohorts were banned from membership of the Theatrical Fund.

George Wieland was the leading pantomimist of his generation and now hailed as the best Clown since Joseph Grimaldi. Essaying new roles as goblins, elves and devils, his performances as an ape became far fewer. As wonderful and prodigious as these roles were, they are outside our study so we can merely give them a nod as we pass by, briefly noting further performances of *The Devil on Two Sticks*, the new *The Little Hunchback* in which his antics 'are infinitely diverting; though he has no clownish humour, his comical gestiloquence is whimsical in the extreme'[23] and the return of *The Daughter of the Danube*.

In the summer break from the major London theatres Wieland toured the provinces cashing in on his success by performing non-stop everywhere, plus the minor London theatres like the Queen's where J S Grimaldi died, and the Royal in Whitechapel Road. In November, he went to Dublin where 'it was painful to see our national theatre degraded by the Bartlemy Fair mountebankism, now all the rage.' Though, having made this complaint, the *Dublin Morning Register* had to concede that the manager had booked the best of the buffoonery, and that he was the principal attraction. It also conceded he was a clever and extraordinary performer in his way, but it strongly objected to Wieland being given the honoured name of 'artiste'.

Wieland's opening play at Dublin was *Daughter of the Danube* and just before the close of the first act, he suffered a wound from a sword in the palm of his left hand during a phantom fight. He remained in Dublin several weeks going through several pieces from his standard repertory, and stayed on at Dublin for the pantomime *Harlequin and Peeping Tom*. This seems odd; in the light of his tremendous success as Clown at Drury Lane the previous year, one would have expected him to return to London to star at one of the two major theatres. One local comment was that Wieland was better as Peeping Tom in the opening, rather than Clown in the Harlequinade.

The Dublin public must have liked George better than the press as he stayed on after the pantomime again playing most of his repertory. Then back to England for more provincial engagements, including Manchester where 'his flexibility, muscular exertion, his hops, skips, and jumps, with his constant, inexhaustible humour, place him immeasurably before Grimaldi, Barnes or any other mime in England.'[24] As both these were now dead, one presumes it was intended to mean in their heyday! To rate Wieland above Grimaldi was very near to theatrical treason.

For the 1840/41 season Wieland signed up with the Adelphi theatre. This was one of the main minor theatres that had proliferated in recent years, and at one time it would have been seen as a comedown for a performer to move from a major to a minor theatre. However, the two major theatres were in the doldrums, legitimate drama was in crisis, and the managers of both had of late incorporated into their shows wire-walkers, performing lions, and so forth, the distinctions between the majors (legitimate drama) and the minors (melodrama and musical pieces) barely existing. In fact, the differences long held via the patent system inaugurated by Charles II had for many years been wearing very thin, to be finally abolished in 1843 putting all theatres on the same footing. Now the minor theatres could put on drama, legitimate actors were finding more opportunities throughout London. The two major theatres both with capacities exceeding 3000, were turning more to music, with Drury Lane giving itself over to promenade concerts.

Covent Garden, after the bankrupt management of Charles Mathews and his wife Madame Vestris, stood virtually unused for three years apart from brief lettings, orchestral concerts and, one year in place of the annual pantomime, an exhibition of curious shrubs and plants from around the world. So with no work at Covent Garden for Wieland, he looked elsewhere, finding four consecutive seasons at the Adelphi.

The first new item devised for him at the Adelphi was called *The Flip Flap Footman* which was

> an extravaganza for Mr Wieland, whose engagement is likely to be one of the hits of the season. The incidents will not bear sober telling, and altogether indescribable are the antics of Wieland. We wish he would not talk. Talking is quite beneath a man of his attainments.[25]

In his new billet, Wieland played as a comedy actor as well as a pantomimist thus eschewing the very talents that lifted him above the commonplace. When the pantomime *Harlequin and the Enchanted Fish* was staged, Wieland played Clown and the Harlequin was Tom Ellar.

Ellar, who had so recently helped his old friend Barnes, had been having a rough time himself, and it is a tribute to him that he shared what little he had with his chum. Ten years previously, he was attacked by theatrical papers for his slowness, but by 1836 Ellar, who was then 56, looked a decrepit old man, and in the wings it was painful to note the physical exhaustion which followed even his slightest exertion. Apparently a jealous cast-off mistress had administered a mercurial poison which had turned his face blue while enfeebling his frame.

TOM ELLAR in his heyday as Harlequin to Joe Grimaldi.

By 1839, Ellar was unable to get work anywhere, and even sacked from a low dive in Shoreditch where he danced one night, picking up a few half-pennies that had been thrown from the 'gods'. He was reduced to singing and dancing in pubs for pennies, and was arrested for performing in an unlicensed penny gaff. Thackeray wrote:

> Our Harlequin Ellar, prince of many of our enchanted islands, was at Bow Street the other day in his dirty, faded, tattered motley – after having well nigh starved in the streets, where

nobody would listen to his guitar. No one gave him a shilling to bless him: not one of us who owe him so much.[26]

Yates had then engaged Ellar for the pantomime at the Adelphi at four guineas a week and offered him an engagement for the following season. The decrepit Harlequin managed to accomplish the necessary 40 performances but that was his last flowering. Ellar died in 1842 aged sixty-two. Coincidentally, James Parsloe, the one-eyed prompter and champion of the Theatrical Fund, acted as prompter at the Adelphi from January to September 1840 so would have been there at the same time as Ellar and Wieland.

GEORGE WIELAND as the Spirit Oberkin in Hexen am Rhein.

The only time George Wieland played a monkey role during his four seasons at the Adelphi was from 4 October 1841 to 16 April 1842 when he played 66 performances as The Devil's Ape and the Spirit Oberkin in Hexen am Rhein.

Between his seasons at the Adelphi, George played an assortment of venues both in London and the provinces. At Sadler's Wells he reprised his renowned Monkey in The Dumb Savoyard and his Monkey with an actor as the Savoyard rather than an actress in a breeches role.

In March 1844 one of Wieland's children had an operation to cure a hare lip carried out by the celebrated surgeon Mr Liston in the exceptional and extraordinary short time of two and half minutes! Charlotte, George's daughter by his first wife, was now ten, and there were now three more children by Sarah his present wife – George Jr who was seven, Henrietta aged four, and the two-year-old John who was presumably the patient in the operation.

Wieland now signed up to be one of a new company at the City of London theatre where the 'new and spirited management' had assembled a motley crew of names from an assortment of other London theatres. The admission prices were very low – Boxes 2/-, Pit 1/-, Gallery 6d. These were half the standard prices at the Adelphi. Wieland gave his Imp in The Daughter of the Danube then at Whitsuntide went to the Surrey Theatre, south of the river.

His debut at this house was as the Sprite Zimmeir in *The Sprite of the Snow-Drift*

> in which the inimitable Wieland made his bow to a Surrey audience, and twisted and grimaced to their entire astonishment and satisfaction. This piece was well got up, and the scenery excellent. One scene in particular, in which a smiling corn field is in a moment covered with snow, at the bidding of the Snow Sprite, was much and deservedly applauded.[27]

Alfred Bunn, now in charge of Drury Lane, deciding that drama would be entirely eschewed, opened for the season with Grand Opera and Grand Ballet Companies featuring performers recruited from the capitals of Europe, and an orchestra augmented by players from the Philharmonic Concerts. Back on his old stamping ground, Wieland was among his old pantomime colleagues.

The format of the evenings was an opera followed by a ballet of action, such as *The Deserter of Naples* in which George played the Mazurier role of Simpkin.

That year's pantomime was *Puck's Pantomime; or Harlequin Robinson Crusoe* with George as Man Friday in the opening, and Harlequin in the Harlequinade with Howell as Pantaloon, and Tom Matthews as Clown forming a triumvirate comparable to the old Grimaldi trio. The opening night was packed and the only dissent was a scene sneering at baths and wash-houses for the poor which was decidedly hissed by the galleries.

In the autumn, Drury Lane opened again with a company very similar to the previous year, Bunn once again relying on opera and ballet, dragging out much the same attractions as the previous season. One new work was *The Princess That Was Changed Into A Deer* in which 'Mr Wieland was seen tumbling about'. This production was extremely poor and suffered heckling and barracking while in progress, with facetious remarks hurled by the audience. Lines like 'These senseless revels amuse me not' were greeted with cries of 'Here, here!' and when Harley was labouring to make a long speech funny, a wag called out 'You know it won't do, Harley.' The gaps in the audience's sallies were filled with ironic laughter, hisses and general mockery, with the performance becoming nothing more than a target for its wit.[28]

At Easter 1846, *La Perouse* was restaged with Wieland in the role of the Chimpanzee, causing one newspaper to comment it must have been a temporary fit of desperation on the part of the manager. The piece was 45 years old, Covent Garden first staging it in 1801 with

Master Menage. In 1825 it was brought out by Drury Lane to combat Mazurier at Covent Garden with the fourteen-year-old Wieland playing the Chimpanzee role, which he had been doing intermittently ever since.

> Not even the clever pantomime of Wieland as the real original monkey of the ballet—a miraculous monkey, gifted, as all stage monkeys have been since the days of Monsieur Gouffe, with the heart of a man and the mind of a philosopher—could relieve the intense tediousness and cumbrous absurdity of the piece. Unless it was revived as an especial insult to Easter Monday, its reproduction is a matter of very questionable policy. That it was not hissed off the stage, was probably owing to that respect which the good English people always feel for the wisdom of their ancestors; for the piece truly belongs to that class of dramas which were once to them a kind of dramatic gospel, and so was held sacred.[29]

It looks as though the old war horse had had its day, and not even the talents of George Wieland – the 'new Mazurier/Grimaldi' – could do much with it.

Drury Lane Theatre where George Wieland came to fame, and where he gave his last performances.

In his private life, some years previously George had become the landlord of a public house. This was the White Hart in Market Street, Oxford Market, which is no longer there but was situated just off Oxford Street near the present Oxford Circus – which was then called Regent Circus – the rebuilt area is now called Market Place. No doubt the experience of seeing colleagues dying in reduced circumstances encouraged him to provide a business for his retirement and a source of income in his old age. Presumably he was able to manage the pub with his wife's assistance and a few staff while he pursued his performing career. The couple's last child Sidney was born in 1846.

Alfred Bunn continued his exclusive opera and drama programme for the 1846/47 season, retaining mostly the same company. The pantomime was *Harlequin and St George and the Dragon* with Wieland as Harlequin, Matthews as Clown and Howell as Pantaloon.

> ... the introductory part was burdened by a very short dialogue of no merit, and, notwithstanding the rapidity of its action, was so confused and wanting in drollery as to draw down frequent busts of hissing. ... very unequivocal symptoms of displeasure and weariness were exhibited by the audience ... and the mythic personages seemed to be under the influence of the general drowsiness.[30]

It seems to have been a rather lacklustre affair. It is not surprising that Wieland was spiritless as he had been labouring under illness for the last two years, no longer reliant so much on his famous leaps and contortions. He had also suffered not infrequent accidents throughout his career.

He died on 6 November 1847 of 'rapid consumption' at the age of thirty-seven, having been on the stage for 30 years. Mazurier, J S Grimaldi, E J Parsloe and now George Wieland all died at an early age while still working; the Theatrical Fund would not have had to hand a penny to any of them.

As a performer of gnomes, imps and sprites Wieland had no equal, but for the theme of the present book he takes his place as an outstanding exponent of the art of the man-monkey, having first donned a skin at the age of ten, played in many monkey plays, but most of all created the role of Marmazette the Monkey in *The Dumb Savoyard and his Monkey*.

Chapter Seven
MONSIEUR GOUFFE

THE NAME OF GOUFFÉ has already been mentioned several times. Of all the man-monkeys that flourished in the past, without a doubt the most well-known, both in his own time and to history, is Monsieur Gouffe. Many people who have vaguely heard of 'Gouffe the Man-Monkey' assume he was unique, not realising that he was merely one of many. Gouffe flourished alongside Wieland, and died within a year of his rival. He was also a contemporary of E J Parsloe, Klischnigg, Martini and Harvey Leach.

The reasons for Gouffe's supremacy are not hard to find – he never played anything other than a monkey, whereas the Parsloe brothers, Wieland and their confrères also appeared in other roles, and their monkey life-span was more limited than Gouffe's. Neither was Gouffe attached to one theatre for regular seasons, but toured widely and non-stop year after year ensuring that he was seen in person by a great number, whereas the man-monkeys tied to major London theatres were known in the provinces mainly via reputation, or much more limited occasional appearances. And, most importantly, Gouffe was an acrobatic speciality act inserted into plays, rather than an actor or dancer adept at gymnastics.

Whereas E J Parsloe and George Wieland had first played as monkeys when they were still boys before the world had even heard of Mazurier, Gouffe was created especially to compete with the French ape in the craze of 1825 and kept working non-stop until 1846. His repertoire was limited, and it is likely that his monkey creation performed pretty much the same antics whichever play he was in. Gouffe was the forerunner of the man-monkey as a variety act.

There are many playbills, press advertisements and reviews of Gouffe as a professional performer, but an almost complete lack of material about Gouffe the man. We do not even know who he really was, as Gouffe, or Gouffé, was a name created for him by the prolific playwright and manager Charles Dibdin. Part of Gouffe's mystique is caused by the fact he publicised himself as 'Is he a man? Or is he an ape?' but judging by press comments one would have to be very naive to think he was a real animal. Although the performer does not seem to

have gone out of his way to conceal his identity or put on any kind of special off-stage persona, there arose a selection of ideas about his true self:
- 'Mons Gouffe, the man-monkey, was one of Ducrow's productions. His right name was Goff, and the bills of the day metamorphosed him into a Frenchman. He was a London cockney.' *Brown's History of the Circus*
- 'Gough, or Monsieur Gouffe, as he is foolishly enough called in the bills . . .' *Every Night Book*
- 'Sam Todd, originally a pot-boy, amused the customers of the house by climbing and running round ceilings, shelves, and every available place in tap-rooms, and imitating in a most natural manner monkey tricks, utterances, and habits.' *Old Drury Lane*
- 'he appeared with Monsieur Gouffe the man-monkey (previously known to Coppin as Mr Wilson the equilibrist) in an act that teamed Coppin as Fabrioletta Dunderhead with Gouffe's Jocko the Island Ape.' *The Multifarious Career of Coppin*
- 'Gouffé whose real name was Gough . . .' *Lincolnshire Chronicle 1846_02_12*
- 'a Portuguese'
- William G Knight in *A Major London 'Minor'* thought Gouffe was two different men.

It is necessary to cut through all these and similar rumours to get at the real man. As we proceed chronologically through his career (for there is little else to go by) we must do the best we can with the material we have available.

It will be recalled that when Mazurier set all Europe alight with his Jocko, it was 'copied' by many who had not even seen him. Charles Dibdin was, at the time, the manager of the Surrey Theatre, one of the three so-called 'transpontine houses' in close proximity across London's Waterloo Bridge. These theatres catered for a rapidly growing population of labouring folk housed in the area south of the river. They did not have an elevated sense of theatre, and revelled in melodramas, circuses and general buffoonery. Not many people of the upper classes or intelligentsia visited these theatres, except for a few slumming toffs.

Always on the look-out for novelties for his audience, Dibdin, who was an accomplished playwright with over 200 works to his name, decided that his customers deserved to see this new play about a clever ape. As there were no copyright restrictions at that time, English hacks would snatch at new French and German plays and hammer out an English version that may or not be a close translation. Quite often there would be plays of the same title swimming around London in several versions as produced by different authors.

CHARLES DIBDIN The Younger.
Manager of The Surrey Theatre
1824 – 1826 who invented
Monsieur Gouffe

So when this amazing new play and performer came to Dibdin's attention he had to write a version for his own theatre, calling it, as in the original, *Jocko; or The Ourang-Outang of Brazil*. The name orang-utan comes from the Malayan *orang* meaning person and *hutan* meaning forest, hence 'person of the forest' often rendered 'wild man of the woods' in English. The orang-utan is only found in the jungles of Borneo and Sumatra so hardly likely to be roaming on a remote desert island off Brazil.

However, since travellers in the previous century brought back descriptions, throughout the 18th century all great apes were known as orang-utan, which is somewhat better than the catch-all term of monkey. Dibdin, claiming he was the first in England to receive a copy of the play, produced it on 6 June 1825. In fact his brother Thomas also put on the play at Sadler's Wells commencing on the same date, with J S Grimaldi in the role of Jocko.

Of course, the Surrey did not have a performer of the ability required, so the part went to the resident ballet dancer and choreographer M Simon, who had the doubtful advantage of being a genuine Frenchman. He had been playing the part for several days with 'infinite *eclat*', which all came to a sudden stop on 13 June when, attempting a leap from one branch to another, he fell to the stage breaking his ankle, and was carried off home in a senseless state attended by Sir Charles Aldis.

So that was one down already, and the replacement was John Kirby, who often played Clown, and was a stalwart at the Surrey, coming and going for years before finally emigrating to the USA. Kirby took over the role for the first time on 20 June, presumably playing the part more sedately because as an added attraction on 4 July:

> In the course of the Piece, Mons. Gouffé from the Continent, will, as a Brazilian Ape, introduce extraordinary specimen of the

MONSIEUR GOUFFE

> Mimic and Gymnastic Arts, his first appearance at any Theatre in England.[1]

So the piece had, in effect, two apes – an acting one and a speciality acrobatic one. On the 7 July, one newspaper opined that the play was 'still high in the public estimation'. In light of what was to come, that was the underestimate of the decade!

On 11 July, Kirby gave way to Ridgway, who became the third player of Jocko in little more than a month. Tom Ridgway, the pantomime supremo at the Surrey, was one of the Brothers Ridgway, a trio of pantomimists who often furnished Clown, Harlequin and Pantaloon, keeping it in the family until going their separate ways.

So where did Dibdin find this talented Monsieur Gouffé from France? As related in a passing reference in William G Knight's *A Major London 'Minor' Theatre*, he auditioned and contracted one John Hornshaw, invented the name Gouffé and made Hornshaw a star. This Gouffé retired at some unknown date, and a new Gouffé called Sam Todd appeared in 1836. Mr Knight was basing this on paragraphs he had found in the memoirs of Charles Dibdin and Edward Stirling. Mr Knight was writing a history of the Surrey theatre so there was no cogent necessity to verify these paragraphs but, as a result, the story of two different men being Gouffé has gained purchase. What follows is my attempt to add clothes to John Hornshaw and dismiss Sam Todd altogether as a red herring. I do hope I am not creating a new myth!

The name Hornshaw was not common in London at that time, it seems to be a Yorkshire name. The man that Dibdin booked was John Finchet Hornshaw born on 29 November 1796 and baptised at St John in the East, Stepney on 6 June 1797. His parents were William and Sarah Hornshaw, the father's occupation described as 'gentleman'. There was also a William Hornshaw born 27 December 1794 who was baptised at the same place on the same day, presumably this being John's elder brother. On 28 December 1819, having gained the age of twenty-three, John Hornshaw married Elizabeth Saunders at St Bride, Fleet Street. This must have been the irresponsible alcoholic wife who was to cause him so much trouble later. Thus Hornshaw would have been in his twenty-ninth year when he was transformed by Dibdin into Monsieur Gouffé. Dibdin does not say why he chose this name, but it is a well enough known French name, being attached to a famous chef, a quality furniture emporium, a politician, and the victim of a notorious murder, to name but a few.

John Hornshaw had never worked in a theatre, and scraped a

living busking for pennies in the tap rooms of London. He was of unprepossessing appearance, being down-at-heel and scruffy, limping because one leg was shorter than the other. The interview took place in the scenery dock and, when asked what he could do, Horncastle leapt up on to the paint frame, bounding and leaping from one girder to another, jumped from great heights on to the floor, immediately springing up to the other side of the stage and so on. Moving into the auditorium, this odd but amazing man ran along the box and balcony fronts, and up and down the pilasters of the proscenium.

Immediately, Dibdin saw that the man would make an ideal Jocko in the place of Ridgway. However, when they tried to rehearse him in the role, it became clear he was only ten pence to the shilling. When given instructions, he gawped vacantly, whilst chomping at a lobster in his hand. Eventually, Hornshaw, or Gouffé as we must now call him, came up with his own method. Ridgway showed him each action required and Gouffé noted it in a little pad in a series of hieroglyphics featuring pin men. The plan was fruitless, Gouffe being 'slow of study'.

MONSIEUR GOUFFE'S *playbills were often ornamented with woodblock illustrations of incidents in the play.*

Realising that the real attraction for his regular customers was the clever acrobatic ape rather than the play, Dibdin asked Tom Ridgway to invent a one-act play with a suitable setting for what was in essence an extended variety act. Ridgway devised a pantomime ballet with the title *Juan Fernandez; or The Island Ape* which had its debut on 18 July 1825. This was imaginatively based on the real precursor of Robinson Crusoe, as Ridgway tipped his hat, calling his hero Lieutenant Selkirk and his island Juan Fernandez – the real names of the true castaway and his island upon which Defoe based his story.

Whereas E J Parsloe was originally a posture-master, and Wieland a peculiarly flexible dancer, Gouffé was an equilibrist – a balancer, who performs handstands, posing his body to defy the logic of weight and gravity, and perhaps walks the tightrope. This is different from a tumbler who rapidly somersaults, does handsprings, flip-flaps etc. The catchall term 'acrobat' was only just coming into use at that time. Although reviews often highly extol the skill and cleverness of the man-monkeys, actual detail of what actions they perform is scant.

All the more valuable, therefore, is this blow-by-blow description of the ballet-pantomime *Juan Fernandez; or The Island Ape* starring Gouffé as the ape. It must be noted that the reviewer, obviously considering himself above this sort of thing, sniffily condescends to the Surrey's working-class audience, but finally admits he is totally in awe at Gouffé's act.

A MAN-MONKEY.
(From a London Literary Journal.)

We were last week attracted to the Surrey Theatre by the marvels we had heard of M. Gouffe, a Frenchman, who performs the part of a large ape, in a ballet-pantomime affair called *The Island Ape*. Zoological accuracy obliges us to protest against the objectionable want of precision which the managers of this theatre exemplify either in their play-bills, or in the "simian" costume with which they have invested M Gouffe. They have altogether cashiered that magnificent appendage of the tail, with which the monkeys of Asia and South America perform all Capt Clias's *gymnastics* upon *the poles* of their native forests. Correctly speaking, therefore, M Gouffe is the representative of either an ape or a baboon, and *not* of a monkey. The doubt we have as to his preferable title to either of the two former shapes is not at all enlightened by the ambiguous declaration of the managers in their bill; who declare of the Frenchman, that his "accurate delineation of the *character*" is such as frequently to occasion doubt in the audience, whether he is a man or a monkey. The piece itself, which introduces this quadrumanous counterfeit to the good citizens of London, has little other merit to recommend it. The principal *human* character is a Lieut Selkirk, who makes believe to have been shipwrecked on a desert inland, and, by one of those happy contrivances which are so familiar to the management of the minor theatres, has written up, or rather painted, in large white letters over his cavern, "I have been on this desolate island for five years;" a piece of intelligence of which it is difficult to say whom it was meant to be addressed to, seeing that the whole society of the island (for anything to the contrary, at least, that is divulged to the audience) consists of two great ugly birds, who do not read at all in these climates; the monkey, who has learned almost all other tricks but reading, the Lieutenant himself, who must have been perfectly conscious of the fact without troubling himself to resort to such a memorandum, and two wild savages, or Indian chiefs as they are called (gentlemen named Karraboo and Pattaboo) who, most likely, were very accomplished men, but knew nothing of English. The principal object of Lieut Selkirk's introduction, appears to be in order to be pelted at by the ape, with some very clumsy imitations of tropical fruits; the birds are, of course, destined to be shot; and Karraboo and Pattaboo *club* together two or three bloodless combats for the edification of the pugnacious gallery. In the last scene, the intelligent Pattaboo is smitten with a sudden propensity for knocking Lieut Selkirk on the head. The Lieutenant, who has been represented in the early part of the piece to be very badly off for eatables and drinkables, is, of course, marvellously strong; the two savages, of course, set on him together; and just as he has killed one of them, and is about to balance the account by falling a victim to the other, that other "Boo" is, of course, shot through the head, exactly in the nick of time, by the leader of a party of Selkirk's comrades, who have, of course, landed on the same desolate inland, and come up, of course, at the precise instant of the Lieutenant's embarrassment. Pattaboo and Karraboo being thus demolished according to the most constitutional forms of melo-dramatic proceeding, the curtain drops, and all the world is content, including the monkey. And we now proceed to speak of that astonishing individual!

M.Gouffe (if it be really he, and not a monkey, which the managers have managed so slily to make a matter of uncertainty) is short, thin, and spare, even meagre in his make. One of his legs appears to us to be shorter than its fellow. He wears a mask sufficiently hideous to be very like his frightful prototype and is clothed with a light hirsute dress, that not unaptly represents the hairy covering of the *simia satyrus*, and other species of apes, as well as monkeys. Through this disguise, the most careful and even anxious observation will fail to detect any external developments or evidences of peculiar strength or muscular power. The outline of his arms and of his legs is apparently free from almost any undulation, and there is an absolute deficiency of the usual proportions that mark the superior and inferior parts of the trunk of the human body. The waist presents no sensible attenuation, the width over the shoulders, the thorax, and the pelvis, seems to be one common and unvaried measure. His arms are decidedly long, as compared to the rest of his stature, and his hands seem to partake of the elongation without being broad or *"patulous"* as the botanists have it. We have felt it necessary to be thus minute in the portrait we have endeavoured to give of M Gouffe's personal frame; because, among the many extraordinary properties that it possesses, none it more astonishing than the little apparent relation between the prodigious bodily powers which he displays, and the unpromising aspect of his small and slight figure. The first tricks that he performs, are so many admirable imitations of the habits and feats of the animal he undertakes to represent. He jumps upon and off a table with an incessant, rapid, whirling motion, that is really so like that velocity of action which one observes in these beasts, that the spectator becomes at last almost a convert to Mr Dibdin's doubts. Afterwards, he affects to find among the valuables of the shipwrecked Lieutenant's sea-chest several pewter pint pots (pardon the alliteration!) and having coquetted with and knocked about these measures in a very monkey fashion, he jumps upon two of them (with his fore feet, we had almost said) or, in plainer terms, he seizes a pint pot in each hand, and stretching his palms firmly over them, raises himself by degrees into an exact perpendicular, with his head downwards, and his feet in the air. Without returning to his feet, or planting them on the ground again, and supported only upon the same insecure and singular basis, he absolutely perambulates the stage, lifting up each hand and pint pot alternately, with the same motion as if they were hands and feet. He then increases the velocity of this motion, raising his arms as well as his hands alternately very high from the ground, and beating time, as if he were dancing, with wonderful precision and exactures. For his next feat, he constructs a pillar of five of these pewter pots, which describe a line about three feet in height ; he then places his hand upon the top, and gradually raising himself upon that single support, he elevates his feet from the ground, until his feet, his head, and his body are all in the same horizontal plane; and then, as if this wonderful achievement were not sufficiently marvellous, he strikes out with his feet and his disengaged arm in the manner of one who is swimming. So prodigious an exertion of strength, and so nice a preservation of the body in *equilibrio*, could only be surpassed, as we thought, by his next effort; which was successfully to repeat the same achievement, encumbered by the weight and impediment of a boy of twelve or fourteen, whom he bore upon his back! In the course of his performances he mimicked the chattering and squeaking (rather of the monkey than the ape) and the mischievous grinning of the original with hideous fidelity. There are some other habits of the same creature (who is, unhappily, still ignorant of the uses of small tooth combs) which M. Gouffe depicts with a degree of exactness as well as *enjouement* that he might, perhaps, omit, without impairing the spirit, whilst it certainly would not detract from the delicacy of his *more* or *less* than human imitation. At a subsequent period of the evening, he pretended to regard one of the stage-boxes with that sort of malign inquisitiveness that is so natural to the ape, and, making a sudden spring upon the exterior ledge of the box, he looked into it, to the almost fatal horror of a wandering dandy, who had strayed thither, and who flew from the dreadful apparition to the back of the box, exclaiming, "Oh! for God's sake, don't!" and "G—d d—n it, get out!" to the infinite amusement of everybody else in the house, and the vociferous delight of the inhuman company in the gallery, and the heartless audience in the pit. When M. Gouffe, in his brute capacity, had sufficiently amused himself by contemplating the terrors he had inspired in this young unfortunate, he darted off upon his astonishing race round the fronts of the boxes and gallery, from one side of the stage to the other; and this daring achievement he accomplished with no other support for his feet than that narrow ledge which runs all round the fronts, even with the bottom or flooring of the boxes; and sustaining himself as he runs, or rather leaps along, by the inconceivable rapidity with which his hands alternately beat the cushions, from which he manages, with great dexterity, to snatch up all the play-bills. In a little time he repeats this giddy race round the upper tier of boxes and the gallery, vaulting as he goes over and through the two parallel brass rails or rods which defend the front of the latter, with more than cat-like agility and serpentine suppleness, terrifying some of the spectators, delighting others, and astonishing all.

It is but justice to say, that he manifests throughout the most perfect good humour, and the greatest anxiety to entertain his audience. We have scarcely room left to allude to other feats which he displays, though they are, perhaps, in themselves, more difficult and amazing than those we have yet noticed. For example; grasping two wooden pegs, which project horizontally from an upright pole, but beyond which (if we were not mistaken) a *portion* of each hand entered a small socket, he raised himself until his whole body was at right angles with the pole, his feet representing the further point from it. He afterwards, inserting the toes of each foot into a small groove, sustained himself in a position exactly inverted, that is to say, his head was at such furthest point; and while his body was in this horizontal line, his arms described a perpendicular. A still more wonderful effort he exhibited, when, having with singular activity placed his feet in a slip-knot or noose at the end of a line, suspended from the top of the stage, he swung himself backwards and forwards, and twisted himself with that rapid whirling motion which can only be imagined by thinking of the impalement of a cockchafer at the end of a string; and then he positively raised himself, without any lateral supports whatever, and by an effort that seemed to one rather of volition than of bodily strength, until his face and body were in a sitting posture, and in a line opposite to, and parallel with, the perpendicular cord to which his feet were attached. This marvellous effort was, of course, but momentary; yet it certainly surpassed, as an exhibition of bodily power, anything, without exception, that we have ever witnessed. M Gouffe is, certainly, a worthy compeer for his extraordinary compatriots, M Davoust and the French Hercules. Perhaps the absence of any indication of bodily power renders M.G. the most extraordinary individual of the three.[2]

Few critics today would devote so much space to a one-act play. It will be noted that already the accent in Monsieur's name has been dropped, from now on he will be Gouffe. Also from this review we can make several deductions, firstly, the piece is executed entirely in mime with any necessary information conveyed by notices – the forerunners of silent film captions. Secondly, Gouffe – like all the man-monkeys – does not have a tail which would have got in the way of his acrobatics.

Thirdly, Gouffe was an out-and-out equilibrist. His act of doing a handstand grasping pewter pots and 'dancing', and performing a lateral balance with a boy on his back, twists and spins on a vertical rope and so on were in the repertoire of all such acrobats in those times as they still are today, and if Gouffe had been clad in the spangled tights of the era would not have been considered particularly remarkable. He did not walk on a tightrope, but the same balancing skills would be needed for his cavorting around the auditorium, and he was lithe enough to include leaps and springs in his routine.

Gouffe, or his director, gave an extra fillip to these audience-roaming antics by planting a stooge 'toff' in the stage box who squealed in fear when the monkey clambered in and gave great merriment to the crowd. It does not say so in the review, but Gouffe caused laughter and mayhem by swapping people's hats, kissing jolly women, and snaffling their sweets and fruit. This aspect probably swiftly developed over time.

Gouffe's unique selling point was that he did it all as a 'monkey'. By adding monkey-like antics to what probably had been his standard routine up to this point, he added a character. M Gouffe *was* the monkey.

Juan Fernandez; or The Island Ape was a tremendous hit and ran virtually every night until 19 November. Advertisements soon dropped the baffling *Juan Fernandez* and the piece was simply known as *The Island Ape*. Thus Gouffe was well established long before M Mazurier even arrived at Covent Garden, having preceded the foreigner by five months. Gouffe was one of the sights of London and full houses were the norm. People who had never crossed the river before flocked to see this wonderful prodigy at the Surrey.

Quite early on in Gouffe's season, the great and good were wending their way to the Surrey. The newspapers were eager to print the fact that in one week alone the following people had attended performances: Their Serene Highnesses the Duke and Prince of Brunswick and suite, Marquis of Hertford and party, Prince and Princess de Bourdeschi and party, Marquis de Espinard and party, Earl and Countess Foulett and party, Comte and Comtess San Martien and party, Lord and Lady Petre, Lords Molyneux and Kennedy, Sir James and Lady Langham and party, Sir Henry Rycroft and party, Sir Henry and Lady Strachan and party, Sir William and Lady Dobrie and party, the Hon John Sanson, The Hon Henry Rowley, the Hon Mrs Binning and family, Colonel Cooke, Colonel Roper, Colonel Jayson, the Hon Henry Rowley, General Pearson, Mr and Mrs Orby Hunter, Mr and Miss Knight, etc. etc.

It became a weekly feature to print in the newspapers a list of the eminent people who had visited the Surrey to see the remarkably talented M Gouffe.

The transpontine Surrey Theatre which became briefly fashionable during MONSIEUR GOUFFE'S six months sojourn.

On 21 November, Gouffe took his benefit and for the occasion appeared in 'Two Characters for the First Time'. This meant he actually played Jocko in *Jocko; or The Ourang Outang of Brazil* which he had taken so long to master, and his familiar *The Island Ape*.

One presumes that Jocko was now quite sedate, as Gouffe would need to keep his speciality gymnastic material for showing in the other piece.

During the week commencing 5 December, Gouffe performed in *Jocko; or The Ourang Outang of Brazil* introducing the 'principal features from *The Island Ape*'. The manager thus tacitly admitting his gymnastic stunts rather than the play were the audience pleasers.

In his memoirs, Charles Dibdin says that Mazurier came to see Gouffe at the Surrey and bore testimony to his merit. Of course Mazurier would have publicly praised a fellow performer in the same line, not to do so would have looked like sour grapes and lowered him in the esteem of the public. Dibdin added 'Mazurier could accomplish things which Gouffé could not; and *vice versa* but the latter possessed an advantage over the former, in his extraordinary strength.' As a perceptive critic noted, Mazurier's ape had an accurate and beautiful costume, an aura of superiority and elegance, a university educated ape, whereas Gouffe's costume was like a scruffy tramp ape, and his behaviour coarse rough-and-tumble, but he was much more entertaining and far more fun.

Preparations were then under way for the Christmas attraction:

> At this theatre, as a substitute for the usual Christmas pantomime, an entertainment was exhibited, called *Crom a Boo*, or *The Ape and the Infant*, which contributed to the amusement of a crowded house, by the introduction of a person in the character of *Jocko* who went through his part with considerable dexterity. The risible muscles of the audience were considerably relaxed when they saw him go round the boxes and exhibit his amatory propensities by attempting to kiss some coy ladies, and occasionally disengaging them from their cloaks and bonnets. This attempt to sustain the Mazurier rage, from its success, bids fair to be as attractive here, as it has been in another quarter.[3]

Gouffe was too good a draw to let go, but as he had been performing non-stop every night since his debut back in June, Dibdin thought his repertoire should be expanded as *The Island Ape* was getting a bit stale. In February, he devised *The Knight and his Page; or the Ape of the Forest*. In March, he adapted the serious and aged *Philip Quarl and His Monkey* into a melodramatic romance called *The Isolate and the Ape*. He wrote it on a Friday morning and it was performed on the following Monday. Not surprisingly, Dibdin was not pleased with the result, neither was the audience and it was only suffered for three performances. Dibdin's next attempt to provide something for his unusual star was a two-act romance called *The Savage Lovers*.

Gouffe, parting with Dibdin and the Surrey at the season end in March, immediately went to Dublin for Easter Week, with Gallott the stage-manager from the Surrey who staged *The Island Ape* for him.

> A Pantomime, consisting of one Scene, professing to be founded on Alexander Selkirk's well-known story, gave an opportunity for an exhibition of the powers of the Man Monkey. This individual is certainly very agile, wonderfully so at times, and in dress and chattering closely resembles his great original. His feats, which were prolonged to a considerable length, appeared to ravish the senses of the groundlings. Indeed it is but fair to say, that his performance, in which there was nothing so antic or grotesque as to offend delicacy, seemed to be applauded in every part of the House. There was a well-conceived, though clumsily painted, Sea Scene used in this entertainment.[4]

Thus Gouffe started his peregrinations round the provinces, appearing for limited periods as a special star guest attraction. As these went on for years there is little point in giving a blow-by-blow account even if that were possible. We shall dip in and out when there is something of special interest.

Birmingham (July 1826) had little foreknowledge of Gouffe, but decided he was one of the most curious and perfect specimens of mimicry ever exhibited, and the excellence of his performance totally eclipsed the efforts of his great rival Mazurier.[5]

In Grantham (March 1827) Gouffe was invited to astonish some fashionable visitants at the noble residence of the Duke of Rutland, and also to exhibit his skill at Belvoir Castle.[6]

Gouffe had added some new stunts to his act including putting his head in a rope noose and swinging from the gallery to the stage. In October 1827, he came a cropper. It was reported thus:

> Monsieur Gouffe lately met with an accident at the Leicester theatre, which nearly proved fatal. He was swinging by his neck on a rope, from the back of the gallery when, owing to a sudden jerk, the sling by which he was suspended slipped from its position and when he reached the stage he was so far exhausted, as to cause the greatest alarm. He however recovered. [The real name of M Gouffe is Gough; he is an Englishman, and was originally a shoemaker.][7]

In April 1828, Gouffe went before magistrates to make a complaint

against his wife. He said she was an incorrigible drunkard who broke the furniture and crockery in temper, and nightly took other men home to his bed, in consequence of which she had contracted a loathsome disease. Mr Hone the magistrate pointed out that he had married 'for better or for worse' and could not offer assistance. His only remedy was to divorce her if he could prove he had valid grounds. Gouffe said he had the strongest grounds of any man in England but it was very expensive following that process of law. Mr Hone told him his only other remedy would be by allowing her separate maintenance to which Gouffe replied that would be his greatest joy but she refused to leave him, sticking as close to him as the shirt on his back. When he caught her in bed with a big fellow, and threatened to turn her out, she said she would hawk periwinkles round the bars nearest the theatre telling everybody she was the wife of Gouffe the famous performer.

The poor fellow's anger had come to a head when he lost a £20 a week contract at Drury Lane through the noisome drunkenness of her carryings on.

Presumably, he abandoned her at home when he went on his endless forays into the provinces. He had inordinate pulling power and many theatres did their best business for years on the nights he appeared. However, critics in more upright areas were often very grudging in their own responses, as at Bury St Edmunds:

> ... curious as an instance of muscular strength and elasticity, which would have done honour to a fairground booth; but what is the dramatic critic to make of it? How is he to describe the twirls and rolls and leaps and postures of a man in a hairy skin, and who wanted only the tail and a *little difference in the head*, to be a perfect ape? But all this is a sad degradation of the stage.[8]

The dig about a difference in the head is clearly aimed at the fact that Gouffe was 'not all there', so it must have been widely known. Several stories grew up around this odd man with the half-witted manners and conversation, and it is not known which are apocryphal. The following anecdote does have a ring of truth, although Wallett the famous clown known as the Queen's Jester tells a similar tale about himself as an unknown playing the man-monkey. Gouffe was very proud of his dying scene at the end of Jocko, and at one performance in a provincial theatre he was put out by the fact that the orchestra did not start playing his dying music. Hoping that they would take up the cue, he gave several nods and winks to the musical director which were all ignored. Eventually, he crawled forward, hung over the footlights and said 'I say, you mister, why don't you play something sollum, don't you see hi'm going to die?'⁹

In order to stay for several days or weeks at a venue, Gouffe had to have a repertory of plays. His stand-bys were *The Island Ape, Jocko the Brazilian Ape, La Perouse,* and *Jack Robinson & His Monkey,* plus, of course, his extended act which when not partly incorporated into a play was presented as a stand-alone attraction. The titles were often mangled on playbills and press adverts so it is never really precise as to what the audience was actually seeing. It did not seem to matter, as all were entranced simply by what was then considered a life-like portrayal. It was not to be expected that Gouffe would differentiate his various simians any more than the audience, and his monkey, ape, orang-utan, and chimpanzee acted identically in the same hairy skin. But it was certainly impressive to the people of his time and, even after five years, when the dead Mazurier was but a distant memory, his performances were still being dragged up to be belaboured with the superiority of Gouffe:

> Monsieur Gouffe . . . is here, astonishing every one with his agility and wonderful strength of muscle. His performance certainly is more natural than Mazurier's, and his feats more extraordinary. Unrivalled as he now is, we think no one could have studied the nature of monkeys more accurately: he has their manner – their squeak (which Mazurier had not); and his monkey's dying scene, without ape-ing Kean, is certainly as good a piece of pantomime-acting as the other's Richard.¹⁰

In August 1829, Gouffe was engaged for a series of some 30 performances including *The Monkey of Arragon* and *Quadrupeds* as well as his familiar repertoire already noted. This was at the West London – the same theatre to be re-named the Queen's – where J S Grimaldi was to breathe his last. In March 1830, Gouffe played a season at the Royal Coburg, the rival house to the Surrey which launched him to fame. The manager was Davidge, later to manage the Surrey. Gouffe was now advertised as making a descent from the gallery to the stage, suspended by only three fingers and holding two flags, followed by a second descent, suspended by his neck, supporting a boy, and waving two flags.

This took place at the beginning of the show and was followed by three assorted plays, culminating in Gouffe in a new ballet pantomime *The Baboon of Paraguay*. In the Easter programme, Gouffe played Sapajou in *Easter Fair; or the Monkey and the Murder*. He must have done a lot of furious scribbling in his pin-man notebook because yet another new piece followed – *The Wanderow of Malabar*. This monkey is usually about two feet high and has very black hair with a long white beard. I wonder if Gouffe changed his monkey suit accordingly?

In May, Gouffe had moved to the Royal Pavilion in Whitechapel where he adopted the guise of yet another simian. This time he was *The Mandrill; or the African Ape*. During this contract, his wife was causing more trouble. She was hauled up before Mr Hone for being drunk and disorderly in the middle of the Waterloo Road. A constable had seen her dancing and capering about, hatless and hair flowing wild, her dress so disordered that he feared her petticoats would fall down exposing her person to mockery as she was surrounded by an amused crowd of bystanders. The constable, failing in his

This stunt by a later monkey performer was very similar to GOUFFE'S rope descent by the neck. In this version the artiste is gripping a pulley in his teeth rather than a neck noose. Illustrated coloured poster 1893.

attempts to persuade her to return quietly to her home, finally thought he must intervene when, attempting a somersault, she fell on her face in the gravel. Her frogmarch to jail was followed by a crowd of 200 people. It transpired that she habitually swigged large measures of gin and beer, and had already spent five nights in jail during the past week.

Mr Hone said there was little doubt that Mrs Gouffe was addicted to liquor, but it was her husband's duty to afford her assistance. Mrs Gouffe agreed she was an alcoholic, and was separated from her husband but 'was still virtuous'. The magistrate said he would discharge her but she must go to the parish officers and apply for relief. They would ensure that her husband would maintain her, or else he would go to jail.

Gouffe had now moved to Sadler's Wells for two weeks where he gave his Mushapug in *Jack Robinson*. His competition there included Chabert the Fire King, and Mons Petit, the French Hercules. Both were genuine French performers – Chabert was a fire-eater but his big thing was standing in an oven being heated to 600 degrees with a steak and a leg of lamb, stepping out with the meat duly cooked and himself unharmed.

Gouffe was back at the Coburg in 1831 with another variation *Pitcairn's Island; or the Mutineers of the Bounty*. Times were changing in the London theatre and although the two patent houses of Drury Lane and Covent Garden were supposed to have exclusive rights to legitimate drama, those regulations had long been worn away and, although not officially abolished until 1843, actors of the stature of Edmund Kean had been appearing at the minor theatres for some time. It was not at all unusual for a tragedy such as *King Lear* to be followed by Mons Gouffe in *Jack Robinson and his Monkey* as happened at the Coburg.

Hornshaw/Gouffe did not retire. The reason he disappeared from the English theatre is that he spent fully four years in America. In July 1831, Stephen Price the American impresario – no longer manager of Drury Lane but a leading promoter in USA – visited England to sign up viable attractions for the USA. One of them was Mons Gouffe. He arrived at Boston on 25 November off the ship *John A Bates*. His name on the passenger list was given as John H Gouffe – the H possibly standing for Hornshaw?

Gouffe made his debut on 29 November 1831 at the Tremont Theatre, Boston as Mushapug in *Jack Robinson and his Monkey*. His New York debut was on 13 December at the Bowery Theatre in *The Island Ape*, and he hit Philadelphia on 2 January 1832 in the same play. As we have seen, E J Parsloe made his ill-fated American debut at New York's Bowery Theatre in February 1832. Surely the two men must have met? Or did they deliberately avoid each other as rivals? We will never know, but it appears that poor Parsloe died without the

STEPHEN PRICE
American impresario
and ex-Manager of
Drury Lane 1826 - 1830

comfort of friends or colleagues.

Now here is a mystery – we are told in *Amphitheatres and Circuses* that Mons Gouffe had a wife who made her first appearance on January 24 at the Camp Street Theatre in New Orleans playing the role of Mysa in *Jocko, the Brazilian Ape*. He must have been relieved to leave his actual wife pouring gin down her throat in London. This may even be the reason he decided to flee to the USA. He certainly would not have taken her with him, so the Mrs Gouffe who popped up in America was probably a recently acquired paramour, and was most likely an actress.

E J Parsloe's brother C T Parsloe, who emigrated to the USA the year before either his brother or Gouffe appeared there, soon got established and by 1836 he was no longer playing the monkey business, and when M and Mme Gouffe appeared at his theatre he was content to let the expert play the monkey roles while he merely played supporting ones. The fact that Gouffe remained four years in America is a tribute to his popularity, especially as he had much competition, America having gone 'monkey mad'. In the States, Gabriel Ravel was considered the 'top banana' of all the imported man-monkeys, and Master Blanchard was the most prominent up-and-coming indigenous one. Gabriel Ravel who first appeared as part of the Ravel family troupe, broke away to form his own show comprising the Martinetti family of pantomimists headed by himself. This caused a rift as Gabriel still called his show the Ravel Family, thus two separate troupes toured America under the same name.

GABRIEL RAVEL
1810 – 1882
The natural successor to Mazurier

After Gouffe's long absence in the USA during which his subsequent publicity claimed he was witnessed by crowded audiences at every theatre on the vast Continent of America, he returned to his home country and carried on his professional business exactly as before. In October 1836, he returned to the Surrey, the theatre that had first promoted him, which was now managed by George Bolwell Davidge. His repertory was just the same as previously, the only change being his 'wife' played Eliza in *Pitcairn's Island* and Mysa in *Jocko*.

At Liverpool he was described as the man-monkey *par excellence*

On his return from the USA, GOUFFE was extensively touring Britain. Typical playbill from Margate 10 August 1837.

but that his face was now made up all red and not as it used to be.

In Sheffield, for his benefit he offered *The Two Monkeys* with himself and 'the Infant Gouffe - his first and only appearance'. The obvious inference here is that 'Mrs Gouffe' had presented him with a child during his American sojourn, and for the occasion he had dressed up his toddler. However, in King's Lynn he repeated this at his benefit there, the newspaper describing his son as 'a youth about nine years old'. This would seem to indicate that the relationship had started some time before he departed for the USA, unless the son was a gift from the authentic alcoholic Mrs Gouffe. Possibly the youth was no relation, being the son of his paramour or an apprentice.

Pavilion Theatre

On THURSDAY, March 9th, 1837 the performances will commence with the popular Drama, called

KING LEAR

Kent..Mr.HESLOP. Cornwall..Mr.BRADSHAW. Glo'ster..Mr.SAKER.
Albany..Mr.THOMPSON. Edmund..Mr.LAWS King Lear..Mr.ELTON
Edgar..Mr.GREEN. Oswald..Mr.PEDDIE.
Goneril..Mrs.DANSON Cordelia..Miss STILSBURY Regan..Mrs.SAKER

After the first piece on THURSDAY and FRIDAY, the admired Drama of

JOCKO.

Jocko (the Brazilian Ape) Mons GOUFFE. Marco (an Overseer)...Mr.SAKER
Fabrioletta (his Son)..Mr.W.West Governor of the Province..Mr.BRADSHAW
Julian (his Son)..Miss Norman
Lauretta (the Governor's Daughter)..Miss STILSBURY
Mysa (Her female Slave)..Miss Cooper

On SATURDAY after the first piece, a new Extravaganza, called

TWO MONKEYS
Or JOCKO and his SON

Jocko the Elder, Mons. GOUFFE. Jocko the juvenile, Master GOUFFE
Other characters by Messrs. PAYNE, SHOARD, SAKER, PEDDIE, Miss
Stilsbury and Mrs Gaskell

---

*On his return from the USA, GOUFFE started appearing with his son.
Playbill Pavilion Theatre, London 9 March 1837 (Detail)*

To add to the difficulties of sorting out Gouffe's private life, on 21 November 1838 John Finchet Hornshaw, widower, married a spinster called Phoebe Girdler. His rank or profession was given as Comedian, that of his father solicitor. The term 'comedian' was the current overall term for any stage player, whether man or woman. I have not been able to find any actress, singer or dancer called Girdler, so it has not been possible to further identify this lady and ascertain if she is the same Mrs Gouffe billed as supporting Mons Gouffe.

Gouffe's son started appearing more often as the Norton Folgate theatre advertised 'a monkey piece for old and young Gouffe' called *The Web of Fate*. This new play was also performed at the City of London theatre during which 'Mons Gouffe and his Infant Son, will personate a Man-fly, a Baboon, a Spider and a Monkey'.

At Taunton the local newspaper thought it in the public's interest to inform its readers:

> The Theatre opened with Mr. Davis's Company, reinforced by M Gouffe's *monkeyfied* performance. The agility and animal adaptation of this exhibitor to the character he assumes is very surprising; and the more so, since, off the boards, M Gouffe, as he calls himself, though an Englishman, is unhappily labouring under a deformed organization, apparently quite inconsistent with his stage adroitness. The House has been extremely well attended.[11]

In March 1839, Gouffe was hired to appear in Ryan's Royal Amphitheatre in Birmingham presenting *Jocko, or the Brazilian Ape*. Ryan was an equestrian and his show was basically a circus. Also on the bill was the Original Gnome Fly. We shall be looking at this gentleman a little later for he too was a man-monkey. As will be seen, Gouffe was inspired to take the role of a fly himself, or to phrase it in the language of variety artistes: 'He nicked my act!' We saw that Gouffe or his son played a man-fly in *The Web of Fate*.

Gouffe regularly returned to the Surrey with his constant repertory of pieces. The residents south of the river must have regarded going to the local theatre to see Gouffe as Jocko as an annual autumnal event. After his season there, in the New Year he appeared at the Garrick Theatre in Whitechapel. He had added to his repertory 'Mons Gouffe will introduce his wonderful feats as the GNOME FLY'.

Unlike his contemporaries E J Parsloe and George Wieland, who played the major theatres in London and provinces, Gouffe worked anywhere. By the 1840s legitimate theatre was really in the doldrums with even the biggest stars unable to pull in the audiences. London and its environs had minor theatres springing up all over, and music halls were taking over from the drama. Country theatres that had formerly opened for several weeks of regular seasons of plays by a resident company were now functioning on an *ad hoc* basis, and a manager would risk taking on a theatre for a month or so, booking anything that he thought would attract. Gouffe was an ideal novelty as he ostensibly appeared as an actor in a play, though it was his monkey acrobatic antics more than his dying scene *à la* Edmund Kean that the public wanted.

On 18 November 1840, at the Victoria Theatre, Gouffe once again nearly hanged himself, and were it not for two of the company rushing forward to cut him down, he would likely have lost his life, being totally insensible when rescued.

In 1841, Gouffe re-visited many of his former triumphs – Sadler's Wells which was quiet at first but packed after half-price; Cambridge where the press thought his real name was Gough and his antics out of place in a legitimate theatre whatever they may be at Stourbridge fair; and Dublin where Coppin played Fabrioletto in *Jocko* and claimed he knew Gouffe when he was an equilibrist called Mr Wilson. In 1842, a playbill for Inverness introduced another piece *The Ourang Outang; or the Monkey and His Double*.

Gouffe also started appearing in outdoor venues – in Dublin at the Rotundo Gardens as *The Runaway Brazilian Ape* scrambling among the trees on suspended ropes; Hull Zoological Gardens had M Gouffe's Terrific Descent, and the Zoological Gardens at Liverpool where the management tried to put an educational slant to his stunts:

> MONSIEUR GOUFFE
> THE INIMITABLE PROFESSOR OF
> ANIMAL PORTRAITURE!
> Whose distinction of character between the wild and domesticated state of the Ourang Outang has been considered by Naturalists and thousands of delighted spectators the most correct representation in the capacities of Man.
>
> Great amusement may be anticipated from Mons Gouffe who will doubtlessly play such "fantastic Tricks" as will not only make his rivals weep, but declare in the climax of a monkey's grief that their "occupation's gone." We Understand Monsieur will commence his grotesque performances in the cage allotted for those animals, surrounded by a multitude of astonished pugs, leap with indescribable celerity through the enclosure and exhibit a series of humorous hair-breadth 'escapes' among the trees and various erections with which the gardens abound. After numerous pranks, characteristic of the eccentric original, he will ascend to a platform, erected for the purpose and portray his inimitable scene the death of Jocko. The exhibition will prove highly amusing from the fact that the place possesses unusual facilities for the

exercise of this gentleman's peculiar talents, as they will be seen to greater advantage than within the confined space of a theatre.[12]

Work at outdoor galas was gradually coming in as a lucrative source for many acrobats of the aerial variety. Many of the small country theatres were ceasing operations altogether, the buildings being converted to other uses. By 1850 most of the country theatres had gone. The Victorian era had ushered in many changes in life-style, scientific curiosity was popular among the rising middle-class and attending lectures was displacing a night at the theatre. This paragraph sums it up:

> There was a time when Ulverston was noted for its Theatre, when each night the house was crowded to an extreme, by persons from different parts of the country, as well as the town itself. But a great change has now taken place, and Mons Gouffe, the Man Monkey, along with his brother comedians, have been performing, for some time, to little more than bare walls. Mons Gouffe, in the capacity of a monkey, is an extraordinary person. He occasionally astonishes the few who visit him by walking on the ceiling with his head downwards, with many similar feats, which he performs with great agility. The other performances are very interesting to all who delight in dramatic compositions.[13]

Theatre work was now only to be found in the industrial towns, and Gouffe, to keep on working, had to diversify. We now find him at circuses, zoos, pleasure gardens, and so on, as well as theatres. The point arises – did he need to keep on working? He must have made a small fortune in the 18 years of constant toil. Soon after Charles Dibdin first discovered him back in 1825 he was earning large sums and 'has long starred it about, at provincial theatres, with his white hat and gold rings, and travelling attendant.' Gouffe's £50 a week days may be over, but there were long years when he was on top money. Why did he not retire at his ease? It looks as though theatre managers were now resorting to a hard sell, when once the name Gouffe alone, in large type, was enough to draw the crowds.

> The celebrated MAN-MONKEY, MONSR GOUFFE, who will make his First Appearance in a Melo-Dramatic Romance entitled *JOCKO! The Brazilian Ape*. The extraordinary Performance of this inimitable man during his engagements at the Principal Theatres in London drew forth the admiration of enlightened and judicious audiences for upwards of Three Hundred Nights. His Personation of the character was considered by the Public, and the Press of London, to be the finest effort of Dramatic Genius ever attempted; the Dying Scene of the Tyrant

> Richard, or the Jealous Moor of Shakespeare, represented so admirably by the late Edmund Kean, or the immortal Garrick, never made a deeper impression on the Public than did the Dying Scene in *Jocko, or the Brazilian Ape,* a piece produced at the London Theatres, to show the peculiar abilities of Mons Gouffe. No person can have the least idea of the character unless they witness his Performance.[14]

Did the Leeds audiences fall for this eulogy? The press did not:

> During the latter part the week, the province of the legitimate drama has been invaded by an uncouth visitant, – Monsieur Gouffe, the man-monkey – whose ludicrous and remarkable eccentricities have afforded amusement, certainly very inferior in quality, though perhaps more than equal in quantity; to that derived from the performances we have before noticed.[15]

and at Gainsborough:

> Mons Gouffe took his farewell of Gainsborough in the play of *Jack Robinson and his Monkey.* As this was announced for the benefit of Mons Gouffe, it was naturally thought by the admirers of the ludicrous, that all the physical energies of which his nature was capable would be brought forth on this occasion to produce, if possible, additional *éclat* in playing his peculiarly "fantastic tricks." The exhibition, however, turned out a poor one, and gave evident dissatisfaction.[16]

In 1844, Gouffe appeared in Cork in a new piece called *The Nondescript of the East* with Madame Gouffe in the role of Mysie. As the character sounds akin to Mysa in *Jocko*, the play may also be a mere variation of one already in his repertoire. Back in London at the Pavilion Theatre in Whitechapel for the first time for eight years, Gouffe offered his entire repertoire including '*The Return of Perouse* in which he will take his terrific flight round the gallery.'[17] There is no evidence that Mrs or Master Gouffe appeared with him.

In 1845, Gouffe once more toured round the East Anglia circuit, finally ending the year at Gravesend where he performed his familiar repertoire. It was evident to all that he could not continue performing much longer and these were his last performances. Gravesend was a ghoulishly prophetic label as he died in his forty-ninth year at Charing Cross Hospital and was buried on 7 February 1846. His address was the workhouse.

Questions remain that may never be solved. Did he really almost die, by hanging himself, on more than one occasion? There are at least

> **Mons. Gouffe's Wonderful Feats.**
> *On the Bamboo Tree and the Rope!*
> CONCLUDING WITH
> **HANGING HIMSELF by the NECK!**
> (A Feat that is acknowledged to surpass any thing ever attempted in this Country.)

Although age and exertion were taking their toll, GOUFFE re-visited many of his previous haunts repeating all his extensive repertoire including the hanging routine which was obviously fraught with danger. Playbill New Royal Pavilion 2 September 1844 (Detail)

three recorded occasions when he seemed to have strangled himself to insensibility yet survived. This was discussed in an article by Dr R B Tracy in *Popular Science Monthly* of July 1878:

> Hanging for Amusement.
> Two remarkable examples are on record of persons who allowed themselves to be hung for the entertainment of an audience. An account of one of them is given in the London Lancet of April 17, 1847. The man's real name was John Hornshaw, but he performed throughout England under the high-sounding title of M Gouffe. He was an athlete, and among other feats it was customary with him to exhibit the process of hanging. In this performance he relied for security on the strength of the muscles of the throat and neck alone. He had a rope with a fixed knot that would not slip, and passed both ends of the loop up behind one ear. The whole act was so adroitly managed that he prevented any pressure of the rope upon the windpipe or the jugular vein, and could even sustain a weight of 120 pounds in addition to that of his own body. On three separate occasions Hornshaw mismanaged the rope and became unconscious, but was, luckily, rescued each time. Dr Chowne, who writes the account, says truly: It cannot be doubted that as far as sensation and consciousness are concerned, Hornshaw passed through the whole ordeal of dying; and had he been permitted to remain hanging until actually dead he would have passed out

of existence without further knowledge of his misery. Hornshaw said, not with particular reference to any of the accidents, but in speaking of his performances collectively, that he could recollect nothing which happened to him after the rope tightened, and that he lost his senses all at once. The moment the rope got in the wrong place he felt the change and could not breathe; felt as if he would like to loosen himself, but never thought of using his hands. He experienced the heaviness of legs and arms mentioned by others who have been half-hung and then rescued, and the rattling sound in his ears, but never saw sparks of light, which are the usual phenomenon.

Two other questions are also intriguing: How idiotic was he? And what happened to his money?

When Charles Dibdin discovered Hornshaw and turned him into Gouffe he described him as 'could hardly speak intelligibly, indeed he scarcely seemed to possess his intellects thoroughly. . . . So idiotic did he appear . . . he could understand nothing'. A Sussex newspaper said 'His half-witted manners and conversation, would lead to the belief he was almost an idiot.' Stirling recounts this anecdote in his memoirs:

> Gouffe, a coarse, uneducated fellow, fell deeply in love with Miss Tree. Down our monkey (dressed to go on) threw himself at her feet.
>
> "I likes you, miss, yes, I does, better than nothing else in the world. I'll marry ye, if ye likes. Mind, I ain't always a monkey; I earns lots o money, fifty and sixty puns a week: you shall have it all, goold real earrings, saton gownds, an a one oss shay to ride up and down in."
>
> Miss Tree, perfectly astounded at this odd declaration, laughingly declined Monsieur's liberal offer, preferring Charles Kean to a man-monkey.
>
> Gouffe unfortunately found a lady who did listen to his 'goold' and 'satons', and that to his cost. She spent his money, and when the poor monkey's attraction ceased, eloped, and left him to die in a workhouse.

As in most theatrical memoirs of the time, the author is no help in dating his events. He says that this incident happened when he was manager at Birmingham, after Davidge had booked 'the new Gouffe' at the Surrey. This would place the event between Gouffe's return from America in 1836 and his second marriage in 1838. Ellen Tree did not marry Charles Kean until 1842. As Stirling is the author who perpetrated the myth that this was Sam Todd, a Gouffe reincarnation, probably the entire tale can be dismissed as a fiction.

Though it could well be true that the second Mrs Gouffe married him for his money, and she may well have eloped, as after Gouffe's death 'Phoebe Agatha Hornshaw or Girdler' married one John Brumhall on 7 November 1847.

One further intriguing point arises regarding Gouffe's two marriages. In an age when many illiterate people made a cross on legal papers, for a man who could not read or write, he wrote a strong bold signature on both marriage documents.

Chapter Eight
EDWARD KLISCHNIGG

EDWARD KLISCHNIGG'S FAMILY hailed from Austria though he was born in London on 12 October 1812, or possibly 1813. His parentage is unknown, and he himself found it expedient not to elaborate on his antecedents. One story has him taken in a school party to see a pantomime, and being so impressed with the antics of the acrobatic Harlequinade, the next day he entered his classroom by leaping through a window, subsequently leaving the same way. Being dismissed for these antics, his family moved to France where he trained as an acrobat. Another rumour says he served as a sailor, thereby gaining his astonishing agility. He must have been a very young sailor for this to be true as he appeared on the London stage at an early age. The most likely explanation for his English birth is that at least one parent was a circus performer who took up residence in England for a period.

Klischnigg is very likely to have been 'The Young German' at the Olympic theatre in the 1825/26 pantomime *Harlequin & Golden Eyes* in which he gave 'some excellent imitations of Mazurier'. He would have been no more than twelve or thirteen at the time.

EDWARD KLISCHNIGG

In June 1829, Klischnigg (now sixteen or seventeen) was at the Coburg theatre billed as 'The Wonderful Performance of the young German Gymnasiast Mynherr Von Klischnig'. He stayed for several weeks during which he also appeared in 'a novel and splendid masquerade' held at the Drury Lane theatre on 15 June 1829 where 'Mynheer Von Klishnig' made several appearances throughout the evening in different characters. He also presented a 'Grand Fantoccini'. These were usually Italian trick string puppets akin to the skeleton mentioned in an earlier chapter, though in this case it could possibly be that Klischnigg himself dressed as puppets in the manner that Mazurier acted as Punch.

EDWARD KLISCHNIGG

According to Klischnigg, he first donned a monkey costume when asked to take over from a sick colleague at Drury Lane. Presumably the colleague was Wieland on the occasion when 'Mynher Von Kleshnig' was prominently billed in the 1829/30 Drury Lane pantomime.

The scenic effects were particularly splendid that year with a rolling diorama showing Windsor Castle, Virginia Water etc and a magnificent cascade of 70 tons of water pouring from a height of 30 feet. These wonders did not swamp the enthusiastic response to Klischnigg:

> The extraordinary activity of the phenomenon, Mynher Von Klishnig, excited universal astonishment. He appears as a monkey; and in truth his wonderful suppleness of limb and pliancy of body would do honour to any of the simia genus. His limbs appear to be as much at his command as the thoughts of other men are at theirs.[1]

> a very extraordinary person in every way. It is worth the trouble of a long journey to see with what facility he throws his limbs into a variety of positions which one would suppose to be utterly inconsistent with the capabilities of the human frame. It is perfectly immaterial to him whether his legs are over his shoulders — in a straight line with one another — or placed upright against his sides. Were his joints composed of Indian rubber they could not be more pliant; indeed some of his positions were so utterly out of nature that we were at a loss to ascertain how he had disposed of the component parts of his frame.[2]

Considering the number of man-monkeys the critics must have seen over the last four years they do still seem to be extraordinarily impressed by contortionists in monkey skins. However, Klischnigg does not appear to have stayed around very long, his work being more international than most covered in this book. In 1832, he was in Paris billed as the 'First Mime of Covent Garden' and the 'English Mazurier'. There is a glimpse of him in Rome in 1834, and Naples, Venice and Milan seem also to have been visited. He toured throughout France, including, in January 1835, the Théâtre de la Porte-Saint-Martin in Paris where Mazurier came to fame. A press report stated he had 'recovered' *Jocko* and added new business, conceding he was less graceful than Mazurier but had greater strength and flexibility. He was considered more extraordinary than anything seen so far in this genre.

A report in a French newspaper claimed that the manager of Drury Lane was suing the French manager for detaining the performer when he was due to be at the English venue. During these peregrinations Klischnigg found time to marry Miss Preschl who was in the choir of the theatre in Vienna.

'Monsieur Klischnig' was in Dublin in December 1835 where he played *Jocko, or the Monkey of Brazil*, with complete success

> displaying great muscular powers and activity, as the monkey. His imitation of this animal was so close to the original as to almost give some probability to the opinion held by Lord Monboddo that man is a species of the monkey, but without the tail.[3]

The novelty aspect being in his favour, he stayed to play other pieces, though the Dublin critic sniffily complained that minor pieces from 'the Coburg, the Surrey, the Victoria, and other two shilling and one shilling establishments of the sister metropolis' were imported in vain as 'the people of Dublin will not stand this.'[4]

In 1836, Klischnigg finally approached the manager of the leading theatre in Vienna. Having gained an interview with Karl Carl to announce he performed as an ape, and would like to do it Vienna, Klischnigg received the typical smart-alec reply that Vienna was full of men behaving like monkeys. However, on leaving the room, Klischnigg put his left leg up behind his ear, thus arousing the manager's interest, leading to a demonstration of his talents. The result was a commission for a new play from the leading Viennese playwright Johann Nestroy who was also an actor and singer.

The Monkey and the Bridegroom – *Klischnigg's passport to fame.*

The piece was called *The Monkey and the Bridegroom* which was a huge success with Klischnigg playing the role of Mamok the Monkey some 50 times. This play was the big breakthrough for the man-monkey, and from then on Klischnigg was a major star, in constant demand throughout all the leading capitals of Europe, embarking on several multi-city tours. He was the man-monkey most cast in the Mazurier mould, probably because of performing mainly in continental countries. His fame firmly attained, Klischnigg's British appearances were very rare, perhaps because England was well stocked with rival man-monkeys – Gouffe, Martini, Plimmeri, Bernaskina, were the most well known then flourishing, with Wieland still the king of them all.

Klischnigg was back in Dublin for April and May 1838. He gave his interpretation of *Jocko the Ape of Brazil* as well as the Nestroy piece *The Monkey and the Bridegroom*. Other plays given were *The Monkey Servant*, and *La Perouse*. The advertisements reminded the audiences of 'Monsieur Klischnig whose performances were received two years ago with distinguished applause'. However, much as the crowds loved him, the local critic was still depressed that such performances should desecrate the hallowed stage:

> In the next piece, the only prominent character, Jocko, the Monkey, was represented by Monsieur Klischnig. We confess he displayed almost un-exampled ability, and evinced a perfect knowledge of the various peculiarities of the monkey tribe; but though we willingly accord this praise to him individually as a very clever artiste, we cannot refrain from expressing our regret that those boards in which the genius of a Kean or a Macready was wont to exhibit itself, should be put to such vile uses, or made the arena for such ridiculous and fantastical representations. We would have laughed heartily at some of Jocko's tricks, if we saw them in a locality suited to them — if we saw them at Donnybrook; [a notorious annual fair] but in consequence of the circumstances under which we last night witnessed them, they produced strong feelings of sorrow and disgust.[5]

'Klishnig' moved to London for June at the Royal Surrey, where he gave his other major work called *The King of the Hills; or The Frog, the Tortoise, and the Sapajou*. This was based on a traditional tale from the Hariz Mountains of Hanover. The celebrated visitor enacted all three creatures with 'wonderful agility' and the 'exhibition of this performer drew down reiterated applause. He is exceedingly clever in his way.'[6] Apart from his English rivals, during that season Klischnigg was in direct competition with Harvey Leach, the so-called Gnome Fly.

In the autumn of 1839 he spent several weeks in France, after which he planned to go to London and thence to America.

On 27 April 1840, 'Klishnig' made his debut at the Bowery Theatre in New York and was soon making quite an impression with the ladies, perhaps because he was now calling himself Monsieur rather than Mynherr. *Jocko* was to the fore, and his other principal work had now become *Gig Gig; or the Frog, the Tiger and the Sapajou*.

As his name disappears from English records, it is likely Klischnigg remained in America for some time, before returning to Europe for more touring. He was in France in 1844 and 1845 and constantly returned to Vienna, which he regarded as his home city, and over the years embarked on new parts in new plays.

In 1852, he played the Monster in the farce *The Monster; or Mr Baldock's and Mrs Nanni's Adventure in Pumzenstadl*, and in 1853, the Clown in the pantomime *Harlequin in the Flower World*. A revival of *The Monkey and the Bridegroom* in 1857 after 18 years proved that both play and actor, continuing to defy their age, had been admirably conserved. Other roles included *Zambuko; or The Monkey and the Gypsy* (1861), *Albo, the Monkey from Malicolo* (1862), and the frog in *Kwang-Kiang-Fui* (1863). In 1864, Klischnigg was rated still a very good gymnast in *Iago; or the Monkey of Peru*.[7]

A composite showing Klischnigg as the monkey Muri and the frog Buri in The Monkey and the Frog; or Hudriwudri's Magic Curse.

Though Kliscshnigg had not appeared in England for decades, an advertisement for the London Pavilion in November 1865 proclaimed 'Klischniggs in a new Pantomimic Sketch'. A review of the show enlarges on this:

> The Klischniggs, a troupe of pantomimists, are now engaged, and appear in an interlude of a quarter of an hour or more in duration. The acting family is constituted about as usual, and the whole entertainment exceedingly droll. There is a 'heavy father' with stiff knees, the fool of the family in a short pinafore, the daughter of the house, a China ornament-looking, but graceful lover, and an interloper with a monkey. The monkey, of course, escapes, frightens everybody into convulsions, and is at length shot. Which Klischnigg personates that abominable animal we cannot say, but must congratulate him on his performance, which is extremely true to nature in details which might be overlooked by less conscientious artists. He actually makes believe to eat his own fleas. The utterly untameable Zoological nuisance also makes an irruption into the Hall, passes the check-taker on the stairs, peers into the ladies' faces, and walks along the front of the gallery, till he leaps on the stage, and is immediately shot. The entertainment is a very amusing item in the nightly list.[8]

This would seem to be the great Klischnigg and his daughter with supporting company. Unfortunately, as we shall see in a future chapter, the theatre world in those days was tainted with copycats who often passed themselves off in the name of other more established artistes. That may be the case here, but I tend to think that this is a rare genuine appearance by the aging Klischnigg. For one thing, he was still working in Vienna as mentioned above and, from the description, the monkey role would have been within the old man's compass. Also, the name is spelled completely correctly – not a proof in itself but it is the *only* incidence I have found in English newspapers and playbills of such a thing. The reader will have noted I have kept the various spellings as used in each case within quotation marks.[9]

In 1866, Klischnigg gained a stage partner in his daughter Eldora who played acting roles. In 1873, he appeared in the farce *The Wild Man of Hütteldorf*, where his elasticity for monkey jumps and gestures was considered downright phenomenal for a sixty-year-old man. His last stage appearance was in 1875 in *Around the World in Eighty Days*.

Edward Klischnigg died in Vienna on 17 March 1877 aged 65. His name lives on as it has been adopted by modern contortionists as a technical term for a 'forward bender'.

Chapter Nine
HERVIO NANO

IF YOU THOUGHT Monsieur Gouffe was a trifle odd, prepare yourself for a man who was even more peculiar. Harvey Leach was born in Westchester County, New York in 1804 and grew up to be an arrogant man with an unstable temper. To say he grew up is a bit of a misnomer as while his top half was fit and muscular better than most, his legs did not develop properly, and as a grown man he had very stunted limbs. Instead of normal legs, somehow the thigh bones had not developed at all, and it was as though his knees were attached to his hips. His feet were normal but the left one was splayed somewhat sideways.

> The defect of the lower extremities has led naturally to an increased development of the powers of the upper. The arms, being continually in exercise, have acquired great power, and the body, being unencumbered with the weight of the lower limbs, it is the more easily lifted. Hervio accordingly, rides on horseback, poised on his hands as steadily as other equestrian performers on their feet. He runs on his hands nearly as fast as other men on their feet; in tumbling he drops as lightly on his fingers as others do on their toes. The same strength of arm, and comparative lightness of body, give him wonderful facilities in climbing. If he had the power of grasp in his feet, he might set up for an actual Chimpanzee; as it is, the power of grasp in his hands enables him to personate the part with singular fidelity.[1]

All this gave him extraordinary leaping power but an ape-like shape as his arms dangled almost to touch the ground. It is no wonder that he became short-tempered and litigious.

Coming to England at a very young age, Leach spent many years on the fairgrounds performing freakish stunts. Graduating to circuses, he established himself as an unusual equestrian, able to race along the ground and spring up on to a galloping horse. There is a playbill for Mr Clarke's New Olympic Circus at Hull dated 22 September 1827 which is a benefit for Jocko, the Brazilian Man Monkey. I suspect this may be an early attempt by the twenty-three year old Harvey Leach to cash in on the Mazurier craze, as also on the bill is "The Celebrated Equestrian Dwarf who will go through his Antipodian Act on Horseback ON HIS HANDS."

Working on the continent, it was in Italy that he gained the name Hervio Nano as *nano* means dwarf, runt, manikin, or midget. Thereafter, he dubbed himself in this Italianate form of Harvey the Dwarf, while still being widely known by his real name. He flourished alongside the older Wieland, Gouffe and Klischnigg.

His London heyday was in 1838 when he was engaged by Frederick Yates for a season at the Adelphi Theatre. He opened in a play called *The Gnome Fly* of which he has been credited as the author, although it is likely it was a joint enterprise with a reliable local wordsmith. The opening night was on 31 January 1838 and there can be no better description than the review of that night (ending with a couple of excruciating puns!):

> A performance which may be truly described as curious, was exhibited at this theatre last night, and the vehicle for its display is a piece entitled *The Gnome Fly*, which is called in the bills, "a bizarre flight of fancy." The principal performer, Signor Hervio Nano, is mentioned as an illustrator of the doctrine of the Metempsychose, and in truth he does undergo some strange bodily changes. . . Signor Nano certainly is a most excellent representative of a baboon. His movements, his gestures, and his tricks, were such perfect imitations of the animal, that were he to exhibit them in the neighbourhood of the Zoological Gardens, some of the tribe would assuredly claim kindred with him. As the Fly the Signor was still more successful, and the audience were very much excited and moved to laughter, but the most astonishing part of the affair was his flight from the stage to the tower where the Princess was confined. He then descended, ran up the side of the stage, and crossed the ceiling with admirable dexterity. The Signor is a curious little fellow, and though be exhibited many an astonishing *feat*, he has scarcely any legs. Nevertheless he is likely to have a *run* for some time, as the applause was very great and hearty at the close of the piece, which was announced by Mr Yates for repetition every evening till further notice.[2]

Metempsychosis is the doctrine of the transmigration of souls, rather on the principle of instant reincarnation. To make this clear to the gallery (which is always assumed to be inhabited by the uneducated working man), Hervio appeared as himself in the guise of the King of the Gnomes, the plot then requiring that he shoots his soul into the body of the King's baboon, and in that disguise performed every trick that a baboon can perform, showing how closely man and the monkey are linked. 'Mazurier himself could not play the ape with more agility.' Critics were still banging on about the great French man-monkey ten years after his death. Hervio, then changing into a fly, clambered around the proscenium arch and flew with the aid of a wire, but that is outside the scope of the theme of this book.

Hervio Nano played 46 performances up to 7 April 1838. Presumably in an attempt to increase Nano's repertoire, Yates introduced *The Mayor and the Monkey*, a silly romp attributed to Joseph Coyne which played eight times from 26 March to 7 April. In this far-fetched nonsense the mayor of a French town seeks to win his fair lady by dressing as a monkey at a fancy dress ball. Coincidentally, a real monkey has escaped from the menagerie and the mayor is caught in its place. Hervio Nano, of course, is playing the real monkey 'and he plays his part with such extraordinary truth, that some of the audience were contending whether he was of the *genus homo* or the *genus simian*'. Presumably this portion of the audience was in the uneducated balcony! Between them the man-monkey and the monkey-man kept the audience in jolly laughter.

At that time, few London theatres played continuously all the year round. Through historical circumstances, theatres were licensed on a seasonal basis. When the Adelphi season closed, manager Yates together with Mrs Yates – both well-known actors – and Hervio, set out to play several provincial dates. The custom was to stay at a venue for anything between a week and a month offering several different plays. If a certain star was particularly popular, 'hot' as we would say in modern showbusiness parlance, he might descend on a town for one or two nights only, whizzing off on a tight but intensely lucrative schedule, having a benefit at each venue he played.

FREDERICK YATES
Lessee and Manager of the
Adelphi Theatre
1825 - 1842

The Yates/Hervio troupe first played Birmingham with a programme comprising *Valsha the Slave Queen*, *The Gnome Fly*, and *Paul Clifford the Highwayman*. All three were hits from the Adelphi, the first two being played at every venue visited.

> The acting of the baboon was perfect. Every act and motion of the animal were faithfully given, and the actual baboon could hardly have shown more agility than did its representative. One

trick – climbing up the one side scene, and passing round the rail of the gallery, and then descending by the other – afforded the gods very high delight, though many of the tricks on the stage struck us as equally curious.³

Leeds was the next port of call where Hervio performed *The Gnome Fly* eight times, and another item not previously noticed advertised as

> *La Mouche a Miel or, King of the Honey Hive*! and Fly from the Top of the Ceiling! crossing the Gallery, the Pit, the Orchestra and the Stage and Alight on a Village Spire! A distance of 200 feet! An Act of Volition peculiar to himself, and never attempted by any other Artiste.⁴

Presumably all this exclamation-marked hyperbole meant he was going to slide down a rope tied to the back wall of the gallery that led over the audience to the stage where a scenic prop of a church spire anchored the bottom end.

HARVEY LEACH
known as
Hervio Nano

THEATRE, LEEDS.

SURPRISING ATTRACTION!

Sig. HERVIO NANO,

The Wonder of the World!!

THE MAN FLY!!

MR. YATES!
Mr. Collins.—Mrs. Hooper.

3rd. TIME, a Tale of Enchantment, constructed expressly to display **Signor Hervio Nano's** peculiar powers, entitled THE

GNOME FLY!

INTRODUCTION.

THE GNOME!

Mine Palace of Alnain, in the Centre of the Earth.
Alnain, (King of the Gnomes and Dives,) **SIGNOR HERVIO NANO**
Deverley, (his Prime Minister,) .... Mr. BUTLER—Cobolt, ... Mr. HOWELL
GNOMIC APPEARANCE, AND DISAPPEARANCE OF ALNAIN.

PART FIRST.

THE BABOON!

Æthereal Descent of Meerjehan—Conference with Alnain.—Valley of Dates, and Romantic Landscape near Lahore, with the COTTAGE OF SIDI.
Meerjehan, (Queen of the Peris,) .... Mrs. H. MELLON.
Chittygong, (Messenger extraordinary from the Grand Cham of Tartary to the Great Mogul,) .... Mr. HERBERT——Sidi, (a supposed Orphan Peasant) .... Mr. FITZJAMES
Sapajou, (Baboon to the Prince of Tartary,) **SIG. HERVIO NANO.**
GRAND HALL OF AUDIENCE IN THE MOGUL'S PALACE!
Solomon Ben Solomon, (the Great Mogul—Emperor of all the Moguls) .... Mr. CROUCH
Mustapha Gobemouchi, (his Grand Vizier,) .... Mr. JOHNSON
Princess Felima, (Daughter of the Great Mogul) .... Miss HAMILTON
Ladies of the Court, Officers of State, Guards, Slaves, &c.
THE GRAND BRIDAL PROCESSION of the PRINCE SHAMUCKDA.

PART SECOND.

THE FLY.

TOWER of the WINDS on the Hanging ROCKS.
Wonderful Flight of the Fly.
Magical Deliverance of the Princess—Appearance of the Peri, and DISAPPEARANCE OF THE FLY.
The Spell fulfilled—The Charm wound up—Union of Sidi and Felima.

Playbill for Hervio Nano at Leeds 4 July 1838

HERVIO NANO

The troupe moved on to York, which was on the same circuit as Leeds, repeating the same repertoire. In August they were at the Queen's Theatre, Manchester playing to full houses where Nano's performance both as a monkey and an insect, were rated natural and astonishing.[5] Thence on to the Stoke and Potteries Theatre:

> The performances of the Signor are spoken of as most astonishing, and some have actually, doubted (until demonstration took place) whether the professed transformations were real, and supposed that they beheld the wonderful doings of a genuine ape, and not the dextrous exploits of a clever man, assuming for a time its form and habits. The appearance of the Signor off the stage is not a little remarkable. The trunk of his body, face, head, and arms, are of a full size, and well proportioned, whilst his legs and thighs are as diminutive as an infant's, so that when his arms hang downwards his fingers are within a little distance of the ground.[6]

Then on to Brighton . . . the tour proving to be a great success with full houses, enthusiastic audiences and jangling money tills – then they returned to Birmingham.

Having played another successful week, ending with a gorgeous spectacle which was most likely *Valsha the Slave Queen* which required a large number of extras, Mr & Mrs Yates left, leaving Mr Hooper their leading man and Harvey Leach to complete a second week. At 4pm on the Monday, Leach set up his equipment for a new play *The Demon Dwarf* which was to be the afterpiece following *Romeo & Juliet*. During the course of the play, Leach went to ask Simpson the resident Stage Manager for £10.14.6 which had been deducted from his pay the preceding week. Simpson pointed out that his agreement was with Mr Yates who had contracted with Mr Monroe the theatre manager for the entire visiting company on a sharing arrangement. The Adelphi people were to receive a third of the gross takings each night except Saturday, when they would receive a half. Yates also agreed to be responsible for extra supernumeries etc. On that particular night there were exceptional charges because of the increased cast and splendour of the production. Mr Yates had examined the theatre's books before leaving and declared himself satisfied, and in any case the dwarf's contract was with Mr Yates, the theatre itself not having any responsibility for Leach's wages.

All this threw the little man into a rage and he made a mild assault on Simpson which was prevented from becoming more severe by several persons entering the room. Leach then went and sat in a box with his wife to watch the ongoing show. When it was time for him to do his stuff, his wife having left, he was sent for but refused to leave his seat until he was paid his money. This necessitated Simpson having to go onstage and explain to the audience the reason for the hold-up. This explanation was greeted with shouts from Hervio in his box of 'Liar!' 'Where's my money?' and so on. Mr Hooper then went on to reason with his colleague pointing this deal, having been agreed when contracts were signed, was all in order.

By now, the audience were taking sides, shouting out advice on a matter of which they knew nothing, while Hervio was whipping them up into a frenzy. Some gentlemen suggested to him that if he were given the money he should perform, which is what the screeching Leach tried to explain was his position, but they would not pay him. Simpson then sent some men to drag him away so that a substitute entertainment could take over. The gallery resented this, and when Hervio either jumped out or fell out of the box (it is not apparent which) and vanished behind the front curtain masking the stage, they started a riot pulling up the benches and, shouting out 'Clear the pit!' throwing them into the pit below, smashing glass chandeliers on the way. Flying wooden planks hurtling down was a major threat of injury if not death, so not surprisingly, the pit emptied immediately. The riot eventually ended when police arrived, Leach being led off in handcuffs shouting, and the theatre emptied by dousing all the lights.

Hervio was bailed and the Adelphi actors proceeded on their tour to Cheltenham and Gloucester. Of course, Hervio was duly called upon to answer at the next Warwick Sessions.

> Harvey Leach, known in the theatrical world by the cognomen of Signior Hervio Nano, was charged, together with divers other persons unknown, with unlawfully causing a riot and disturbance at Birmingham Theatre, on the 1st of October, with the intention of forcing James Monroe, lessee of the establishment, to pay Leach the sum of £10 14s, 6d which he claimed to be due to him; in the course of which tumultuous proceedings, twenty chandeliers, twenty seats, and twenty benches, value £100, the property of Mr Monroe, were broken and destroyed. There were other counts charging the defendant with a riotous assault upon Mary Ann Walton, and with inciting others to commit the said riot.[7]

The proceedings seem certain enough as Leach shouted to the gods 'Will you stand by me?' and was handcuffed by the police and led away shouting 'Hervio Nano's handcuffed: men and boys won't you assist me; where are my friends?' Miss Walton and Miss Crisp were two actresses valiantly trying to struggle on in *A Roland for an Oliver*, the substitute that Simpson had put on to replace the missing play. They were assaulted with fruit and vegetables including an apple and a turnip. The case hinged on whether the first item (a bottle) had been thrown while Hervio was in the auditorium as he had skipped off behind the curtain, and doubt was caused by nobody knowing for sure whether it was thrown in the dwarf's presence or absence. As nobody knew who James Monroe was except he was 'the boss', whilst Hervio was a favourite performer, the twelve good men and true duly acquitted him.[8]

A free man again, Hervio carried on with his engagements, appearing at the Pavilion in November, back at Sheffield in December, then the Royal Victoria from late December and January. He expanded his repertory with *The Shipwreck; or The Captain and his Monkey*, *The Egyptian Fly*, *Bibboo the Island Ape*, and a new version of *La Perouse* as well as repeats of *Queen Bee*, *Demon Dwarf* and the inevitable *Gnome Fly*. He moved to the Pavilion again in February and March, billed alongside Mons Bibin the Belgian Giant.

Unfortunately, amongst all this lucrative work, Hervio managed to be brought to court again. He had been driving a lady – probably his wife – in a post-chaise along Ludgate Hill when a young man called Williams, riding a valuable pony, and seeing an opportunity to pass, overtook him. For some reason this angered our hero and he assaulted Williams with a horsewhip, dragging him off his mount, damaging both pony and rider. As the *Theatrical Observer* observed: 'The Dwarf is of a very pugnacious disposition.'

The result of this latest escapade was a fine of £20 to the court, with an option to mitigate the penalty by paying the prosecutor (ie Williams the victim) £10 compensation instead. The spiteful little Nano preferred to pay the full fine rather than half the sum to his opponent.[9]

That ended the affair for Hervio, but not for poor John Williams. Sometime later at the Court of Aldermen, Alderman Harmer presented a petition on behalf of Williams over the offence, as he had not only sustained injury from the assault, but had also lost his job for letting the pony be damaged. The petition stated the object of the Court at the time of the trial was to obtain some remuneration for the injury inflicted by the assault; but the Court's offer to Leach to make some amends being rejected, Williams now appealed for the Aldermen to make some order that would offer some part of the payment due to him as, having lost the situation which he possessed at the time, he was now penniless and out of work. Fortunately, there was a fund out of which the corporation could make remuneration to the poor man, and it was unanimously agreed to award £10 as the court had intended. The decision gave a great deal of satisfaction to all concerned as the ruffian's spite was thus defeated.[10]

In April 1839, the nasty little man decided, rather than let sleeping dogs lie, he would resurrect the trial at Warwick – where he had been acquitted of causing affray – by claiming against Simpson and Rook, the police constable, for ill-treatment and wrongful imprisonment. So another trial was convened, this time with Hervio as prosecution, Simpson and Rook in defence. All the details were gone through again in minute detail, all duly reported in the national press. This time the theatre men had a more effective lawyer who argued that it had been necessary to handcuff and remove Leach to maintain good order. Simpson would have been highly culpable had he not done his uttermost to do so in such a large building with a hot-headed crowd. Again it was left to a jury to make the decision and, on this occasion, they found in favour of the defendants.[11]

Alas, this did not satisfy Harvey Leach, the famous Gnome Fly, and in June he challenged the verdict on the grounds that the judge had not directed the jury sufficiently in the matter of whether there was any justification for putting him in handcuffs. So the same prosecution and defence lawyers took up their opposing cudgels yet again, and in short order Simpson and Rook's lawyer soon convinced the bench of the righteousness of the judge's conduct of the case, and it was ruled that there were no grounds for re-opening. [12]

It may be that all these court appearances undermined Harvey Leach's popularity, or it may be for other reasons that he decided to return to America. He first appeared as Hervio Nano in America on 27 January 1840 at New York's Bowery Theatre in *The Gnome Fly*, exactly four months before Klischnigg made his debut at the same theatre with his trio of frog, tiger and monkey. In December, Leach was appearing in Philadelphia.[13]

Leach's USA sojourn lasted until late 1842 during which he played several New York theatres, and visited other eastern states with an entertainment that included piano recitals by his wife.

Leach was back in London on 10 November 1842 advertising that he was to petition for bankruptcy, strangely stating he had resided 19 months at London addresses. From evidence at the insolvency hearing, it appears that during his English absence he had toured various European countries with his own troupe of eight people. His business methods were such that he had no accounting books to show, though it was believed he had lost £400 in that year alone. Leach explained this money was spent paying expenses for his troupe. He now had no assets, his only security for paying off his debts was the future engagements at theatres. Leach's debts totalled £266 (over £22,000 in today's money) entirely arising from law proceedings against Mr Simpson of the Birmingham Theatre and constable Rook. An order was made allowing the performer's future wages to be set against his debts.[14]

Leach was soon back at work again, in February 1843 appearing at Sadler's Wells supporting the American Giant, Charles Freeman.

In this picture (reproduced from a coloured painting) HERVIO NANO looks very docile and almost effeminate. It certainly does not convey the angry and irascible character regularly portrayed in press reports.

They appeared together in a play by Leman Rede taken from a Calabrian folk tale called *The Son of the Desert and the Demon Changeling*. This then transferred to the Royal Olympic where they packed the audience in, regardless of stuffy critics saying 'The piece is worth no further notice than as a vehicle for introducing these freaks of nature upon the stage, for which purpose it is well adapted.' March was spent at this venue, adding *The Ourang Outang; or the Indian Maid and Shipwrecked Mariner* which may well be Leach's updated version of *La Perouse*.

By May, he was appearing at Astley's as the Equestrian Ape, where he had an indisposition that prevented his appearing, to the chagrin and dissatisfaction of the audience.

In July, he was at Sheffield with Tourniaire's Cirque Royal Francais, again as an equestrian ape, or as it was more elegantly billed: 'His Equestrian Comedietina of Monkeyisms, riding on his Hands.'

Leach cannot be blamed for turning back to the circus for his work at this period. Theatres were going through a very difficult time with few star actors having the drawing power to warrant their inflated salaries. Indeed, many large towns had their theatres closed for much of the year, as few managers were willing to take the risk of opening them. Hence, in August we find our hero at the Abbey Street Theatre in Dublin where 'We wish he may prove attractive, for, of late, empty benches have stared the actors in the face'.[15]

In October, he arrived at Tunbridge Wells where he found the theatre, after a long struggle with poor business, about to close. The prospect of playing to empty benches so much alarmed Hervio Nano that he did a runner. Again, he can hardly be blamed when the three highly-regarded thespians Mrs Nisbett, Jane Mordaunt and Samuel Phelps together only played to £8, and the famous Helen Faucit and her brother played four nights for a gross of £10.16.0.[16] The Tunbridge Wells theatre had been built in 1802 by Mrs Sarah Baker and had been very successful in Regency times when the town was a fashionable resort but, like many provincial theatres, the hard times got worse, and a few years after Leach's abortive visit, it closed to be converted into the Corn Exchange, though the original facade still exists.

In March 1845, Leach returned to America and in May was back in New York where a fire in the Bowery found him on the roof of Bartlett's Hotel dashing about calling for those below to send him up a hose so he could save the buildings. He was ignored, and no doubt he was setting up a clamour to call attention to himself and his heroics.[17]

After performing at Palmo's Theatre and the Bowery Amphitheatre, Hervio Nano toured with Howe's Circus where his 'incredible feats of horsemanship make him an object of special wonder.'

Leach seems to have crossed the Atlantic back and forth several times during his career, as once again he turns up in London in 1846. This time, abandoning the idea of a stage career, he persuaded a promoter to display him at the Egyptian Hall as a 'What Is It?' This venue, a well-known London landmark built in 1812, originally housing a museum, was later transformed into a group of exhibition halls. It was used to display scientific marvels and inventions, and exceptionally large paintings, as artists could hire halls, charging an admission price to view their work. The halls were also rented for what we would call 'freak shows'. At Easter 1846, the artist Benjamin Robert Haydon rented a gallery to display his latest masterpieces, as he was in financial straits and needed a commercial success. At the same time the Yankee showman P T Barnum was showing the midget known as General Tom Thumb, an extremely popular attraction seen by 12,000 people in Easter Week alone, while Haydon's religious-themed paintings attracted just 133 admirers. Haydon shot himself – unsuccessfully, then cut his throat.

Not long after Tom Thumb had departed from his several months stay, new advertisements proclaimed that *The Wild Man of the Prairies* or '*What Is It?*' would be shown for three 90 minute periods through the day at a fee of 1/-.

The come-on blurb read:

> 'Is it an animal? Is it human? Is it an extraordinary freak of nature? or, is it a legitimate member of Nature's work? Or is it the long sought Link between Man and the Ourang Outang?'[18]

The exhibition opened on 31 August, and by 2 September everybody knew what it was – a correspondent to the *London Evening Mail* soon told them:

> Yes, there "what is it" was with its keeper, playing "toss" with an indiarubber ball. What was my surprise when, at the first glance, I found "what is it" to be an old acquaintance – Hervio Nano, alias Harvey Leach, himself!

Some of the stories regarding this quick exposure grew more fanciful, with the 'visiting old friend' turning out to be Carter the American lion trainer who is supposed to have said 'leave the gnawing of bones and get dressed, and I'll take you for a slap-up meal.' Others claimed the visitor was Barnum himself but, whatever the apocryphal stories, the deception was widely disseminated causing the exhibition to swiftly close.

If Leach had travelled fairgrounds charging the country yokels a penny a time he might have got away with it, but how he expected to do so in the middle of London when he had been a star attraction in the minor theatres not many years before, and been prominent in several court cases, beggars belief. He died six months after the exposure on 16 March 1847 – some said from the shame of being found out, which seems unlikely, as according to the report below he continued pretending to be a missing link.

According to an obituary in the New York press, Leach was fluent in English, French, Spanish, Italian and Portuguese, and had a head full of statistics and rare stories. He had once been married in France and had two fine children currently being educated in Paris.

> Death of Harvey Leach,
> The mortal career of this remarkable individual, who earned for himself considerable reputation both in this country and abroad, for his clever personifications of the habits and eccentricities of the monkey race under the assumed name of Signor Hervio Nano, terminated, after a short illness, on Tuesday evening, at his residence, George-street, Shoreditch. A short time ago the deceased exhibited himself at the Egyptian Hall, disguised as an extraordinary animal captured at the Cape of Good Hope, "supposed to be the link between the human race and the ourang-outang," and called "What is it?" The last place the deceased performed at was the Standard Theatre, in December last, where, notwithstanding the deception having been discovered and made public, he continued to represent "What is it?" He was about to start for Lisbon when he was

taken ill. He was a native of America, and in his forty-sixth year. The last request of the deceased was that his body should be presented to Dr. Liston, the eminent surgeon, not to be buried, but embalmed and kept in a glass case, as the doctor had been a particular friend to him.[19]

This piece would make a fitting end to the story of Harvey Leach except to say his body was not treated in the manner described but, by right of Leach's will, dissected by an eminent surgeon. The results were published in the *Literary Gazette*. The head and top half of the body were described as 'particularly fine – a perfect model of strength and beauty' but in place of legs were two limbs – one measuring 24 inches from hip to point of toe, the other only 18 inches. A plaster cast was made of the whole body. The true end to the story is related in this paragraph from the *Morning Post* on 25 May 1847:

> It will be in the recollection of our readers that the late Harvey Leach, the celebrated gnome fly and man monkey, left orders that after his decease his body should be given to Mr Liston, of University College Hospital, for disposal. Mr Liston handed the body over to his most intimate friend and companion, Mr Potter, for dissection, who, whilst engaged in his labour, pricked his finger with the lancet. This caused little care beyond placing his hand in a sling for a day or two; but on the third day Mr Potter was attacked with fever – abscesses formed on his hand, which extended up the muscles of his arm and over his chest, causing great agony; death eventually put a period to his sufferings, and on Saturday his remains were interred in the Kensal Green cemetery.

Truly a poison dwarf.

Chapter Ten
FREDERICK MARTINI

THE HUGE SUCCESS of Mons Gouffe tempted other performers to emulate him by donning an ape skin and clambering around the theatre. One of these was a Signor Mortini, who appeared at Lincoln in October 1830.

> The spirit and confidence with which SIGNOR MORTINI performs
> HIS TRICKS, LEAPS,
> ESCAPES FROM HIS PURSUERS, ETC.,
> Keep the spectator in constant good humour; nor can any emotion of fear, for one moment, disturb the pleasure excited by his varied feats, as they are performed with that apparent ease which characterizes the Animal he is so happy in his imitation of.

In *The Island Ape* Mortini

> will exhibit his
> WONDERFUL TRICKS, LEAPS, BALANCING, &c,
> Which have excited the curiosity and astonishment of the Metropolis, and raised a doubt in the minds of thousands,
> Whether he be a Monkey or Man ! !
> And conclude by RUNNING ROUND the Front of the BOXES and GALLERY, and performing some most extraordinary feats of human dislocation.

This hyperbolic language was typical of the man-monkeys' publicity, and not only did the performers copy the actions of each other in their routines, they also shamelessly stole each other's bill matter.

Mortini next surfaced in a March 1831 advertisement for the theatre at Sherborne. He claimed to be from Drury Lane and Ducrow's Amphitheatre and 'the greatest Novelty of the Age!' The 'unrivalled Phenomenon and wonderful Physiognomist' promised he would perform the whole of his 'astonishing Feats, wonderful Postures,

Equilibriums, Evolutions and Attitudes.'

Like all the other man-monkeys he relied on the play *Jocko; or the Brazilian Ape*, introducing within it the usual gymnastic antics with which we are now very familiar. In other words, a Gouffe facsimile, although he did offer the addition of a *Pas de Grenouille* in which he imitated a frog.

In May, Signor Mortini had progressed to Birmingham where he was a special Whitsun attraction along with Mr Wilson on the tightrope. In September, he was plying his trade at Andover. After that he seems to have disappeared for good, unless he is – with a change of vowel – the same man as Signor Martini. There was also a Monsieur Martine at Stratford-upon-Avon in January 1832 according to three extant playbills.

Frederick Martini is probably the man-monkey who flourished for the longest period of all, commencing his career while E J Parsloe was still alive, and not ending it until 10 years after Gouffe's death. Martini is first recorded at Leeds in 1829 playing Mushapug in *Jack Robinson & His Monkey*, next surfacing at Edinburgh in October 1832 where he performed along with Mr Cony, a strong pantomimist, and his dogs Hector and Bruin. All four arrivals were deemed extremely clever in their way, 'particularly the quadrupeds.' Martini was dubbed 'one of the most extraordinary posture masters we almost ever beheld' which is not much more than damning with faint praise, but the 'whole exhibition was loudly applauded.'[1] Needless to say Martini's main contribution was *Jocko, the Monkey*. This little troupe then moved on to Aberdeen where 'notwithstanding the heavy but indispensible expence of the novel engagement, the terms of Admission will not be advanced'.[2]

Then we lose track of Martini until February 1839, but presumably he had been constantly touring the provinces. In company with Ellar the famous Harlequin whom we met in an earlier chapter, he entertained the good people of Aylesbury. Ellar was not just a Harlequin, he gave a sample of his dramatic pantomime artistry as *The Dumb Man of Manchester*. Martini's Man Monkey 'afforded much amusement' and the pair had a crowded audience

February 1840 saw Martini at Petworth theatre. People are often astonished today to learn that in those far-off days when the populations were so much smaller than they are today, places like Petworth and Sherborne had theatres. In 1788, a new Theatres Act had

THEATRE, LEEDS.

The Managers have the honour to inform the Public in general, that at their earnest solicitations, they have prevailed upon

Monsieur Martini,

That unrivalled PHENOMENON, and wonderful CONTORTIONIST, (whose Success in Leeds has been so triumphant that at the fall of the Curtain, he has been greeted with Reiterated bursts of Applause) to remain a few Nights longer, and will appear (by the kind Permission of

A. DUCROW, Esqr.

of the Royal AMPHITHEATRE, LIVERPOOL,) on

Wednesday, & Thursday, March 3rd & 4th,

In the most popular Pieces of MONKEYANA ever produced on this Stage.

The Performance will commence with (by Desire,) a grand Spectacle, called

Will Watch.

Will Watch, (a Smuggler,)	Mr. GATES.
Rob Rudderley, (Captain of the Smugglers,)	Mr. SHEENE.
Hugh Mallison, (the Black Phantom,)	Mr. DIRK.
Levi Lyons,	Mr. CLIFFORD.
General Harcourt	Mr. BALLENTYNE.
The Stranger	Mr. PATON.
Arlington	Mr. MILLER.
Michael	Mr. JONES.

Smugglers, Villagers, Soldiers, &c. &c.

Mary, (supposed Daughter of Rob,	Mrs. SCOTT.
Edward	Miss WYATT.

A VARIETY OF SINGING, DANCING, &c.;

To conclude with

Jack Robinson
AND HIS MONKEY.

Jack Robinson,	Mr. GATES.
Mushapug, (his Monkey,)	Monsieur MARTINI.
Muley, (a black Boatswain,)	Mr. BALLENTYNE.
Sebastion,	Mr. JONES.
Diego,	Mr PATON.
Fernando,	Mr. HEWITT
Jose Romerio,	Mr. MILLER.
Juan Fernando	Miss GATES.
Thomas,	Mr. CLIFFORD.

Sailors, Smugglers, &c. &c.

Emmeline,	Mrs. SCOTT.
Captain's Wife,	Mrs. PATON.

Admission—Boxes, 2s.—Pit, 1s.—Gallery, 6d.—Half Price at 9 o'Clock.—Boxes, 1s.—Pit 6d Doors open at half past SIX, and Performance to commence precisely at half past Seven o'Clock.

EDWARD WOOD, PRINTER, 80, BOAR-LANE, LEEDS.

This early playbill of 3 March 1829 shows MARTINI 'hitching his wagon to a star' as the famous Andrew Ducrow gets bigger billing for giving permission than the performer himself!

given control of licensing to local magistrates encouraging a boom in country theatres, over 300 small playhouses being built immediately following. Alas, with the ending of the Napoleonic Wars in 1815, a great slump descended on the country towns and those theatres – once thriving on a seasonal basis – were now in desperate straits. The repertory of plays had become stale, money was tight, and there was now a rapid turnover of managers. Indeed, as we have already noted, many country theatres had already given up the ghost and closed down, the buildings being stripped of theatrical fittings and converted to other uses, with many becoming non-conformist chapels.

Martini kept the Petworth people amused with his apish tricks, and also added the well-known Grecian Statues. These poses purported to be living copies of famous classical statuary – the discus thrower, the dying gladiator, Ajax defying the lightning, and so on. One assumes Martini had a particularly well-developed body. This gimmick, first launched by the equestrian Ducrow and widely copied, professed to be an educational presentation of authentic ancient sculpture appealing to students of the fine arts. Many actors seized on the idea as a method of both extending their repertoire and titillating their female fans.

Martini ran into a little bit of bother at Windsor in April 1842 as he was accused of a most unprovoked attack on a respectable inhabitant of the town whilst in the theatre. This brought the show to a sudden stop, and Martini was hauled up before the local beak and mayor. The complainant was a stonemason called Stanfield who, accompanied by Mr Fred Turner and a youth named Hask, were occupying one of the boxes. The accused, in the guise of a monkey, ran along the mouldings outside the gallery and boxes. When in the gallery, he seized hold of the hat of some person (a monkey's trick) and threw it into the pit. Descending quickly from the gallery to the boxes, he alighted on the box containing Stanfield and his party, knocking back Mr Turner in the violence with which he jumped in. He then snatched off the hat from the head of the youth, Hask, placed it on his own head, and grinned over the box to the rest of the audience. Stanfield, naturally indignant at such conduct, snatched the hat back, whereupon Martini immediately struck him a most violent blow on the eye, which produced the marks that were still visible – Stanfield appeared to have been severely injured, he had a black eye, which was greatly swollen, and over his eyes were pieces of plaster where the skin had been cut.

In his defence Martini said it was the practice adopted by Mazurier at Drury Lane Theatre. As it was now 17 years since

Mazurier had appeared at Covent Garden (not Drury Lane), and 14 years since his death, it is likely that everybody had forgotten what Mazurier actually did, or even who he was. It is doubtful that Mazurier left the stage, though certainly most of the other man-monkeys inspired by Gouffe performed in this way. To take off a hat from a person's head in the performance of the character was usual, said Martini, and it had never been objected to before. In any case, he had merely taken up the lad's hat which was on the seat, and not off his head, and put it on his own head, when Mr Stanfield struck him behind the ear. He admitted that he then certainly had returned the blow.

Martini called witnesses to prove that Stanfield gave the first blow, but they differed materially in various parts of their statements. Mr Clinton the manager had tried to calm both audience and performer but Martini, who was greatly excited, threatened Mr Clinton, who was in fear of personal violence from him. What is it about these man-monkeys that makes them so aggressive? Do they actually begin to adopt the characteristics of the animal they impersonate?

It was stated that such conduct was not to be tolerated in a person who sought the means of subsistence by the patronage of the public. The magistrates agreeing the prisoner had been guilty of most shameful conduct, ordered him to pay a fine of £3 and 9s 6d costs or, in default of payment, one month's imprisonment. The prisoner said he had not got the money, but Mr Dodd, the lessee, was indebted to him, and he hoped he might be allowed to send to him. The mayor said 'Yes, you can send to him for the money, but in the meantime you must remain in custody.'[3]

In August, Martini was at the Ashton-under-Lyne theatre for race week but played to 'indifferent success'. From now on the glimpses of Martini, although very occasional, indicate that he had an ongoing career even if it was not proceeding as smoothly as he would have liked.[4]

In January 1844, Martini was at Deptford in *Jocko*, in March at London's Royal Albert Saloon playing Marmazette in the by now well-worn play *The Dumb Savoyard and his Monkey*.[5]

August 1845 saw him at Littlehampton on the south coast where, to drum up business for his benefit night, as a publicity stunt he sailed on the sea in a washtub pulled by four geese. He failed to take heed of the tide ebbing, and the whole lot was swept out to sea. The waiting boatmen did not know what was supposed to be part of the escapade, and stood watching as he disappeared. Somewhat slow to realise that the stunt had got out of hand, and that the biggest goose was Martini, they did not go to his rescue until he was a mile offshore. But that night he filled the theatre for his benefit.[6]

On 19 January 1846, Martini appeared as a guest artiste during the last week of the season at the Tenterden theatre. However, on that occasion he performed only his living versions of classical statues, the playbill listing by name 14 different poses, 'concluding with the beautiful Position of the DYING GLADIATOR'. It is quite likely that Martini stayed over and performed his monkey tricks later in the week.[7]

Martini ventured over to Ireland in May 1846. He was engaged for the Cork theatre where business had latterly been very poor. It was hoped that Signor Martini would improve attendances, the manager deserving far better at the citizens' hands than apathy, or rather more accurately 'almost utter neglect'.[8]

In October 1846, Martini tried his washtub pulled by geese stunt again, this time at Dover. He announced he would navigate the wide waters of the Pent in a tub drawn by six geese. The banks were crowded by eager sightseers when Martini set out at nearly dusk. The geese were tied to the tub, but instead of the geese pulling the tub it was actually propelled by the navigator himself which resulted in pushing the startled birds before it. Martini had not proceeded far when the two leading geese broke away from their harness, and watching the fleet of small boats giving chase to the runaways was much more fun than watching Martini himself.

By dint of paddling, Martini managed to get safely ashore. The point of this stunt was to woo customers to the Eagle gardens where Martini in his ape suit was the prime attraction. Evening came, but not the public. Having been gulled by the geese stunt they were not so foolish as to flock to the Eagle. Martini, having taken the money at the door, realised that he had not taken enough to cover his expenses so resolved to keep all the takings himself, duly bolting as soon as the supporting show commenced. Dear, oh, dear![9]

For a manager to decamp with the takings was not a rare event in those days – and for the next 150 years – but how he got away with it, I do not know, because he was still in the area in February 1847 being engaged at the Canterbury theatre where he was billed as 'the successor to Gouffe the monkey professor'.[10]

In December 1847, Martini was at Portsmouth and Landport

drawing good houses with enthusiastic applause.[11]

In February 1849, Martini played at the Liver Theatre, Liverpool where he appeared in *Jack Robinson and his Monkey, Jocko the Brazilian Ape, The Dumb Savoyard and his Monkey* and a new Comidetta *Captain Charlotte* which may have been a version of *The Captain and his Monkey* often performed by other man-monkeys. Then in April he moved to the Adelphi Theatre, playing the same repertory garnering good houses even though he had recently done them all at the rival venue. He then went on to Wigan in July where the theatre was under the same management as the Adelphi, and performed the same plays there.[12] February 1850 saw our man at Macclesfield where he gave his Mushapug in *Jack Robinson*, and presumably the other plays in his repertoire. On Martini's benefit night the 'celebrated violinist J Tate played one of Paganini's solos in a style seldom if ever equalled in this town.'[13]

In May 1851, Martini was giving his Mushapug at Hastings and creating a favourable impression.[1]

In June 1852, Martini had a short season at the Queen's Theatre with *Philip Quarl and his Monkey* being a prominent feature of his stay. He then moved on to the Royal Marylebone Theatre where he performed in *Peter Wilkins; or the Flying Indians*. This play, it may be recalled was the big success of E J Parsloe back in 1827. The part is a Nondescript or Wild Man rather than an ape.

On SATURDAY, Dec.8th, and MONDAY, 10th, 1855, & during the Week

JACK ROBINSON!
AND HIS MONKEY

Jack Robinson ... ... (a Shipwrecked Sailor) ... ... Mr HENRY DUDLEY
Muley (a Mariner) ... Mr. C. Morton, Captain Romerio ... Mr. Hayes, Thomas ... Mr. Howard,
Old Gammer ... Mr Hamilton, Sebastian ... Mr Bennett, Diego ... Mr W Stevens, Henrique...Mr Jameson

Musha Pug ... ... **Signor MARTINI**
Who, in the Course of the Piece, will Introduce his Celebrated CHIN MELODY

In December 1855, MARTINI was yet again bringing his Mushapug before the audience – 26 years after we first spotted him playing the role at Leeds.
Playbill Pavilion Theatre, London (detail)

In December 1855 he was reprising his Mushapug yet again at the Pavilion, Whitechapel. And that would seem to be the last trace of

Signor Martini, but (assuming he is the same Signor Martini) he pops up again in Wombwell's Menagerie as late as July 1863 billed as 'Gorilla – Mr Martini the original man-monkey'. Even if he had continued no longer, Martini must have laboured for over 35 years in his monkey outfit, which is considerably longer than Gouffe himself.

After retiring from the arduous life of a man-monkey, Martini became an agent fixing circus artistes with managers. Lacking an office, he carried out business in the bar of the Pheasant pub which was situated near to the Westminster Bridge Road, an area where many circus performers congregated.

Once deals were done and contracts signed the artiste would inevitably ask what Martini would care to drink and his standard reply was 'Two without' which signified a twopenny nip of neat gin. As he was treated to several of these throughout the day he soaked them up by nibbling plain dry bread which seemed to be all he ever ate. A concerned friend urged him to have some oysters which he reluctantly did, partaking of a mere one or two. A few days after, Martini was taken ill, blaming it on the unaccustomed rich food of the oysters to which his stomach was unaccustomed and more than his system could stand. The friend relaying this tale seemed to think it something of a joke but, as the poor agent died shortly after this whole escapade, it seems unfortunate rather than amusing.[15]

Chapter Eleven
HARVEY TEASDALE

WE HAVE SEEN HOW some man-monkeys tend towards the irascible, but none has been driven to the desperate measures of our next subject.

Up to now our man-monkeys have been London based, or imports from the continent or USA, but Harvey Teasdale was born in Sheffield, Yorkshire in 1817 and remained faithful to the area. He was an active and mischievous boy, preferring to play truant rather than attend lessons. After failing with several day schools, his desperate parents sent him to a boarding school where he delighted in stupid pranks including clambering on the school roofs. As he grew older he was often in scrapes and scraps, and indulged in petty crime such as shoplifting. Teasdale trained as a table-knife cutler, but his heart was not in the trade as he was a stage-struck youth who aspired to tread the boards, being inspired by the shows at the local Theatre Royal.

In the early 1830s he took to hiring rooms in pubs and putting on shows wherein he usually played the clown. Gaining a local reputation, he decided to become a professional performer and struggled for many years to make a living joining various fit-up and fairground companies in the north of England. During this time he learned a great deal of the lowly levels of the theatre world, not only acting but management too. It was during this period that circa 1845 at Grantham he became the man-monkey which would be his main occupation in future years.

Teasdale married around the age of 20, and had two daughters Bolyna and Harriet. This family he was obliged to leave at home while pursuing his somewhat vagabond-style life. During 1847, he was summonsed for the second time for abandoning his family without means of subsistence and ignoring official letters sent to him. In fact, during that year he returned to Sheffield to carry out a series of shows at the Adelphi Theatre, and to boost audiences for his benefit night arranged the publicity stunt of floating down the river in a washtub drawn by ducks. He claimed that 70,000 came to watch him perform this feat which must have been somewhat of an exaggeration as that would have meant half the population of Sheffield was present. As these stunts so often seem to do, the 'marvellous and unprecedented sight' became a complete fiasco as the ducks, totally unmanageable, left Teasdale floundering about getting drenched as he paddled furiously for the bank, and a wall collapsed throwing a number of spectators into the water.

Having decided that he would henceforth be a German, our hero became 'Herr Teasdale the celebrated Man-Monkey and Wonder of the Age'. Gouffe had not long been in his grave, so perhaps Teasdale thought there would be room for a replacement, although Martini was still in his heyday, as was Shentini. In March 1848, Teasdale was in Carlisle, and in November at Bradford. He was emulating the typical repertoire of all the other man-monkeys – *Jack Robinson and his Monkey*, *Jocko the Ape of Brazil*, *The Dumb Savoyard and his Monkey*, etc but like a third-rate Gouffe he relied mainly on scrambling around the auditorium and swinging on ropes. Unlike Gouffe, however, he also appeared as an actor without his monkey skin, his showpiece being *The Dumb Man of Manchester* a favourite mime part of many pantomimists including the late Tom Ellar.

In the summer of 1849, Teasdale applied for a licence to erect a temporary theatre in the Sheffield Cattle Market for the performance of legitimate plays. The building, of substantial wood construction, cost £200. In those days, annual fairs regularly had travelling theatres as part of the attractions; when the fair was in progress they performed as many short shows as they could cram into the day, drumming up audiences on a walk-up basis. It had become a regular tradition that when the fair was over, a mobile theatre would be allowed to stay on alone, often for several weeks, functioning as a proper theatre with full evening shows changing often. These theatres usually operated without a licence but, as Teasdale was actually applying for one, the magistrates could hardly refuse without placing him at an unfair disadvantage, thus granted him a licence for one month. Later in the year he was appearing at Sheffield's long established Theatre Royal and

> The mirth-exciting exploits that followed in every scene in which the monkey appeared, kept the house in continued roars of laughter. We may add that, in our opinion, Herr Teasdale stands unrivalled as man monkey.[1]

Teasdale, very loyal to his home town and the north in general, kept returning to the same few towns on a regular basis. He was at the Theatre Royal in Sheffield again in 1852 and it probably gave him satisfaction to play in the town's principal theatre where he had spent much of his youth watching the shows from the gallery, wishing he could be down there on the stage.

In 1853, Teasdale took over the lease of the Grimsby theatre which functioned as a legitimate playhouse. He then added the theatres at Driffield and Burlington Gap (Bridlington). This did not stop him performing elsewhere in his man-monkey guise, and he did a few nights back at Sheffield while he was organising his new circuit. In October, he was back in Bradford, this time at the Colosseum.

In November, he was engaged at the Britannia Theatre, Hoxton, probably his first time in a London venue. He was retained beyond his original contract, and for several days the show ended with Herr Teasdale in *Pulverino Pongo*. However, he did not like London, and did not aspire to work there, possibly because it was said that he received poor reviews on his visit.

Last 6 Nights of Herr Teasdale
The Celebrated Man Monkey

The whole to conclude with the highly successful Serio-Comic. Melo-Dramatic Romance, entitled

PULVERINO
PONGO!

Lucien............Mr. Fitzwilliams	Domerino............Mr. W. H. Newham
Valerio.....Mr. H. Carles Cartouche......Mr. Sinclair	Josef.....Mr. Lucas

Pulverino (the Island Ape)   **Herr TEASDALE**

Gomero....Mr. W. Rogers	Michel....Mr. Cushion	Carlos....Mr. Davison
Janette........Miss Pettifer	Rosina........Miss Grithes	Erica......Miss Green

Soldiers, Attendants, Sailors, Planters, &c. &c.

A rare London appearance of Herr Teasdale the Sheffield man-monkey. Playbill Britannia Theatre 5 December 1853 (detail)

For his pantomime season, Teasdale was at the Adelphi, Liverpool as Clown in *Sinbad the Sailor*.

Teasdale also dabbled in running a low-class bar in Sheffield which may be why he kept returning to the town for theatre work, not wishing to stray too far from the area. As Teasdale was a hardened drinker himself, it was probably not very profitable. In February 1855, he was at Halifax where he appeared in *Jack Robinson and His Monkey*, *Dumb Man of Manchester*, *Far at Sea*, *Dumb Boy of Brussels*, and *Don Juan*. Business was stated to be good.

When Egerton of Liverpool's Liver theatre took the lease of the Adelphi, Sheffield in March 1855, Teasdale was amongst the company engaged. Alas, as was increasingly common at this period, theatre business was often poor, and projected seasons often abruptly curtailed. Egerton only lasted until July before he failed. The theatre was then taken over by Teasdale himself who ran a varied programme including a week of opera before he too threw in the towel in October. In December, he was at Bradford Theatre Royal where he was engaged for the pantomime. It was the first pantomime presented there after three absent years and it sounds as though it was not too well cast: 'Herr Teasdale's Clown is not admired, while Mr Spacey as Pantaloon and Mr Glanville as Harlequin, when the novelty of their debut has worn off, will no doubt improve on their present doings.'[2] The show had a longer lease of life by transferring to Huddersfield and then Halifax. For his benefit at the latter venue he played the lead role in *The Monkey That Has Seen the World* the play that E J Parsloe introduced in 1831.

Pantomime 1855/56
Playbill 26 February 1856

In May 1856, Teasdale was at Hull playing the Wild Man in *Peter Wilkins* which claimed to be staged with 'all the original Scenery, Machinery, Music etc as produced at the late Covent Garden'. That theatre had burned down in March. It will be recalled that *Peter Wilkins* was E J Parsloe's first starring vehicle at Covent Garden in 1827, so with the theatre gone, that production must have been available for hire elsewhere. The Hull venue was the Queen's Theatre which had been granted a licence in spite of opposition from the far longer established Theatre Royal. Prior to the act of 1843 Theatres Royal were able to quash opposition theatres as they had legitimate monopolies, but after that date the old rules no longer applied, and upstart theatres all over the country were granted licences. In this case the magistrates amended the conditions so that the strength of the Queen's opposition was diminished. It must not charge lower than 6d in the Gallery with no half-price, nor open in December, January and February.

In March 1857, Teasdale appeared at Dewsbury where the young Misses Teasdale were worthy of favourable notice. He then went to York where, for his benefit night, he enlisted Sam Wild, an old colleague of the touring fairground theatre known locally as 'Old Wild's', who related an anecdote regarding that night. When Mushapug the monkey was supposed to defeat the character called Diego in a fight, it seems the actor playing Diego, bearing some grudge against Teasdale, refused to be defeated. Teasdale did his best to slay him, but Diego leapt off the stage and disappeared under the benches with the monkey chasing him. Not having much success, Mushapug returned to the stage and addressed the audience: 'Ladies and gentlemen, I have to express my astonishment at the conduct of that man Diego. It was his duty to be knocked down by me, and, as you have seen, he resolutely refuses to be. He has left the stage, and I am unable to go on with this scene in consequence, but should he return again he shall have cause to remember his conduct.' That must have been the first monkey ever known to speak directly to the audience. Teasdale's *amour propre* may have been injured but no doubt the £70 his benefit raised smoothed him down.[3]

For much of April and May, Teasdale was back at the Adelphi in Liverpool. In August he was at Blackburn with Mlle Bolino and Mlle Clari (Harriet) on the bill. These were Harvey's daughters who would be 19 and 15 at this point, and obviously dragged in by their father as general song-and-dance girls. In September and October, Teasdale was at Manchester with the monkey piece *Life in the Indies* and other plays in his repertoire. At the end of the year he was back at Bradford to play Clown again in their pantomime *Harlequin Ogre; or the Invisible Princess*. The Teasdale daughters danced a pretty clog dance.

At the end of January 1858 the pantomime moved to Halifax, but the dancing Teasdales received censure: 'there is room for improvement, a little carelessness being discerned in their performance.'[4] Teasdale's benefit night was 'a bumper'. The show then visited Huddersfield where it was the first successful show held there for some weeks.

Whether Teasdale was swayed by his success as the Clown in the pantomime or whether he shrewdly noted an opportunity in Huddersfield is not clear, but he started putting on shows in the Gymnasium Hall advertising them as 'Cheap Amusement for the People' where the best talent would be engaged and the performance would change nightly. Admission prices were 1/-, 6d and 3d – cheap indeed! Within a month he was advertising 'crowded houses and immense success'.

By the following year Teasdale had gained the lease of the proper Huddersfield theatre and in a *volte face* took a travelling theatre to court for violating his vesting rights. This was based on the fact that the mobile theatre had opened the day before the fair. As previously noted, it was the practice of travelling theatres to perform at fairs without a licence and then stay on for several weeks alone. This manager had simply got fixed up early and put on a performance on the day prior to the fair. The magistrates, who evidently sided with the itinerant, fined him a mere 1/- plus expenses.

Teasdale was determined to make a success of the Huddersfield New Theatre Royal which was re-erected in place of the former one. The new version had an increased capacity and a more magnificent interior than had previously been seen in that town. It also had three separate doors for boxes, pit and gallery where previously there had been one communal door. The superior theatres of the time deemed it necessary to keep class distinctions. The later doyen of theatre architecture Frank Matcham was expert in designing separate entrances, stairs, bars and circulation spaces which maintained class distinctions from entrance to exit throughout an evening at the theatre.

Teasdale's policy stated 'the dignity of the stage is to be preserved throughout the season by a due regard to the legitimate drama, as well as to the lighter productions of the dramatists of the present day'.[5] It opened on 24 September 1859 for a winter season. The programme followed the time-honoured system of a main play and an afterpiece, changing nightly, with a resident company bolstered by limited engagements of principal actors. The Misses Teasdale danced between the items.

All the stops were pulled out for the pantomime *Sleeping Beauty in the Wood* with new scenery painted by Mr R Gordon who produced a Grand Transformation Scene, a Banqueting Hall which was greeted with applause nightly, and a Fairy Lake with a beautiful fairy ballet. Harvey's daughters were now taking the principal roles of Harlequina and Columbine, although their father was not appearing as Clown or anything else.

Our hero really went to town by engaging star actors Mr and Mrs Charles Kean for a special night. This was so successful that he rebooked them a short time later. In April 1860, the manager produced *Kenilworth* with new scenery and costumes, and a pantomime for the Easter holidays which was reported to fill the place every evening. Alas, much of this turned out to be bluff as on 21 April 1860 the theatre abruptly closed. Much of the disappointing business can be attributed to a common situation – to boost business the manager engages an expensive star who pulls in booming business for a night or two, but takes most of the profit, and then when he goes the customers stay away until another star attraction arrives; people were no longer satisfied with merely the resident company. Stars were expensive, sometimes even the increased business not covering the cost. During the latter weeks business had been so bad that often the audience numbered no more than 30 people. The management was taken over by Thorne of Leeds and York.[6]

> TO MANAGERS OF FIRST CLASS THEATRES
> HERR TEASDALE, Clown, at liberty for next Christmas;
> also Mdlles Bolina and Clari, Columbine and Harlequina
> HERR TEASDALE open to engagements as
> the Man-Monkey from the present date.

From August 1860, the above advertisement began appearing in the showbusiness newspaper *The Era*. Unfortunately, nobody wanted the Teasdale family for pantomime, and in December they were to be found at the Monster Saloon, Crampton Court off Dame Street in Dublin. This was a music hall with various 'turns' and the programme was headed by Herr Teasdale, 'the greatest Man Monkey in the World', Mdlle Bolena, the beautiful Soprano Vocalist, and Mdlle Clari, the fascinating Danseuse, all making their first appearances. Why a German Herr should have French Mdlle daughters troubled nobody.[7]

In March 1861, Teasdale was back in Sheffield appearing at the Theatre Royal for a few nights with his *Dumb Man of Manchester*, *La Perouse*, and *Don Juan*. He had a good benefit night. Shortly after, he was in court for ill-using his wife. She said he habitually struck her and wanted to be separated from him. The court pointed out they did not have the power to grant divorces. The defendant was bound over to keep the peace, Mr Smith telling Mrs Teasdale 'to mind and always do right to her husband'. She replied that she always did. Mr Smith: 'Well it's the first time I ever met with a woman that did.' Laughter in the court.[8] Shortly after this the couple separated.

In November, Herr Teasdale was advertising in *The Era* that he had lost his pantomime engagement as Clown at Christmas as the theatre had suddenly closed and he was urgently in need of a substitute place. In the meantime he was playing man-monkey plays at the Queen's, Manchester, then the Adelphi, Liverpool. Fortune smiled on him and at the last minute he got a job as Clown in *King of the Busybodies*, the pantomime at Cardiff. 'Herr Teasdale as Clown is almost inimitable, he is both nimble and humorous in the highest degree.'[9]

In March, Teasdale was back in his old own area playing the New Amphitheatre, Leeds, with daughter Mdlle Bolena; and in July at St Helen's. But soon all his engagements were to end.

Harvey Teasdale fired the contents of a pistol at his wife, and then made an attempt to commit suicide. Teasdale had gone to a house occupied by one Henry Hewett, where his wife was lodging. Hewett was sitting on the door step, but Teasdale walked past him into the house, bolting the door behind him. Shortly afterwards Hewitt heard the report of a pistol, and throwing up the sash window jumped into the kitchen. There he found Teasdale attempting to cut his wife's throat with a razor. Hewitt struggled to stop him, calling out for help, but in the meantime Teasdale tried to cut his own throat. Help swiftly came enabling Teasdale to be subdued and taken to the Town Hall, where it was found that his injuries were actually of a trivial character. The injuries he had inflicted upon his wife were thought to be more serious, but, after her wounds had been dressed at the Infirmary, and found to be not life threatening, she was allowed to return to her lodgings.[10]

When the committal proceedings took place, Teasdale's defence was that, though he loved his wife dearly, she hated him and kept leaving him, but each time he wooed her back. On the last occasion she had left him at St Helen's and returned to Sheffield to lodge with Mrs Hewett. The Teasdales had been married 26 years but throughout that time she had acted as a common prostitute, sometimes residing in a brothel. Teasdale's statement was very long and rehearsed all his grievances with his wife, but was summed up as 'she was bringing up our daughters to the same mode of life. Here I am who has earned as much as £30 a week walking about in rags, whilst she and her daughters are going about in silks and satins'. He did not intend to fire at her, the gun was not loaded but was a stage prop filled with powder only, it went off in their scuffle. He bought the razor two minutes prior to entering the house. The prisoner was committed to the Assizes at York on the charge of attempting to murder his wife. There Harvey Teasdale was sentenced to two years with hard labour for attempting to cut his wife's throat.[11]

On his release he tried to take up his career by placing advertisements in *The Era*. It appeared that he was lodging with fellow performers Mr and Mrs Harry Garside as his plea for work took the form of an afterthought in their advertisement: 'PS – Herr Teasdale, the celebrated Clown is at liberty for Christmas. Address as above.'

Having failed to obtain work for Christmas, Teasdale underwent a sudden conversion and found God. He allied himself with a Sheffield organisation called the Hallelujah Band which was holding a series of evangelical services at the Temperance Hall. Crowded houses gathered to hear 'convicted felons, prize fighters, pigeon stealers, poachers, wife beaters etc etc' giving their experiences. In January 1865, posters proclaimed that Harvey Teasdale the converted clown would publicly destroy his stage dresses, playscripts, music and pantomime tricks. To meet the expenses of this 'extraordinary engagement' charges were made for admission and the place was packed for the event.

After a hymn sung with gusto by the audience, and a prayer, an address akin to a sermon was given but impatiently attended to, as it was punctured with calls for 'Harvey!' One of the leaders had to admonish the crowd, reminding them that it was a religious service, as they were behaving like a theatre audience not a congregation. Teasdale then came forward with a bag of his props and introduced Edward Lauri of the famous Lauri pantomime family, who was the clown from the Surrey Theatre, to testify they were the genuine articles. He was there by coincidence, as these props had been offered to him by Teasdale for £2.10.0 the lot, which he had refused. Finding himself in Leeds, Lauri had heard that Teasdale had destroyed the articles there, so had come to Sheffield when he heard the same thing was to happen again. This got a laugh from the audience, and the terse comment from Teasdale that he had 'enemies in Leeds'.

The ritual of destruction went ahead with each costume handed to the brethren to be rendered to shreds with knives and scissors. Finally the monkey costume – filled with straw – was displayed before being pounced on by the Hallelujah Band who tore it to shreds with cries of 'Hallelujah!' That was the end of Teasdale's testimony but, surprisingly, not the 'service', as further converts told the crowd about their conversions.[12]

This extraordinary evening was mulled over in the public press, as some sceptics were dubious as to the authenticity of the dresses that were destroyed, especially in the light of the fact that Teasdale had advertised them for sale, and indeed offered them to Edward Lauri, plus the statement that he had already destroyed them once before in Leeds. What is not in doubt is that being a convert became Teasdale's future career as he toured all over the north addressing prayer meetings – often for fees, selling photographs and copies of his book *The Life and Adventures of Harvey Teasdale, the Converted Clown and Man Monkey* at 1/- a time. This was a best-seller going through several editions between 1878 and 1881 totalling, according to Teasdale, 40,000 copies. As only three copies now appear extant, the figure is probably another of Teasdale's gross exaggerations.

His flyers boasted he was 'once the greatest impersonator of the man-monkey in the world, and late proprietor of 22 theatres and 7 public-houses'. He also incurred the censure of his late profession by maintaining it was full of rogues, drunkards and prostitutes, and they should give up their immoral lives and seek the Lord's way as he himself had done.

In later census returns he gave his profession as lecturer, and at the end of his life he had a fishing tackle shop. For some time his brain became affected, and in June 1904 he was moved to the Workhouse Asylum where he died two weeks later at the age of 86.[13]

Chapter Twelve
MAN-MONKEYS IN MUSIC HALL
"A WHOLE WILDERNESS OF MONKEYS"

THE MAN-MONKEY PHENOMENON was fuelled by a handful of plays with the chimpanzee, orang-utan, or ape as a character integral to the plot. The public did not differentiate between the simians – they were all monkeys. The thing that elevated the animal from being merely an actor in a costume was the casting of incredible acrobats, gymnasts and contortionists in the part. Whereas an actor would strive to imitate an ape as precisely as his talent allowed, the acrobat was a showman who ignored verisimilitude, but displayed his particular talent to the full, performing comic antics and prodigious feats unknown to any species of monkey. This is where Gouffe and the others scored – the people did not want accurate impersonations, they wanted clever stunts and comical actions.

This aspect did not go unnoticed by the lighter side of the theatrical profession, and soon performers who were not actors realised that by dressing in a monkey outfit they could perform a novel speciality act in the music halls and circuses. The story aspect was irrelevant to wire-walkers, trapeze artistes and gymnasts, all they had to do was to put together a routine of tricks already in their repertoire, replace their spangled tights with a mask and a hairy suit, and launch themselves as a man-monkey. Thus, alongside the performers acting in the plays of *La Perouse*, *Jack Robinson & His Monkey*, *Jocko the Brazilian Ape*, and *The Dumb Savoyard and his Monkey* and the like, a host of music hall performers played the monkey as a ten-minute 'turn'.

During much of the Victorian era for some fifty years, from 1825 to 1877, many man-monkeys flourished as well as the stars featured in this book. A number of gymnasts, contortionists and acrobats vied for public attention, some specialising like Gouffe, only appearing as a monkey, with others it was just an extra facet of a clown's or acrobat's business. The pages of the showbusiness weekly *The Era* name many such man-monkeys. To convey a flavour of how much activity involved man-monkeys, I made a trawl through the advertisements and reviews, simply noting names and dates. Music hall performers were usually engaged on a weekly basis, touring from town to town, with weeks out when not engaged. Thus, rather than listing every single week I have noted a sample month and a year to indicate the period when the artiste was performing or touting for work. Where two dates are given they are the earliest and latest noted. The purpose being to provide an overall picture of the general activity of man-monkeys, the following list omits the star names covered in other chapters, and is by no means exhaustive:

Ching Lau Lauro		London (Aug 1827) – Carlisle (July 1838)
Mons. Garcia	A	Brighton (August 1829)
Mr Wells	B	Newcastle (March 1833)
Young Mazurier	C	London (July 1837)
Mr Bonaker	D	Leeds (July 1838)
Signor Bernaskina		Dublin (October 1839) – Stonehaven (April 1847)
Signor Plimmeri		London (June 1835) – London (January 1856)
Signor Nicholi	E	Manchester (October 1841)
Mons. Macarte		Huddersfield (April 1842) – London (Dec 1860)
Mons. Gaipie	F	Cork (March 1844)
Herr Hiram Sugna	G	London (November 1845)
Signor Vinoni	H	Warwick (March 1846)
Mr T Fielding	I	Bolton (January 1848) – Bolton (August 1851)
Mr W Hemming	J	Whitehaven (June 1848)
Mons. Montero	K	Liverpool (Oct 1848) – London (February 1849)
(Signor) Shentini		Burnley (March 1849) – Nottingham (May 1854)
(Mr) Shenton		Liverpool (January 1856)
(Herr) Shentini		Birkenhead (Oct 1858) – Halifax (February 1866)
(William) Shentini		Leicester (December 1864)
Mons. Huline	L	Manchester (March 1850) — Dublin (July 1860)
Herr Adolph		London (February 1850)
Mr Stead	M	Nottingham (December 1850)
Mr Ed Edwards	N	Dublin (June 1852)

Cousens	O	London (July 1852)
Hernandez	P	Dundee (April 1855)
Signor Blitz		Wrexham (March 1856)
Flexmore		London (May 1857)
(Signor) Hunt		Rochdale (November 1857)
(Mr R) Hunt		Leeds (October 1859)
(Huntini)		Swansea (January 1861)
Hunt		at liberty (October 1869)
Mr W Patterson		Leeds (March 1861) — at liberty (December 1885)
Jean Lemaine	Q	Stroud (November 1869)
Mr W Waller	R	Sheffield (December 1869)
Nicole Druelin	S	Liverpool (January 1869) — London (August 1869)
Mr H Braham	T	Portsmouth (May 1870)
Hassan (Van Hare)		at liberty (August 1870)
Mons. Raslas	U	London (January 1871)
Davis	V	Sheffield (May 1871) — Southampton (May 1872)
Harry King	W	Carlisle (November 1871) – Longton (June 1873)
Signor Grovini		Portsmouth (October 1870) — Preston (December 1877)
Sig. Omey (Ohmi)	X	Hastings (March 1872) — Cardiff (February 1874)
Herr Vandenhoff	Y	Huddersfield (October 1875)
Signor Erber	Z	London (December 1875) — Glasgow (April 1877)

The italic capital letters after a name indicate approximately a performer's place on the Time Chart of Principal Performers. Thus it will readily be seen that these lesser artistes were working contemporaneously with the featured man-monkeys. The more visible over several years have a ⟵⟶ lighter in weight and their name in italics on the chart.

Every large city had several theatres and music halls, London abounded with them, so performers were able to go from one to another filling in large portions of their datebooks. The above sightings are taken from newspaper sources, chiefly *The Era* a weekly trade newspaper that ran to 24 densely packed pages reporting on the weekly changes of performers at venues throughout the land. In many cases the entries are culled from what were known as 'Calls' – a classified column listing where artistes were performing in this fashion:

> SIGNOR BELLI (Eric Bell) the celebrated Clown and Man Monkey This: Royal Alhambra, Leeds. Next: Park Theatre, Liverpool. 7th Nov week: Th Royal, Wigan. Letters to the above.

Other names are taken from columns of artistes 'at Liberty' (ie work wanted), in which case the date given is the issue of the newspaper. Not every performer took advertisements, whether in work or out of work, so there were many more busy man-monkeys than those we now know about.

With the Theatres Act of 1843, a distinct division arose between theatre and music hall licensing with the latter permitted to sell food and drink in the auditorium while presenting a series of acts or 'turns'. At first these tended to be singing and musical acts as the name supposes, but soon artistes that we would think of today as circus performers found a home there too. In that way 'music hall' became 'variety theatre'. Also a new source of income for aerialists, including man-monkeys, was an increasing number of galas. These were usually one-day events in the open air that attracted large crowds with fairs, bands and so on. Spectacular high wire and trapeze acts were ideal, and man-monkeys performing on ropes gained a fair share of the opportunities. Many of them were circus acrobats who performed an act in spangled tights, and then donned the monkey skin as a 'second spot' under a pseudonym.

What the above summary shows is how well established some man-monkeys were and the satisfactory careers they had. Ching Lau Lauro who flourished from 1827 to 1839 had a short but intensive career that ended only by his premature death in 1840 at the age of thirty-three. As we saw much earlier, he was already being compared to E J Parsloe when working at Vauxhall Gardens which he did in 1827, 1828 and 1834. Ching was also in the Drury Lane pantomime *Harlequin and Cock Robin* in 1827/28. He followed this with an appearance with Cooke's circus at the Royal Pavilion in Whitechapel Road, where he included the Brazilian Ape in his diverse repertoire.

After this auspicious start as a contortionist and juggler, he also became a magician performing in evening dress. Ching continued with a contortion segment in his shows but most likely did not persist with the ape costume. He claimed to be from Venice but is thought to have actually hailed from Cornwall, but the Chinese appeared to be in vogue at the time so he adopted the dress and name as a character.

> **Ching Lau Lauro,**
> *The Inimitable Posture Master, and Buffo,*
> FROM THE THEATRE ROYAL DRURY LANE,
> will exhibit his
> Wonderful Postures, Equilibriums, Evolutions, Attitudes &c.
> DANCE A HORNPIPE ON HIS HEAD,
> And conclude his Amazing Feats by throwing Golden Balls in every direction while extended on the backs of Two Chairs, in imitation of
> **A SPREAD EAGLE!!!**
> In the course of the Evening he will likewise appear in the Character of a
> **BRAZILIAN APE,**
> and perform all the Tricks and Comicalities attributable to that Singular Animal. The whole forming the most intrepid and amazing Performance ever seen at this or any other place of Public Entertainment.

Ching Lau Lauro included contortionism in the guise of a Brazilian Ape in his early career.
Playbill the Royal Pavilion   19 February 1828. (Detail).

Shentini – who claimed to be a pupil of Gouffe – is particularly visible for a period of several years, if we assume that Mr Shenton, William Shentini, Signor Shentini and Herr Shentini are all the same man. It seems to have taken him some time to decide on his professional character. He was not averse to working abroad as I found this advertisement in the newspaper *L'Entracte Boulonnais* dated 1857:

> *Demain Dimanche* **26** *Juillet*
>
> Mr. **SHENTON**, the **GREAT MAN MONKEY**
> From the Theatres Royal, Drury-Lane, St. James Theatre, etc
> will give a representation to commence by
>
> *JACK ROBINSON AND HIS MONKEY!*
>
> 1o L'AUMONIER DE RÉGIMENT.
>
> 2o DON CESAR DE BAZAN, drame en cinq actes.
>
> 3o JACK ROBINSON ET SON SINGE, (Mr Shenton)
>
> 4o LES CHANSONS DE BERANGER.

MAN-MONKEYS IN MUSIC HALLS

It is surprising, therefore, to find that such a regular standard artiste was sacked by the manager of the Midland Concert Hall in 1864. Shentini took him to court on the grounds that the contract stipulated two weeks' notice, and he wanted his money in lieu, a sum of £5.10.0. The manager claimed that no money was owed because he sacked him on the first night of his engagement and allowed him to work two weeks. The reason for dismissal was that the manager claimed his act was sub-standard and both Shentini and his wife were drunk on stage. As in all these cases, the details are fraught with contradictions and the circumstances seem different looked at from opposite directions. But what it does show is the low pay on which even an established artiste subsisted. Shentini, who was expected to play the ape, do slack-rope vaulting and take part in the ballets, plus his wife who danced the women's roles in the ballets, were on a joint salary of £2.15.0 a week.

When appearing in Wild's travelling show at Hunslet near Leeds, Shentini suffered an accident. While aloft on the *cordes elastique* a pistol in his belt exploded driving part of his costume into his side. He was taken down and three doctors were soon in attendance extracting the wadding and dressing the wound. That put him out of action for some time. One wonders how much a man could save out of £2.15.0 a week to tide him over several weeks out.

Plimmeri also had an accident – the same one that caught out Gouffe. He was performing a trick with his head in a noose and nearly hanged himself.

Another unfortunate accident took place at Leicester in September 1861 when the eight-year-old Master Stevens enacting the part of a man-monkey climbed a rope that was set too near the circus lighting which would have been a naked flame in those days. His padded costume caught fire and he dropped to the ring and was rolled over and over by colleagues until the flames were extinguished but he was badly injured. The circus was crowded with spectators, and 'much excitement was manifested.'

Unlike Gouffe whom we saw in the past, and James Dubois we are still to look at, many man-monkeys, unable to make a living with the ape suit alone, appeared in other guises, many of them also working as clowns. Lemaine was a clown who performed stunts on a velocipede (an early form of bicycle). Edwin Edwards had performing dogs, and performed callisthenic exercises as well as playing the Chimpanzee in *La Perouse*. Hunt was chiefly a stilt-walker with his infant sons. The widely versatile Mr H Braham advertised himself as 'comic vocalist, man-monkey and ballet master'. Grovini, known as 'Iron Jaw' being an aerialist who hung by his teeth, by 1894 had become a family troupe of four acrobats who in pantomime played Dog, Cat, Goat and Monkey – heralding the skin performers who specialised in portraying varied animals that we shall look at later. At this period the troupe appeared as the Grovinis with a second spot as a monkey duo Jacko and Jinnie.

William Patterson noted above, working some twenty years as a man-monkey, was also a contortionist, actor and clown, as well as performing under the name 'Si Slocum the Champion Rifle Shot of the World'. He died in 1907 aged 75.

Most of the man-monkeys were British, many adopting a foreign stage name simply because performers from abroad were more highly regarded than the native species. For most it was only a matter of becoming Monsieur, Signor, or even Herr and adding 'ini' to the end of one's name. Mr Hunt became Huntini, Mr Shenton turned into Shentini, and presumably Grovini started out life as Mr Grove.

This poster is particularly interesting as it advertises a man-monkey duo who claim to be 'the only tew in this line'.

This eccentric spelling of 'two' might indicate a foreign act newly working in an English speaking country.

Illustrated coloured poster circa 1887

Certainly there were also foreign performers who were 'international speciality acts' making their living touring the civilised world, staying in a country for a few months before travelling on, just as some Englishmen sought work on the continent. There is no way of differentiating these names, though we do know that Antonio Bernaschina was an Italian from Milan.

> In the course of a round-trip around Europe, which took place towards the end of the 1830s, and even during the time when Klischnigg was the order of the day, Bernaskina set the world astonished with his art. He succeeded, especially, in imitating the movements of the monkeys. He was greatly supported in this skill by his whole personality. He was thin, with a marked pale face, fiery eyes, black frizzy hair, and the same beard. When he had stained himself blue, red, and brown, and stuck in a monkey's fur, the illusion was striking.[1]

ROYAL
EAGLE THEATRE
Proprietor & Manager, Mr. THOMAS ROUSE, City Road

It is respectfully announced that

Signor BERNASCHINA

The celebrated representative of the "SIMIA" race, who is engaged for a limited number of nights, has met with the most flattering applause, and will make his appearance every Evening.

To conclude with an entirely New Ballet Pantomime, entitled
IL PONGO
Or, The Marriage at Tivoli

Povolo, Owner of a Large Mill and Father to Rosina......Mr GENNAIRE
Cavochio, Comic Servant of Povolo ....Mr FLEXMORE
Dominico,....................Lover of Rosina..............Mr. DEULIN
Three Disappointed Lovers ....Messrs. COLLETT, KERRIDGE, and SMITH
Rosina ....a Coquette ....Miss LANE

IL PONGO, the Monkey ... Signor Bernaschina
Who will perform many Wonderful Feats in his unequalled personification of the Monkey Tribe.

As we saw earlier, America took to the stage man-monkey phenomenon in a big way then, just as in Britain, monkey antics drifted away from the dramatic stage to be taken up by acrobats. The circus tent was invented in America by J Purdy Brown who introduced it in 1825 and it became the norm in that country within ten years, whereas in Britain the tent auditorium was not adopted until 1842 when Richard Sands's American Circus arrived to show us the way. The ease of transportation and erection was a boon for spreading entertainment through the wide open spaces of the USA. So, with the ongoing stage work, opportunities were manifold but I can only mention in passing a few man-monkeys gathered from American circus history – Henry Magilton (circa 1854), Jerome Mascarini (1859), George Derious (1861), Mons Baptiste (1864) Signor Victor (1865), and Edward Mills (1874). Samuel Canby known as Canito was another name in the past but I do not know when he flourished. I have also noted a Frank Donaldson (1872) who may, or may not, be related to Tom, Fred and Leon of the Ardel and Brothers Donaldson act.

A huge boost was given to the profession when Blondin, the hero of Niagara, moved to Britain. Blondin was born Jean François Gravelet in France in 1824. He began performing at a young age and was known as 'The Little Wonder', and with the French Ravel family of acrobats toured America. Blondin made his name crossing Niagara Gorge on a tightrope for the first time on 30 June 1859 on a rope over a quarter of a mile long placed 160 feet above the water. Blondin made several more crossings of Niagara, each one more daring than the last. He crossed it blindfold, pushing a wheelbarrow, on stilts, and once he carried a stove, stopped half way across and cooked himself an omelette. His reputation sped all over the world. In all he braved the crossing some 17 times.

Blondin came to London in June 1861, when he appeared for 12 performances at the Crystal Palace earning the colossal sum of £1200 (£100,000 in today's money). He was a high rope walker using a rope of 3 inches diameter setting it as high as conditions allowed. After touring the country, he returned in December to the Crystal Palace to perform high in the transept.

December and January being pantomime time in London, a new pantomime was specially written to star Blondin. This was *Child of the Wreck; or the Faithful Ape* by Henry Coleman. Blondin played the Ape and his small daughter the child. To accommodate this production a special stage 70ft wide by 80ft deep was built with 1700 gas lighting jets and appropriate scenery specially painted. With a large fee paid for the copyright, the total sum for mounting the show was £2000.

This is a brief summary of the plot:
Fernando, the proprietor of a plantation on the coast of Brazil, is awaiting the arrival of his wife and child from England, but the vessel is wrecked offshore. Fernando succeeds in saving his wife alone, both thinking their child has drowned. The child, played by Mlle Adele Blondin, is rescued by the Ape (M. Blondin), who conceals him in a

cave, carefully tending over him and amusing him with monkey antics. The local peasants, in dislike of the ape's activities, set out to shoot it. This means the ape clambers to the galleries and swings on a rope a distance of 120 ft while being shot at by the villain of the piece. I do not think you need to be told any more, do you? Yes, it is the same old Jocko/Jack Robinson story that had been around for nigh on 40 years, with a dramatic death just as the parents have their son restored to them.

BLONDIN, the hero of Niagara, playing an ape in pantomime.

How Henry Coleman dared to claim to be the author of this 'new' play when the piece was so well known, I cannot imagine. But he seems to have got away with it as there are no reports of anybody claiming to have even seen the plot previously, never mind familiarity with the piece. When you are a star you can get away with anything!

Blondin, hailed as acting to perfection, was greeted with much applause. 'His representation of the ape could only have been the result of much observation and study of its habits.' Where have we heard that before?

> Of all absurdities on the stage the ballet is the most absurd. To see a parcel of people going through extravagant grimaces and throwing themselves into extraordinary attitudes in the vain effort to express something or other which could readily be expressed by a few words, always strikes me as buffoonery without wit, and absurdity without fun. There is a good deal of tumbling about, upsetting tables and crockery, falling over one another, and practical jokes of that sort, while the sentimental lovers look inexpressibly foolish. But Blondin's performance as an ape is

really wonderful. That terrific leap of his across the transept is the most marvellous thing I ever saw. But in spite of this I could not repress a feeling of sadness, if not of disgust, at seeing a clever intellectual man dressed up as an ape, with admirable resemblance to this lower order of creation. When we think of what man is "in apprehension how like a god" – it is a repulsive sight to witness one of our fellow-creatures gibbering and mouthing like an ape, and performing an ape's tricks in all their disgusting peculiarities. My feeling, I could see, was shared in by many around me, who, after that one marvellous leap, went away sickened at the other features of this absurd entertainment.[2]

I have located three pictures of Blondin in action as the ape. In none does he look anything like an ape, indeed in one looking more like a naked bald-headed man with a moustache!

The season ended on 6 February 1862 and Blondin went off on his stunts as an individual attraction again. I do not know if he repeated the play anywhere, but it seems unlikely as one newspaper said:

> M Blondin's monkey tricks and terrific leaps are attracting tolerably good gatherings, but the entertainment – a ballet extravaganza, I think they call it – in which Blondin appears, "dressed" as an ape, is one of the dullest, deadest, dreariest, most doleful and dismal productions ever brought forward. The people yawn and are apparently sick of it.[3]

So you didn't like it then?

A scene from the The Child of the Wreck. *Blondin does not look to have taken too much trouble to look like a monkey!*

Wire-walkers, given a boost by the excessive publicity gained by

Blondin, set out to outdo the maestro, attempting riskier stunts than they were capable of, resulting in several performers suffering unhappy accidents.

A rumpus started up with well-meaning people saying 'Blondinism' should be banned, with letters to the press and even debates on the subject:

> Young Men's Christian Association. An interesting discussion was held on Tuesday evening, when the following question was freely discussed "Ought such exhibitions as those of Blondin to be encouraged?" The question was opened by an able essay given by Mr H F Gray, in favour of the opinion that such exhibitions ought not to be encouraged, and the votes at the conclusion proved that the meeting was unanimously of the same opinion.[4]

In 1863, at Cremorne Gardens for some two months, Carlos Valerio a twenty-five-year-old Italian attired in a golden costume, had walked a wire the whole length of the gardens – a distance of some 600 feet – backwards and forwards, sometimes with his feet encased in baskets, at others with his head covered by a sack.

> We have not been horrified so much as formerly with the details of the terribly dangerous tricks of such men as Blondin; but there is, I see, a new sensation-performer of this high-pressure-danger school. At Cremorne – that chosen resort of the fastest young men and the loosest young women of the age – may be seen. How long are these hideously dangerous games to be allowed in the vain attempt to satiate a morbid appetite? The Legislature ought to step in.[5]

On 25 June 1863, when a shackle on his apparatus broke, Valerio fell 40 feet to land on his head. When he fell, crowds gathered in distress, women cried and fainted, and three doctors who happened to be in the gardens that evening hastened to the rescue. Valerio was taken off to hospital, and half-an-hour later, the incident was forgotten, the crowds continuing with their dancing, eating and drinking. Valerio died within hours of having fallen.

As this tragic event followed soon after Selena Young, known as the Female Blondin, was left a mangled cripple, and another aerialist had died when crashing through a chandelier in accidents at other venues, there was a righteous clamour taken up nationwide that such entertainments should be banned by law. Said a commentator in the *Oxford Times*:

> The public are now at the point of disgust at ropewalking and all other man-monkey exhibitions. The death of poor Valerio, who fell from his 'wire rope' at Cremorne has rendered this kind of 'entertainment' peculiarly unpopular, and I trust the salutary reaction will be felt elsewhere.[6]

Valerio – who was actually Dutch – did not work as a man-monkey, but the newspaper was totally amiss in its conclusion; while the popularity of the monkey plays was in decline but still performed, the man-monkey as an aerial acrobat remained a big attraction on the halls, with several different man-monkeys likely to visit the same theatre over the space of a year. Not all man-monkeys were aerial performers, some like the Arley trick-cyclist duo simply adapted their normal stunts and tricks into a comedy act by dressing in ape outfits.

This trick-cycling duo is a typical example of the many acts who donned monkey costumes to cash in on the Pongo vogue.
Illustrated coloured poster 1893.

It may be wondered why the above list of active man-monkeys ends in 1877, as there was no diminution in the employment of these performers. It is simply a convenient place to pause for a cogent reason. We are about to meet Mr Pongo.

Chapter Thirteen
MR PONGO
ENTER THE GORILLA

SINCE MASTER MENAGE played the Chimpanzee in *La Perouse* in 1801, hundreds of actors had climbed into a monkey suit to play a character in that play and others that followed. Most of these took on the part as simply another role, with no more thought than giving thanks they had no lines to learn. The vogue for plays with an ape as a principal character gained a huge boost in 1825 with the play *Jocko, the Brazilian Ape* which led to an entire sub-section of the drama as further works were penned by opportunist playwrights. Because every theatre in the land wanted to stage 'a monkey play' a small clutch of professional ape-players arose who were able to guest star at a theatre, bringing a repertory of half-a-dozen of the principal monkey plays.

Critics showered praise on these expert performers, claiming that their portrayals were indistinguishable from the real animal. As playwrights tried to ring changes on the basic theme of an educated ape, the simians were as varied as monkeys, apes, chimpanzees, orang-utans, marmosets, baboons, and even the wanderow – obscure by any standards.

As orang-utan means 'person of the forest', it is easy to see how this creature was translated into folk lore as 'the wild man of the woods' and started appearing in stories. It is also obvious that playwrights, catering for the uneducated masses, should conveniently transfer the characteristics of apes in general into feral humans and vice-versa, as demanded by the plots of their plays. As far as the man in the gods was concerned they all did 'monkey tricks', and one suspects that the performers always wore their same hairy suit and did pretty much the same sort of routine in whatever play or part they were cast.

Long before Charles Darwin published his *On the Origin of Species* in 1859, scientists and educated people had pondered a connection between apes and humans. Even newspaper reviews of the monkey plays mused on the similarities and differences between the species. It was in 1860 when the famous debate on evolution took place between Huxley and Bishop Wilberforce during the course of which the bishop asked Huxley whether he claimed he was descended from a monkey on his father's or his mother's side.

The observant reader will have noticed one glaring omission in the above list of simians – the gorilla. It seems remarkable in the light of modern general knowledge that the gorilla, now amongst the endangered species, was unknown as other than a rumour until scientifically described in 1847. The first Westerner to see a live gorilla was Du Chaillu during his African explorations in 1856 to 1859, and the wider world saw his dead specimens brought back in 1861. The first live gorilla seen in Europe was Mr Pongo at Berlin Aquarium in 1877. It seems odd to call a gorilla Pongo when *pongo pygmaeus* is the genus of the Bornean orang-utan, and *pongo abelii* the Sumatran species – no wonder the man in the gods was confused!

In July 1877, Mr Pongo was brought to London's Westminster Aquarium and placed on display for a limited few weeks. He was thought to be about four years old and would gain adulthood at twenty. As he was but an infant, only childish things were expected of him. Inevitably, he was a great attraction and many eminent scientists and naturalists flocked to examine this first live gorilla. It was thought that the conflicting opinions regarding the physiological peculiarities of Mr Pongo would be likely to reignite the debate about the descent of man that had raged a decade previously.

MR PONGO

On a more prosaic level it was announced that the owners of the animal valued it at 3000 guineas and an offer of £5000 (£425,000 in today's money) had been refused. Mr Pongo was the talk of the town, drawing up to £400 a week in admission fees before he finally left London in September.

On 13 November, Mr Pongo died at his home in the Berlin Aquarium whose shares promptly fell 3% as a result. Unexpectedly, a post mortem showed that the animal's lungs were in excellent condition whereas it had been assumed that the removal of the gorilla from its natural habitat to an unnatural industrial climate would cause some deterioration. Mr Pongo's other organs were all in good shape too. Only the intestines were disordered, and his death was caused by simple diarrhoea. A bent pin, a button and a bit of wire were also found but not considered harmful. The brain and organs were preserved in fluid for future examination.

The following month 'Pongo' was appearing on the stage in at least two London pantomimes. At the Crystal Palace, 'Mr Fred Johnson was well made up as an imitation Pongo. His monkey tricks were exceedingly good.' The principal man-monkey Pongo, however, was a new Japanese performer called Kotaky who billed himself as 'Pongo Redivivus' (reborn). He was appearing at the rather grand Her Majesty's Theatre in the ballet pantomime *Rose and Marie* which featured a chorus of 300 children. Kotaky was immediately embroiled in a court case caused by the inefficiency of his newly appointed agents Classing & Francis. One of the partners had succeeded in getting Pongo Redivivus booked by Mr Mapleson the manager of Her Majesty's for three months at £30 a week, with an option of a further term of three months at £50 a week. The following day the other partner had made a deal for Pongo to appear at the Oxford Music Hall. Mapleson argued his contract was for the exclusive services of Kotaky, hence the legal dispute. It must be pointed out that in those days music hall performers often contracted to appear at more than one hall a night, dashing in a cab from one venue to another, so the situation is not as obviously ridiculous as it first appears.

When the pantomime season was over, Kotaky duly appeared at the Oxford with great success, and the following review is so detailed that we can see in our mind's eye exactly what his performance was like.

> Pongo is not dead. His identity has gone out of the dead body of the Aquarium ape and has been mysteriously transmigrated into the existence of the clever entertainer who has been received with such triumphant expressions of approval at the Oxford. If ever eyes and senses were deceived they are in this instance; the man disappears, the monkey holds possession of the stage. We do not behold a human being, we see an animal. The illusion is perfect, the acting art is shown in its highest form. The imitation in all its detail, in every delicate subtlety, is

photographic in its completeness, is Japanese in its correctness to established models. When the curtain draws up and Pongo is discovered in his cage all notion of personation disappears. The eyes see a monkey, the mind believes it is a monkey, and both curiosity and amusement are aroused. There on the stage in a wooden barrel cage squats Mr Pongo. He is just such an amusing fellow as we have seen scores of times at the Zoological Gardens and as travellers have met with in distant forests. He grins, he shows his teeth, and with comical curiosity he peeps into the centre of an appetising nut. But when the nut is devoured, and the shell thrown disconsolately away, the attention of the ape is directed to some further article of food, which has been left accidentally on the floor. Here is a chance for further mischief. Mr Pongo at once chafes under his irritating bondage. He wants to be free, and longs for any chance that will release him from captivity. Once more he grins and shows his white teeth; he stretches out his paw through the bars, and exhibits considerable impatience. Meditatively he scratches himself and reflects how he can possibly shorten the distance between himself and the envied object. At last he gets angry, he shakes the bars, they yield to his force, the cage splits and falls to pieces, and Mr Pongo, to his intense delight, is free. Then begins a splendid game, exhibiting all the tricks and eccentric mannerisms of the monkey tribe. Pongo plays with an orange that is rolled to him along the floor. He shows the power of his prehensile toes by clutching the fruit with them as he picks at it. He gambols about the place. He bounds with one movement upon a convenient table, and there squats grinning. And at last, weary apparently of these minor tucks, he takes a bolder flight, and with marvellous agility swarms up a wooden pole as quick as lightning – as quick if not quicker than a monkey — and chatters defiantly on the cross-bar overhead. But this is not all. Bolder deeds are still in store. On the other side of the stage there is a loose hanging rope, by which only a monkey could reach the trapeze aloft. Up the rope goes Pongo with marvellous skill, with that delicacy and surety of foot that only an animal can show, and once on the swing he revels in his freedom. Here, at any rate, is a makeshift for the branches of the primeval forest, here is a pretence for the overhanging boughs amongst which all monkeys love to gambol. If there were cocoanuts up here Pongo would certainly pelt the audience and aim very mischievous blows at the head of the worthy Chairman. He would put many a pipe out and play havoc with the glasses. But he contents himself with free and abandoned swinging, now by one leg now by another, head downwards, feet foremost, every way in fact, according to monkey pattern, except by his tail. The descent of the rope with its toe movement is as extraordinary as the ascent, and Pongo's marvellous exhibition at this point is greeted with round after round of cheers. He has now shown the audience all that a monkey can do and in the best monkey style. It remains for him to prove to demonstration that he is no monkey at all. When the applause is very demonstrative Mr Pongo for the first time in the entertainment stands erect on his human legs and bows like a human being. Even then the audience is not convinced of the deception, so Pongo removes his mask, and everyone sees the marked features of an intelligent Japanese gentleman. This accounts for the fidelity of the impersonation, which may be admired as an exhibition of fun as well as a sincere work of mimetic art. Lovers of natural history and students of fun will alike be loud in their admiration of "Pongo Redivivus". Our curious visitor will certainly be the talk of the town, for it is a fascinating as well as a clever entertainment. Experience teaches us that pretty women are always looking at their features in the glass, and that the most popular corner of the Zoo is the monkey house. Whether the Darwinian theory be correct or not it is certain that everyone will be astonished and amused with Pongo.[1]

It seems a subtle work of mimetic art for a music hall, and the reviewer describes it in the sort of artistic terms that were showered on Mazurier all those years previously. The arrival of Pongo Redivivus seems to have been regarded as a totally new thing with no comments regarding all the man-monkeys who had gone before, many still working at that moment in the nation's music halls and circuses. Gouffe, are you so soon forgotten?

The Japanese Pongo was soon back in court as his agents claimed that he had signed a year's contract with them which he had now broken causing them to lose money by being sued by managers at venues where he was supposed to appear and never arrived. How it was all sorted does not concern us here, it is sufficient to note that he became represented by S A de Parravicini who had continental contacts enabling Kotaky to work prolonged engagements in France, Spain and Portugal.

The big success of Kotaky inspired other gymnasts to don monkey skins. Acrobats used to earning two or three pounds a week hoped to propel themselves into a bigger league. £30 a week just for donning a monkey suit? I should say so! Just as Gouffe had many imitators, so rivals to Kotaky soon sprang up. A trio of dancers called Sterling, Jephson & Sterling put together a fast moving comical sketch with Pedro Sterling as Pongo. The trio of 'Ethiopian comedians and dancers' soon became Sterling, Davis and Sterling with Pedro claiming to be 'the Greatest Pongo Performer and Quickest Character Dancer in the World'.

Kotaky, quite rightly peeved at the appropriation of his name, started advertising in *The Era*:

> THE ONLY ORIGINAL
> PONGO, PONGO, PONGO
> REDIVIVUS
>
> ROYAL AQUARIUM WESTMINSTER
> NB: Caution to Managers – Beware of imitators.
> There is only one
> PONGO,
> who is now playing with great success at the above.

Pedro Sterling seemed to think that this rather mild advertisement was attacking him personally and retaliated with his own:

MR PONGO – ENTER THE GORILLA

> To Whom the Shoe Fits
> The Individual that calls himself PONGO REDIVIVUS who cautions Managers against imitators, happens to be a Japanese. Pongo is an animal. I advertise PONGO REDIVIVUS SKETCH, in which I take the Character of PONGO, and as far as imitating, I should want far superior than a Japanese to copy from. We have only met once last July in Manchester. He played it One Week at the Gaiety; I played it Three Weeks at the People's. Talk is cheap, but it takes money to buy Whiskey.
> PEDRO STERLING

In November 1878, the trio were advertising they were off to Hamburg, Bremen, Rotterdam, Dresden, and Berlin, with Vienna to follow. While they were away, Kotaky was having a spell at the Alexander Palace where critics' reviews did not always chime with the artistic pretensions of the one previously quoted:

> In this part of the comicality, also, appears Pongo Redivivus, whose monkey counterfeit is very clever, but prosy. If he could be less the animal and considerably more comic, we would like him much better. Above all things a man-monkey should be droll, and this is the consideration which influences us when we say, that the monkey of Mr Paul Martinetti or Mr George Conquest is more entertaining than that of the distinguished Japanese, who is pleased to call himself, 'Pongo Redivivus'.[2]

> Pongo's performance is only weak in the sense that it is not very funny; it is more to be praised for its truth to its prototype than for the comic side of its character. Such monkeys as have been made popular by Mr George Conquest and Mr Paul Martinetti have gained their reputation by the amusing exaggerations and funny 'business' with which these gentlemen have decorated their mimicry. Neither of these artistes could, probably, use his toes as does Pongo, but it is within the bounds of probability that either could make more of an entertainment of his sketch of the Monkey character. That Pongo's mimicry is legitimate and true there can be no question, but that there is sufficient fun in it to delight those people who expect, before all things, that a monkey shall be very comic, we have our reasonable doubts. For all this, the 'show' is an interesting one, even if only to see how Pongo uses his feet in descending from the ceiling by a rope.[3]

Conquest and Martinetti were established theatre artistes, as opposed to music hall turns, and appeared as animals in pantomimes and pantomimic sketches. We will be looking at these shortly. Kotaky was clearly in the Mazurier mould where the aim was artistry and accuracy not mere laughable entertainment; the music hall was evidently not the correct environment for his display.

Nevertheless, in the early summer of 1879 Kotaky was doubling afternoons at the Aquarium with evenings at the Metropolitan Theatre where the manager must have thought 'Pongo Redivivus' was a bit too learned for his patrons and billed him as 'Pongo the Japanese Man Monkey'. In late summer he too departed for an extensive tour of the continent.

Pedro Sterling, now back from his continental foray, was touring with new partners as 'Casey, Ball & Sterling in their Screaming Acts and Grotesque Sketches including their great speciality Pongo; or the Missing Link'. Although Kotaky was currently abroad, there were other Pongos competing for work. The act that seemed to be garnering most mentions was a high wire walker – Colleen – who trumpeted that he surpassed all the original Pongos. He, at least, was prepared to admit he was not the originator, and as he was with an established trio of trapeze aerialists 'Colleen's Troupe with Frank Angelle and Mdlle Oza', his Pongo was a second spot billed as 'Pongo, Darwin's Missing Link'.

Yet another trio who put together a Pongo sketch was 'Mr & Mrs Leno with Mr Dan Leno'. Yes, the premier comedian of the late Victorian music hall was once a man-monkey! Dan Leno made his name as a solo artiste as a result of his early success as a clog dancer, but for many years he toured with his mother and stepfather in the family song and sketch routines.

More direct competition for Kotaky was:

> The Wonderful TYCOON TROUPE of
> Real JAPANESE, in their Marvellous Feats.
> PONGO, the Great Japanese Man Monkey.
> All should see this Living Wonder.
> A few vacant dates. Share or Certainty.
> Splendid Posters.
> Address, W Brown, Hyde, near Manchester.

Unlike previous man-monkeys who played as Jocko and promoted themselves under their own stage names, the current crop of man-monkeys all called themselves Pongo. Therefore the difficulty in telling which is which, and even calling oneself 'The Japanese Pongo' does not greatly help. Another trick of the 'imposters' was to copy the style of

Kotaky's advertisements in *The Era* by putting Pongo in triplicate so that many ads for man-monkeys were headed PONGO PONGO PONGO.

Other current Pongos were Master C Lauri (whom we shall discuss later), Professor Jamrack, J M Cowper, Ohmy, and Russell Pongo. The Brothers Poluski became Pongo & Jocko with a double monkey act for pantomime in Birmingham.

Trawling through the Calls from 1884 to 1888 reveals Pongo billed at many theatres and music halls, and lacking any indication whether they are artistes already named or others that we know not of, thus remain unidentifiable.

In 1888, two new 'original' Pongos arose. These were 'Francisco, the Spanish Lofty Wire-walker, and Pongo, the Original Spanish Man Monkey', and 'The Original Man Monkey PONGO, James Dubois'.

Such claims to be the 'original,' 'oldest,' 'foremost,' 'greatest', 'only', etc were commonplace in the announcements of music hall artistes, and just as much as 'favourite', 'by public demand', 'few vacancies' and other statements, were only believed by the incredibly naive.

In April 1889, a Leeds critic picked up on this kind of boast: 'Pongo, the man monkey (why the *original*, we do not know, seeing that Teasdale, the *reformed* man monkey, lived sixty years ago) gave a very amusing entertainment.'

> P O N G O,
> the Original Spanish Man Monkey.
> A dispute respecting Pongo.
> Who was it that made a tremendous hit at the
> Eden Theatre, Brussels, and at Eldorado, Antwerp, In 1881 ?
> Why PONGO, the Original Spanish Man Monkey.
> Who was it that created a Furore at the
> Royal Aquarium in 1882?
> PONGO, the Original Spanish Man Monkey.
> Who was it that performed at the Crystal Palace
> with great success in 1885-86?
> PONGO, the Original Spanish Man Monkey.
> And who is the talk of Islington, now performing at the
> ARCADIA, ROYAL AGRICULTURAL HALL, LONDON?
> Why PONGO, the Original Spanish Man Monkey.
> Permanent address, 13 Ida-road, Stamford-hill, London N

The placement of the above advertisement provided some amusing entertainment for regular readers of *The Era* as the Original Spanish Pongo duelled with Dubois the Original Pongo in the pages of the weekly trade paper as to who was the most original.

Dubois responded with an advertisement stating that not only was he retained at the Belle Vue Gardens in Douglas, but offered proof from his mentor that he had been playing as a man-monkey virtually since the live Pongo arrived on the scene when he was but a small boy:

> The Original Man Monkey.
> PONGO, P O N G O, PONGO,
> JAMES DUBOIS.
> Since Originality is disputed, the following is a Copy of a Document forwarded to me by my Tutor, J. Gingero, Esq,
> Notice.
> I Hereby Certify that James Dubois, late of the Royal Tycoon Japanese Troupe, was the First European to Perform the Man Monkey, and styled himself Pongo, and first appeared in such performance at the Paris Hippodrome during the Exhibition of 1878. (Signed) J Gingero, of the Royal Tycoon Japanese Troupe.

So much for the Royal Tycoon Troupe being genuine Japanese! In 1878 Dubois would have been only eight years old. Spanish Pongo, changing his tactics, was now punting to be the cleverest by letting fly with:

> P O N G O
> the Original Spanish Man Monkey
> acknowledged to be the
> Cleverest Perpendicular Rope Performer that has ever been seen, and the nearest approach to a Gorilla.
> PONGO
> PONGO
> PONGO
> You cannot mistake the Artistic Pongo

The following week James Dubois responded with a repeat of his advert plus the line 'Genuine merit succeeds' because he had been retained for a third week in Douglas. Spanish Pongo, still baiting his rival, instead of trumpeting that he was the original and older established performer, now came up with a challenge:

MR PONGO – ENTER THE GORILLA

> Here is a good opportunity for supposed Pongos, who call themselves Monkey Performers.
> I am open to compete with Anybody in the World in Two of the principal Antics of a Gorilla, viz, Running on all Fours and Rope Climbing, say 100 yards running and 100 Feet Climbing, which is a fair trial for anybody.
> The proof of the pudding is in the eating.
> Come up to the scratch.

James Dubois replied with 'The mere play of a child certainly does not constitute an artistic contest, the winning of which could possibly flatter the vanity of an "artist"'. Spanish Pongo was now more concerned with advertising that he had played seven weeks at the Arcadia Royal Agricultural Hall and fixed a tour starting in two weeks time. One wonders what was the response of both these 'originals' to another announcement: 'Como Tarro, Japanese, is the Original Pongo Performer, and Challenges all Imitators.'

Eventually, this nonsensical banter petered out. Today people do this stuff on Twitter, but in those days there was only the public press and the personal postcard. The telephone was still awaited, and though telegrams were now available they were not yet in common use for artistes and agents. It is significant how adverts in *The Era* always asked people to write – the penny post was in force from 1840 to 1918 – a contract could be fixed up in two days.

Other gymnasts calling themselves Pongo appeared, making it pretty impossible often to sort out who was who. Whereas 'man-monkey' had been the generic term for that kind of performer, now 'Pongo' had become a generic. Agents placed advertisements on the lines of 'WANTED. High and low wire and rope walkers, jugglers, acrobats; also a good Pongo and all lines suitable for Fêtes.' For acts that could work in the open air, fêtes were an increasingly growing lucrative work opportunity, and performers who could provide high outdoor rigging were desirable.

Como Tarro was the new Japanese Pongo, his claim – totally false – was 'the only Pongo performing in the World.' How he thought he could get away with that I do not know, but this book was not available then! After six months in Germany, he had returned to challenge all imitators.

Another was Dick Moss whose card read: 'PONGO, PONGO,

PONGO. DICK MOSS, the Greatest of Man Monkeys, is not a Monkey but his imitation is so natural that people cry "Oh, Lor," and throw Nuts, Pineapples, Bricks, and other Foreign Fruits.'

Other Pongos were Fred Harman and Eugene Salvine. Yamamoto came up with a twist, he was 'the Original Pongo, the Man-Monkey, Ponkey.' Another performer produced the inspired version Pon-Gorilla. This may have been the acrobat John Hester who worked in Sanger's circus, and used The Great Pongorilla as a stage name, or another artiste who adopted a similar name.

PON-GORILLA, billed on this German poster of 1880 as 'the First time in Europe', may have been an Englishman.

The Three Brothers Lomas presented a sketch *Troubles in Monkey-land*, thereafter two of the troupe, harking back to former times for their stage names, turned themselves into 'Jacko & Jocko the

Greatest Monkey Performers now before the Public'.

Similar acrobatic monkey sketches were presented by the Coco Troupe in *Monkeymania*, Johnson, Riano and Bentley in *The Farmer and the Monkeys*, and the Lupino Brothers in *The Sailor and the Monkey*. The Four Senetts were a knockabout acrobatic troupe based round a man and his poodle visiting the zoo getting tangled up in the monkey cage.[4] A troupe called Ardel and the Brothers Donaldson presented what must have been a very similar act called *Scenes at the Zoo*.[5] All these were flourishing at the turn of the century.

There can be no definitive listing of man-monkeys during the Pongo craze, many performers turning to the idea but quickly abandoning it; others bought a monkey suit and mask and simply added it to their existing accomplishments. Other names seem to have flourished for a brief time never to be heard of again.

Truly the last two decades of the 19th century and the first decade of the 20th century provided a veritable plethora of Pongos. These were all different from the man-monkeys of old, they did not perform a part in a play, as a character in a story, but were gymnastic speciality acts just as trapeze artistes or wire-walkers. Indeed, most of the man-monkeys 'on the halls' were former and current acrobats, many remaining so as they often performed two separate acts – one in human form and another in a monkey suit. Typical of these were The Arleys a couple of trick cyclists who also performed in ape skins.[6]

The sketch troupes noted above, were merely monkey-dressed-up acrobatic turns. There were much more established troupes, usually family-based units that had flourished over two or three generations. These were pantomime performers who put together plays up to an hour in length, much on the format of Gouffe's *The Island Ape*. These plays or extended sketches – often developed from pantomime routines – toured the variety theatres, the artistes so having a foot in both sides of the entertainment industry. We shall now have a look at these talented and versatile performers.

One of the popular music hall sketch troupes that flourished during the Pongo craze. This foursome comprised a man, a poodle and two apes. A similar act is illustrated below. *Illustrated coloured poster 1883.*

Ardel and the Brothers Donaldson comprised three man-monkeys and one human character. *Illustrated coloured poster 1890.*

Chapter Fourteen
MAN-MONKEYS IN PANTOMIME AND PANTOMIMIC SKETCHES

AFTER GRIMALDI'S DEATH in 1837, the Harlequinade went into a decline and the first part of the pantomime became longer and longer while the Harlequinade section became markedly curtailed. What had been an opening prologue was now fully ten or twelve scenes and the Harlequinade much like an epilogue that tradition alone decreed should remain. Year after year, critics declared that no clown had successfully replaced old Joey, and the Harlequinade had outworn its time the day that Grimaldi died.

Pantomime had changed and the new form reached its zenith in late Victorian times. On Boxing Day, London had 16 pantomimes all packed to the gunnels, a total estimated at 40,000 patrons. Those were the days when Sir Augustus Harris of Drury Lane thought nothing of having 500 personnel in his annual pantomimes which ran nightly for three months. Major provincial cities also had several competing pantomimes. Most man-monkeys gained employment at panto time, thus providing some stability in their regular diet of weekly changes.

As some pantomime subjects required animals as part of the plot – the cow in *Jack & the Beanstalk*, the goose in *Mother Goose*, the cat in *Dick Whittington* are obvious examples – there were performers who specialised in playing just these parts, others were man-monkeys who were versatile enough to take on these additional roles.

These animal impersonators tended to run in families and the business was handed down from father to son. Also, as in many family businesses siblings preferred to go their own way on reaching maturity, often rival companies developing bearing the same family name, each claiming to be 'the original'.

GEORGE CONQUEST

The Conquest family members were renowned for their animal characters, chiefly in pantomime but also in other pieces. George Conquest was a theatrical polymath being an actor, author, acrobat, scene designer, prop maker, theatre manager, and able to turn his hand to most other occupations necessary to running a thriving London theatre. A complete workaholic, it seems impossible that he could accomplish the workload that he did year in and year out.

George Conquest was born in 1837, son of actor-manager Benjamin Conquest. Instead of being brought up from an infant as a theatre child as were many of his contemporaries, George had a formal education including four years in France and a course at the Royal Academy. His father wanted him to be a musician so he could take over the leadership of the band in his theatre. George had no interest in music but, passionate about gymnastics, spent more time in the gym than the conservatoire. As a result, when he joined the family firm at the age of twenty he was bi-lingual, steeped in continental culture, had a library of French plays and was able to design sets. Moreover, he was a shrewd business man, more practical than his father, and he was an accomplished acrobat.

GEORGE CONQUEST
a theatrical polymath

From 1857, George Conquest dominated the pantomimes at his father's Grecian Saloon Theatre when for the next 22 years the annual event was a vehicle for his startling acrobatics and ingenious contrivances. He delighted in oddities and evil characters such as the Demon Dwarf, Grim Goblin, Rock Fiend and Spider Crab. His breakthrough role was the Nondescript in a version of *Peter Wilkins & the Flying Indians*, in effect emulating the success of E J Parsloe thirty years previously.

At this early stage of his career, George was intensely acrobatic, revelling in flights and transformations with elaborate trap work. In the 1862/63 pantomime *The Spider & the Fly*:

> He plays Number Nip in a style which for fantastic activity eclipses anything that has been seen of the kind since the death of Mr Wieland. For more than an hour he sustains a most arduous performance in which he is constantly appearing and disappearing in all positions through more than twenty trap doors fixed in different parts of the stage. This extraordinary agility reaches its extreme height in a scene called "the phantom fight"[1]

The Grecian pantomimes were becoming a major London Christmas attraction and, although the Grecian was a minor theatre, the Conquest family ran it in a fashion that punched above its weight. Not only were the pantomimes written by George Conquest with Henry Spry, George masterminded the whole production being producer, director and star. In the next year's panto *Harlequin Robinson Crusoe*, George naturally played Man Friday incorporating his usual trap antics.

In a career as a theatre manager and performer lasting over 40 years, during which he produced some 45 pantomimes, and appeared as the star in 25 of them, his man-monkey work was but a small part. The reason is that George Conquest was a protean performer who loved transforming himself several times in the course of one show. In pantomime, he normally cast himself as some sort of grotesque – an ogre, dwarf, goblin and so on, but he did not remain in that character throughout:

> It is the great and exceptional talent of Mr Conquest, son of the lessee of this theatre, that chiefly gives value to the new pantomime, *Rik-Rak the Giant of the Mountains*. Mr George Conquest is one of most remarkable artistes of the day, combining the qualities of actor and acrobat to a degree which could not easily be found elsewhere. He can tumble, jump, execute feats on the trapeze, and walk on stilts to perfection, at the same time allowing an histrionic feeling to shine through all his athletic exploits. As the principal character in the new pantomime, he first appears as a Colossus, not to be represented without the most consummate proficiency in walking upon some support that raises the feet high above the ground, and wearing an enormous head that begins where the natural skull leaves off. Superior powers force this gigantic gnome to become first a human turnip, afterwards a monkey. To assume the former character he is compelled to throw aside the gigantic appurtenances and to cram himself into a spherical covering of small diameter, in which constrained position he dances as lightly as a fay. For the representation of the monkey he is armed with the knowledge of all the monkey tricks for which a precedent can be found.[2]

This sort of procedure was George's standard form, over the years appearing in many weird and wonderful transformations and characters. This is a selection – butterfly, pear, spider-crab, vampire bat, toad, octopus, parrot, porcupine, innumerable gnomes and ogres, a multiplicity of devils and demons, and even a severed head. This last affair was a sort of mechanical floating head called Nix that could change expressions. He also had a predilection for performing as a tree, something that he did more often than as a monkey. But it is as a man-monkey that he deserves his place in this book:

> It is, however, in his third form, as a green-haired gorilla, that this gentleman's peerless daring skill and agility as a gymnastic pantomimist are most fully and astonishingly exhibited. A scene in which are all kinds of gymnastic appliances, in the form of boughs, supplies the arena for his wonderful exploits. Here he runs up poles, swings and leaps in quite an ape-like fashion, and disappears and reappears through the floor and walls with lightning speed, and seems like a supernatural being in his marvellous movements. In an outdoor scene he hops on all fours on rods projecting from the wall. This feat is novel and clever in the highest degree. Applause of a very rapturous degree is indulged in by the crowds which assemble to witness Mr Conquest's deeds, and if ever great talent, ingenious devices, downright hard work, and zealous efforts to amuse and astonish an audience, fairly earned the most glowing thanks and congratulations, they do so in this case.[3]

It soon becomes clear that Conquest has not sent his son to be educated in France, but is training him to follow in his footsteps. In *Nix the Demon Dwarf* Conquest advertised that he and his son execute sixty traps and tricks in fifteen minutes; they both jump out of traps to a height of 27 feet; and they dive into traps head foremost from the same height. At the time George Jr was fifteen. This was the scene known as the Phantom Fight which was included in all George's pantomimes.

Conquest took his sources from anywhere, and with his writing partner bent the story to fit his peculiar demands. It is significant that he turned to old material that we have met previously when discussing other man-monkeys – *The Devil on Two Sticks*, *The Gnome Fly* and *Peter Wilkins & the Flying Indians* were all grist to his mill. Apart from writing the pantomimes, George, partnered by either Paul Merritt or Henry Pettitt, wrote a prodigious number of dramas, comedies and farces to occupy his theatre for the rest of the year. Not only did he write the plays, he usually took a leading role and directed them too.

Like in former times, Conquest ran his theatre with a resident company, and all the scenery and costumes made in house. He kept a tight control of expenses and rarely deviated from the salary list he had drawn up. If one of his actors asked for a raise, he rarely got one, and if somebody told him they had got a better offer elsewhere he would say 'Well done, my boy, off you go. Good luck.'

For the 1873/74 panto season George decided that one production was not sufficient so, as well as playing *The Wood Demon* at the

Grecian every evening, in the afternoons he was at the Crystal Palace as the Ogre in *Dame Trot and her Cat* with son George as the Cat. In the 22 February 1874 edition of *Reynold's Newspaper*, George advertised that between the two venues he and his son had leapt, fallen and dived through 2,448 traps since Christmas Eve, and he had daily played twelve different characters – an Ogre, an Imp, an Astrologer, a Pear, a Dwarf, a Fish, Half a Giant, a Tree, Two Giants and Two Fiends. The Grecian pantomime ran the longest of all the theatres in London, usually running into April.

In 1875/76, he was to do a similar double, this time with the Alexandra Palace. Unfortunately he twisted his spine during the dress rehearsal and was indisposed, with the fear that he had done permanent damage. However, it was not so and he bounced back after a two-day postponement. At the Grecian, the pantomime was *Snip-Snap-Snorum* with George as a bird, a monkey and an oyster!

In 1876, Conquest did a deal for the entire English rights with Walter Dando the inventor of a new flying apparatus that enabled leaps of up to 32 feet, and did not require traps cutting into the stage; the latter a bonus for touring productions. He made use of this in the 1876/77 Grecian pantomime *Grim Goblin* where he played an octopus, a demon and a monkey:

> We have on former occasions noticed the monkey performances of Mr Conquest, and it is only left for us to say now that it is the best exhibition of its kind, and that the imitator must have been a very close observer of the animal to be able to reproduce his habits and antics with so much fidelity.[4]

During 1877, George built a completely new theatre of giant proportions that seated over 4000 people, with 1700 in the gallery and 1800 in the pit, but surprisingly sold it two years later.

In July 1878, Conquest was at Brighton recuperating from an indisposition that had warranted a complete rest from professional duties for several weeks.

In March 1879, now for the first time without his own theatre, George set out on his first provincial tour of 16 weeks with *Grim Goblin*.

In 1880, George, George Jr and other family members set out for America for what was intended to be a lengthy stay. No doubt he recalled the success that Gouffe had found there 50 years previously enabling a four year sojourn. The two Georges opened at Wallack's Theatre, New York with *Grim Goblin* which was greeted with delight by the USA audience who had never seen anything like the Phantom Fight. Alas, during the chase of the two Demons, the wire sustaining George at a height broke and he plummeted some twenty feet to the ground falling heavily into the wings landing on an uneven patch. Immediately afterwards, George Jr too suffered a broken wire and was dropped on to the stage, but managed to land on his feet. George's leg was shattered and he was plainly going to be out of action for some weeks.

Performances were suspended for two days and resumed with George Jr playing his dad's role and Mr Manley standing in for George Jr. Alas, at exactly the same point during the Phantom Fight the wires broke, with George Jr falling into the wings and Manley dropping to the stage. Fortunately both men escaped injury and finished the show. George was convinced that sabotage was responsible as the wires appeared to have been severed at exactly the same place and time on both occasions. At a later performance, Ada Conquest playing a fairy fell to the stage smashing her face and breaking her nose and some teeth.

The English contingent left for home as soon as was practicable. USA had been a disaster.

The new Surrey Theatre of 1866 which for twenty years was the home of George Conquest and his outstanding pantomimes.

On his return, George realised his acrobatic days were over, therefore he could not exist without his own theatre. With Merritt as a partner, he took a lease on the Surrey Theatre south of the river. This was not the same building that had launched Gouffe to become the doyen of man-monkeys; that one had burned down in 1865.

In this new theatre, from 1881 to 1901, George produced an annual pantomime and these became as famous as his Grecian ones had been, but he only ever personally appeared in one, his sons coming to the fore as regular performers.

However, in 1882 he wrote and starred in a sensational melodrama called *For Ever* which one review described as 'a bewildering and a wearying conglomeration of crimes – ranging from poisoning to cutting throats – of the grotesque and horrible, and the loathsome.' The authors had stuck at nothing in order to pile on the agony, nothing was too wildly improbable for them to include, nothing too inhuman, nothing too repulsive, even a scene in a charnel house with sickening and harrowing details about the victims of cholera. The play was a complicated tale based around a man-monkey. The normal point of a man-monkey is that he is a human being exactly copying the mannerisms and actions of a simian, in other words an actor imitating an ape. The part, Zacky Pastrana, obviously created to Conquest's strengths, is actually half man, half ape (a 'missing link') offering an unclear ambivalence between an animal with human passions, and a man who has absorbed the habits of an ape. The play is in seven acts and on the first night lasted nearly five hours. It was eventually pruned to 3½ hours, proving a huge success with the 'gods' who revelled in having George the man-monkey back, scrambling about and performing a cut-down version of his Phantom Fight. It did not all go according to the writers' intentions with Zacky's mad scene raising laughs rather than pathos. The play ran for several weeks in spite of damning reviews:

> Mr Conquest's ape is an exceedingly unpleasant creation . . . so utterly disgusting is the spectacle of this hideous, hairy, chattering monstrosity exhibiting his passion for a comely young woman. . . . simply loathsome . . . a feeling of sickening aversion.[5]

> A "missing link" grotesquely acted by Mr Conquest. The task of entering into details of the horrors contained in a transpontine seven-act melodrama is too herculean for the present writer, whose mental digestion has not yet recovered from the shock of swallowing so much blood and fire.[5]

> Nothing more flagitious or revolting was ever done in public in the days of the vilest corruption of the Roman Empire. Even the most depraved minds of ancient as well as modern times have avoided the hideous subject of monstrosity, which is in this age the latest tit-bit of theatrical sensation. Fortunately, however, as well as sublimity is near neighbour to the ridiculous. Instead of shuddering at the man-monkey, the Surrey audiences laugh at him. What was meant as tragedy is taken as comedy, and the audiences are pleased with a pantomime instead of nauseated with a beastly romance.[5]

The aspect of the play that revolted most people was the heroine's father persuading her to marry the freak. All this was grist to Conquest's publicity mill and his adverts made great play of the adverse comments:

> FOR EVER: The greatest sensational drama ever written or conceived. Seven acts of realism and emotion. It is the most horrible, blood-curdling, terrible, savage, weird, revolting, fascinating, and attractive Play ever produced, so says the Press.[6]

The play was revived for a run in 1884 when George's prowess as a pantomime actor were thought exceedingly clever and interesting but 'the sight of a half-man, half-beast monstrosity making love to a woman is repulsive'. That was the last of George Conquest's career as a man-monkey. He ran the Surrey as a melodrama house with a long-running pantomime at Christmas, but after his wife died in a coach accident in 1890 the spark went out of George. He soldiered on, with his sons Arthur and Fred taking on the trap work in the pantomimes.

In 1896, a touring production of *For Ever* promoted and directed by George Conquest did the rounds with Harry Pleon in the role of Zacky Pastrana.

George Conquest died on 14 May 1901 leaving £64,000 – over £6 million in today's prices.

Zacky Pastrana

George's three sons George Jr, Arthur and Fred took over the theatre and continued for a couple of years but times were changing in the new century. New rules and regulations that were tiresome for theatre managers used to their former freedoms led to the business being given up. The sons went their separate ways, with Arthur and Fred forming separate sketch companies to tour the variety theatres.

CHARLES LAURI Jr

Acrobats who played in the pantomime Harlequinades – which were rapidly losing favour after the death of Grimaldi – had to find similar work elsewhere for the rest of the year as pantomimes were now rarely performed at times other than Christmas. One solution was to incorporate the techniques of trap work, flying and transformations from the Harlequinade to the more modern form of the sketch presented as a feature on a variety bill at a music hall.

One of the top pantomime sketch troupes of the day was the Lauri family who styled themselves the Lauri-Lauris. The head of the troupe was Charles who played Clown in panto Harlequinades and claimed to have been in the last show that Queen Victoria watched before going into purdah on the death of dear Albert. Other Lauris were John, Henry, Edward, Louisa, Master Charles and Master George.

Apart from pantomime, either as a troupe, or individuals in separate theatres, for most of the year they travelled as a troupe presenting a knock-about sketch. An advertisement in 1873 boasted they had spent four years in America with their sketch *Le Diable de l'Eglise* with the Phantom Fight. They had done 634 performances in New York alone. The sketch was invented by John Lauri and all the machinery, traps and effects were 'legally secured by Act of Congress'.[7] Returning from the USA, the Lauris went straight to Paris for 8 months with the Folies Bergère, and other continental engagements. A pantomime act could work anywhere in the world as they had no language barrier and physical comedy is universal, hence the world-wide fame of Charlie Chaplin and Mr Bean in later years.

Returning home in 1876, Charles Lauri was engaged for pantomime at Drury Lane in the role of Clown which he had previously played for eight consecutive years, and was now returning after a gap of nine years. Also engaged were sister Fanny, brother Henry and son Charles Jr. In the pantomime, the Lauris presented their own exclusive kitchen scene which was 'protected at home and abroad'. After which Charles and Henry went straight off to Belfast to perform in another pantomime with Master Charles Lauri ('the little ball of quicksilver'), while Fanny ('the acme of grace and elegance') joined their other brother Edward at Southampton. The troupe spent summer at Cremorne Gardens, a venue similar to the more popular Vauxhall Gardens.

Rebooked at Drury Lane for the following year's pantomime *The White Cat*, Master Charles Lauri gained many plaudits as 'a young man who appears to be equal to any emergency, and to be running over with comicality.' He played the Fiend Cat and 'presented to our notice some of the best pantomime we have seen, and moreover proved himself an acrobat of no mean ability.'[8]

Charles H Lowe, the son of Charles Earith Lowe (Lauri was a stage name) was born on 17 March 1860 at Islington. After joining the family troupe at Birmingham at the age of six he played with them from that point on.

For the 1878/79 season Charles Jr, parting from his family, moved to Covent Garden where Harry Payne was the Clown. Charles, now eighteen, played a poodle in *Jack & the Beanstalk*. In this role he behaved like a real dog including jumping through a hoop and other animal tricks.

CHARLES LAURI JR photographed in St Petersburg

Returning to Covent Garden for the 1879/80 season, Charles Jr, jumping on the new and now booming Pongo bandwagon, played Pongo in *Sindbad the Sailor*:

> Certainly one of the biggest hits of the performance was made by Master C Lauri as Pongo. So active and comical a stage monkey has not often been seen. This monkey's escape from shipwreck, is about as clever and comical a bit of business as has ever been executed, and while it was in progress every spectator was screaming with delight. . . . Master Lauri distinguished himself by running up a rope stretched perpendicularly from the stage to the flies, by taking headers through traps and property frying pans and by a number of antics of an exceedingly droll description, and denoting extraordinary gymnastic skill. That Master Lauri was heartily applauded "goes without saying."[9]

> The laughter for both young and old undoubtedly has its main source in the lively and mischievous antics of a certain Pongo in the person of Master Lauri.[10]

At the end of the season Charles Jr rejoined his family in Paris to play in a sketch called *Tot, Tot, Tot; or the Rendezvous* which, in the family repertoire for 15 years, had achieved 2814 performances. After five months in Paris, the troupe moved on to Germany. The family had also been booked for the next Covent Garden pantomime thus switching allegiance from Drury Lane to be with Charles Jr who was playing Little Bear with the three bears who had been wedged into the old story of *Valentine and Orson*. Charles stated in an interview that he had bought a small bear so that he could watch it closely at home and learn its movements. 'Master C Lauri does wonders; in fact, it may be said that, without his athletic extravagances, the pantomime would be robbed of one of its chief attractions.'[11]

The premiere danseuse was Mdlle Zanfretta with whom our hero obviously fell in love as she was to become the future Mrs Lauri.

After the Garden's panto closed, Charles Jr went to the Grecian and appeared there in *Harlequin King Frolic* once again playing Pongo. It being mid-March, all the other pantomimes had now closed so it was in the nature of a bonus for pantomime lovers.

> Nor must I forget to mention the doings of Master Lauri, who, released from Covent Garden, disports here, in the guise of a monkey, with an amount of agility which is astounding. With this young gentleman's ability I think it quite unnecessary that he should frame the principal portion of his performance on that given by an individual who some time ago was exhibiting his prowess under the *nom de theatre* of Pongo Redivivus. Some of the details of monkey life which are imitated by him, too, might be advantageously omitted, as it tends to unnecessarily lengthen the entertainment. It is a marvellous performance, however.[12]

Not many critics were astute enough to realise when a performer had ripped off another man's material, or at least they were rarely bold enough to say so in print. In later years when Pongo Redivivus had been well and truly forgotten, Lauri bent the truth somewhat by claiming he had been inspired by the antics of a performing monkey called Pongo, and thought that if he had a suit made he could imitate a monkey. By then he was a major star of pantomime renowned for his ability to play an assortment of animals and could tell reporters anything.

The same critic also stated that 'A pantomime that plays four hours is too long.' Pantomimes were no longer afterpieces, following a serious drama, those days had gone and the panto was now the full evening's entertainment – but four hours! Really!

Mr Charles Lauri Jr (now officially an adult) was engaged by Augustus Harris at Drury Lane for his next pantomime season where he played Man Friday in *Robinson Crusoe* and 'may be pronounced wonderful. His rope climbing, his somersaults, his grotesque dancing, his general activity and never tiring pranks astonish as they amuse.'

On 6 May 1882, Charles married Francesca Virginia Zanfretta who had been born in Milan and made her dance debut in Prague. The groom was twenty-two, the bride twenty.

The following season (1882/83), back at Drury Lane, Charles reprised his dog routine in *Sindbad the Sailor*: 'For fantastic fun the performance depends almost exclusively upon the exertions of Mr C Lauri as a performing poodle.'

As customary, Charles went on to the continent after the pantomime season with the Lauri-Lauris Pantomime Company now under the directorship of C & C Lauri Jr, Henry having split off to form his own troupe.

When all the proposals for 1883/84 pantomimes came in, the Lauris were obliged to turn down offers from Covent Garden, Drury Lane, and Her Majesty's, postponing panto engagements until the following year as they were having such a resounding success in Paris where Charles Jr was the 'L'Homme Singe' (The Ape Man) for 300 performances. It was now 60 years since Mazurier had charmed all Paris with his Jocko, the Brazilian Ape.

The company spent the best part of two years in Paris returning to London for the 1884/85 season when Charles Jr was the Cat in *Dick Whittington* at Drury Lane with Mdlle Zanfretta, while his father was with the troupe at Sheffield in *Sinbad the Sailor*. Charles Lauri Jr was now an established star and his animal impersonations were a highlight of any show he was in. However, our theme is the man-monkey so we are obliged to gloss over his many other animal accomplishments, though in the 1886/87 Drury Lane pantomime *Forty Thieves*, whilst Charles Jr played a Donkey he was joined by Paul Martinetti as a Monkey.

In 1889, Charles Lauri senior died, and his son, now riding high, took sole control of the Lauri-Lauris troupe. Although now no longer referred to as 'Junior', in an interview with the *Pall Mall Gazette* the reporter expressed incredulity when Charles revealed he was twenty-nine as he looked like a boy of fifteen. Charles stated that he never played in the provinces between London panto seasons, but preferred taking his own company to the capitals of Europe where he was a bigger star than even in this country. He was now a regular in the Drury Lane pantomime and would be pleased to return annually as long as Mr Augustus Harris was happy to keep him, disclosing that he was paid £50 a week.

CHARLES LAURI
photographed in Paris

The interview included several line drawings of Lauri as various animal characters with two different monkeys. In this interview Charles comes across as appearing rather 'big time'.

In 1891, Charles was engaged at the Alhambra Theatre in a ballet *Oriella* playing Astarte a Chameleon Demon. He also played his famous poodle in a sketch *The Sculptor and the Poodle*. He went straight from that into the Drury Lane pantomime which starred Dan Leno, Herbert Campbell, Little Tich and Marie Lloyd, all the biggest music hall names of the day. The Demon Cat was played by the Brothers Kitchen. Charles was reduced to playing an eccentric waiter until the Harlequinade when Harry Payne, the Drury Lane clown for many years, played with his regular supporting cast, while Charles as a *fin de siècle* version clown performed with his own troupe a sketch called *On the Roof*.

Charles was also becoming an impresario, putting out tours of shows in which he did not appear in person, and while he, himself, was at Drury Lane, his company was playing in Paris. The Lauri family became fragmented with his uncle and cousins going their own way. Charles's brother-in-law Enrico Zanfretta became a stalwart of the re-jigged troupe. At Easter 1892, Charles himself appeared at the South London Palace in a sketch called *The Sioux* in which he played the monkey Chadi. He had played this for several weeks at the up-market Alhambra in the West End, and it was to be his meal ticket when he started touring the English provinces, which was something he had previously not deigned to do. Although set in the Wild West with settlers and Indians, *The Sioux* owed a lot to Jocko.

CHARLES LAURI ventured out into the minor theatres with a new sketch that kept him going for the rest of his life.   Playbill 1892.

Mr Charles Lauri's imitation of the movements and grimaces of a monkey is a wonderful piece of work. He has evidently studied from life, and the truth of his performance must be seen to be appreciated. It is also a gymnastic and aerobatic achievement of a high order, especially striking being Mr Lauri's ascent and descent of a perpendicular rope which he grasps between his first and second toes, only assisting himself with one hand. His leaps, swingings, drops, dartings, climbings, and gestures are simply marvellous; and the death of Chadi is one of the most pathetic things ever seen on the stage; the dying agonies of the man-monkey are so intensely real, and yet so essentially simian It is the essence of dumb tragedy.[13]

PANTOMIME & PANTOMIMIC SKETCHES

Times were obviously changing as Charles, now not only taking engagements at the lesser theatres and music halls of London, set out on his first UK provincial tour of a pantomimic play called *Le Voyage en Suisse*. He was not playing an animal and the piece was a knockabout farce of acrobatics. This 23-week tour took him up to panto time at the New Olympic Theatre where he played the Cat in *Dick Whittington* while his troupe was at the Crystal Palace in *Babes in the Wood* with the *On the Roof Sketch* which Charles had done at Drury Lane.

No longer a stalwart of the Drury Lane pantomime, for the following three years Charles played in matinee-only pantomimes at the Lyceum Theatre, the theatrical home of Henry Irving. In 1895/96 he played Man Friday in *Robinson Crusoe* during which it was promised he would change into a monkey in sight of the audience. In the evening he was with his troupe in an elongated farcical pantomime sketch *The Housewarming* that had been a success for him in Paris. In this Charles played a speaking role, thus eschewing his unique status as the No 1 animal impersonator.

In 1898 Charles went into partnership with Madame Bayet at the Alcazar Theatre, Brussels. This did not prosper and the partnership ended early in 1899. Charles was declared bankrupt with debts of £1200 (£120,000 in today's money). His main activity now was appearing with his Lauri-Lauris company in pantomimic sketches throughout the UK provinces with occasional forays into Europe. The only family members now involved with Charles, were his wife (still professionally Mdlle Zanfretta) and brother-in-law Enrico.

For the 1899/1900 season Lauri was Cat in *Puss in Boots* at the Garrick Theatre, whilst his troupe provided the Harlequinade in *Dick Whittington* at the Borough Theatre, Stratford. Thereafter Charles and his troupe embarked on provincial weeks. They had a good selection of pantomimic sketches in their repertoire which had usually started out as a feature of some past pantomime and, ringing the changes on these, variously provided Charles with a human role, or chance to play bear, cat, dog or monkey. As only one sketch is pertinent to our theme we must ignore these and concentrate on:

> The Garrick of Animal Mimes,
> **CHARLES LAURI**
> In the North American Play without words
> "The Sioux" in
> which Mr Lauri impersonates
> Chadi, the Man Monkey,
> supported by full Pantomime Company.

This music hall sketch, which thrived for the rest of Lauri's life, was dragged out time and time again amongst pantomimes and other offerings. This is a brief synopsis curtailed from the first night review:

> The scene is a picturesque settlement in the "Wild West." The settler's eldest son has brought home some very pretty presents and one very ugly one in the shape of a man-monkey (Mr Charles Lauri). It is to that monkey we have to look for the principal fun, for the man-monkey will set everybody sneezing by playing too freely with the pepper-box, or pelt the Indian enemy with bricks, or walk a perpendicular rope with all the skill of a Japanese funambulist. This rope ascent and descent by Mr Charles Lauri is the most notable thing in connection with *The Sioux*, and on Monday evening it called for a hurricane of applause. There is much leaping through windows, and many sudden strange disappearances through trick boxes and sacks, and in the end, when the monkey has assisted the settler's young daughter to escape from a burning house, and has been shot, the artist gives a remarkable illustration of pantomimic skill in the realisation of the animal's death.[14]

CHARLES LAURI
as Chadi in
The Sioux

The *mise-en-scène* may be different but the plot line is not dissimilar to that of *Jocko, the Brazilian Ape* of 70 years before, in that the hero of the piece is an Englishman surrounded by a hostile enemy. There is a child befriended by a friendly ape who charmingly plays games and tricks with him/her. The sketch ends with the ape being shot, dying a dramatic death that brings tears to the eyes.

There are extant photographs of Charles Lauri as two very different monkeys, the one described here is his costume in *The Sioux*.

Lauri first bound his ankles with a couple of strong, stout strips of linen, then he donned brown socks with a hole for every toe. The costume was put on, and combed out. Making up his face, he put blue eye shadow round both eyes, then with a mixture of lard and burnt umber he covered his face except where the mask would be placed. A little blue added to the brown on the face, and a few wrinkles painted about the eyes in black and red completed the make-up. He also made up his arms and hands.

The mask Lauri wore was made of chocolate-coloured leather which covered the lower part of the face, so as to obtain the heavy, protruding jaw of the animal. The actor had a spring in his own mouth, which worked the mouth of the animal and showed the two rows of large ivory teeth. The mask was strapped round the neck and over the head. Separate movement of the heavy eyebrows was obtained by a thread concealed in his costume, a wig and whiskers completed the operation.

Lauri was playing *The Sioux* until at least November 1901, alternating with *Gelert* – a sketch based on the Welsh legend of a faithful wolfhound that Lauri changed to a collie on the grounds that the human skeleton could not be distorted to resemble a wolfhound.

Charles's bankruptcy was discharged in February 1902 after a three-year suspension. In October, he was reported to be ailing, but in December he opened in the pantomime *Robinson Crusoe* at Manchester playing Man Friday, including the visible change into his man-monkey garb. With a part specially written, the star of the show was the American James E Sullivan who had recently had a big success in *The Belle of New York*.

All went well until Monday 9 February 1903 when Lauri fainted at the end of his spot and had to be carried to his dressing room. He turned up on the following day for the matinee prepared to work, but manager Robert Courtneidge immediately sent him home to rest. He died at his lodgings at noon the next day. He was 42 years of age. His friends knew he had been suffering from tuberculosis for some time but, always presenting a cheerful front, he had expected to make it to the end of the panto season.

Charles Lauri:
The Dangers of Animal Mimicry.
The peculiarly saddening part of the affair is that there is more than a probability that the consumption which killed the great mimic was festered – if not engendered

– by the nature of his art and its trying requirements. He was always laced into a furry skin which fitted close to his body, giving little or no ventilation. Swathed in this leather attire, he spent hours in the terrible heat of the footlights and the gas in the borders. And in these conditions he was performing a variety of acrobatic and muscular exercises – springing, leaping, jumping, – so that when, at the close of the evening, he "peeled" the mimic skin from his body, he was in a bath of perspiration from head to foot. Animal mimicry, there can be no doubt, is a dangerous and merciless profession, and poor Lauri has not been its only victim.[15]

In his latter years Lauri had been working to discharge his debts, but he was still totally insolvent when he died, leaving his wife and daughter destitute. Concerned colleagues agreed to inaugurate a fund to provide for the widow and child, and an eight-man committee was formed which included Arthur Collins the manager of Drury Lane who had succeeded Sir Augustus Harris, Oscar Barrett a promoter who had often engaged Lauri, and fellow man-monkey Paul Martinetti.

The list of subscribers was headed by an anonymous gift of £100, followed by the Eccentric Club with ten guineas. Sir Charles Wyndham and Sir Henry Irving each contributed five guineas. Paul Martinetti gave three guineas, his brother Alfred two. Arthur Conquest gave a guinea and bought the rights, scenery and costumes of Lauri's two latest sketches *The Sioux* and *Gelert* with the intention of presenting himself in the Charles Lauri roles. He also undertook to employ the existing supporting performers.

PAUL MARTINETTI

Paul Martinetti was a pantomimist from the age of seven, being one of the Martinetti family who worked in an American combination with the famous French Ravel family which at its peak was 90 strong. He was the fourth generation of the family who started out in Italy, moved to France and thence to the USA. Paul Martinetti first came to the notice of the English theatre scene via reports in *The Era* newspaper despatched from Australia where the family was touring in 1868. They were back in their home country by 1870, and became involved in a lawsuit with a Boston manager as on their arrival for a four-week engagement the company were two short of the planned personnel making the performances weak. To add to this, Paul Martinetti was taken ill half-way through the first week. The manager cancelled their engagement on the grounds that the troupe was not the same as the one he had contracted. The Martinettis sued for their unpaid salary. The court agreed with the manager and ruled they were entitled to $250 only, this being half a week's salary.

Back at full strength they continued playing 'with distinction that is world-wide' for another three years while making plans to invade England which they did in 1874, after appointing sole agents to arrange suitable bookings for their arrival. The Martinetti repertoire comprised several pantomimic sketches that ran from 40 to 60 minutes each, but the one that was dangled as the principal attraction was *The Brazilian Ape*:

PAUL MARTINETTI

The novelty of the night was the Ballet Pantomime of *Jocko; or, the Brazilian Ape*, originally performed at Covent Garden fifty years ago, with the once-famous Frenchman Mazurier in the part of the Monkey. This is here represented with excellent effect by the American pantomimist Paul Martinetti, whose gambols and antics are exceedingly entertaining, while his command of pantomime expression is remarkable.[16]

Paul Martinetti and his 'Renowned American Pantomime Company', rapidly assimilated into the English music hall scene, became a rival to Charles Lauri's far longer established Lauri-Lauris troupe. As both principals wrote their own sketches the repertoires did not often clash except, of course, in the monkey pieces. Charles Lauri Jr was no longer the outstanding man-monkey, as Martinetti wooed the public with a play called *Mongo* with a plot so like that of *The Brazilian Ape* one wonders how they knew which one they were supposed to be playing that night.

Like the Lauri-Lauris, for great slabs of the year the Martinettis played the capitals of Europe with a repertoire of pantomimic sketches.

Paul Martinetti was described as the 'drollest of the droll' and his troupe also played roles in Harlequinades, though not in the now outworn traditional form as the Yanks believed in modernisation. Apart from the monkey, Martinetti did not play animals, which were the lifeblood of Charles Lauri.

> Paul Martinetti besides superintending the entire performance, plays the part of Mongo, a creature of the gorilla species, whose movements are characterised by marvellous celerity, and who does a vast deal of mischief and causes infinite mirth by upsetting tables and other articles of furniture, breaking crockery, scattering or devouring viands, whirling garments about, and upsetting everybody. Mongo's actions are not all random, meaningless, and hurtful. He displays intelligence, affection, and fidelity in conjunction with the rescue from the ocean of an infant lashed to a floating spar. This child is borne by Mongo on his back when he ascends trees and darts hither and thither. At the last when the animal is wounded, it brings forth from its lair its little pet which is recognised and embraced by its glad mother, as its strange preserver and friend dies. Of Mr Paul Martinetti's agility, industry and ability it is impossible to speak too highly.[17]

It is impossible to know if Martinetti and Lauri were amicable, or professional enemies, their adverts, often being placed in juxtaposition in *The Era* columns, trumpeted their current achievements but without the knocking copy that sullied the 'original Pongos' we saw earlier. Paul Martinetti was certainly popular amongst his colleagues, becoming prominent in showbiz social circles by joining various clubs and charitable orders like the Grand Order of Water Rats which elected him King Rat, serving on the Music Hall Railway Association committee, one year writing a personal cheque for a £250 insurance premium when the Association's finances were stretched, and serving on the committee of the Music Hall Artistes Benevolent Fund.

In 1880, Martinetti injured with a sword thrust to the eye, spent some days in Westminster hospital, but fortunately, unlike poor James Parsloe, his sight was not damaged and he was back onstage the following week.

In 1886, the Lauri-Lauris troupe was appearing for several months at the Eden Theatre in Brussels, while the Martinettis were appearing for eighteen weeks in the same city at the Theatre de la Bourse. In *Jocko, the Brazilian Ape*, Paul M gave such a finished portrait of the monkey that one critic suggested it might well form a companion picture to Charles Lauri's cat. This comment may have sowed the seeds of Augustus Harris's idea of having both stars in the same pantomime. However it came to be, the Drury Lane pantomime of 1886/87 had Lauri, not as a cat but as a Donkey, Martinetti as a Monkey.

One can but speculate how these two worked amicably together as not only were they both accomplished man-monkeys but their pantomime sketch companies played the same continental venues in direct opposition. Was Charles so sure of his position that he did not fear competition, or had he not the clout to oppose it? It must have irked him to read Martinetti boasting in his adverts that he was 'the Greatest of Ape Delineators'. It is to be hoped that they worked in harmony when we read:

> Two characters, whose names are not to be found in any extant edition of the *"Thousand and One Nights,"* are introduced — an extremely clever donkey (Mr. Charles Lauri jun), and a marvellously agile monkey (Mr Paul Martinetti), whose antics, if a little prolonged, create roars of laughter. Both animals are attached to Ali Baba's household, and befriend him in various ways. We may enter a protest against their race round the dress circle, which may not be dangerous to themselves, but is certainly the source of alarm in all those who are sitting below them. These "games" should be discontinued.[18]

Martinetti and his troupe also provided the Harlequinade which the progressive Augustus Harris was annually squeezing into oblivion.

It does not seem as though Martinetti and Lauri worked together again, though their relations would seem to be friendly enough considering Martinetti was prominent amongst the committee charged with raising funds to support Lauri's widow and family.

In 1891, Martinetti returned to tour America with his company, the first time since leaving 14 years previously. A dinner was held for the popular performer at which his many friends and colleagues wished him *bon voyage*. The company was away for 32 weeks and on his return Martinetti took out long advertisements in *The Era* trumpeting his success with detailed press reviews.

There was never a week when the trade newspaper did not carry an advertisement for the Paul Martinetti Renowned American Pantomime Company. His successes throughout frequent seasons in Europe, always lavishly advertised afterwards, launched him into the 'acknowledged greatest mime in the world.' Martinetti created many successful sketches – *Robert Macaire*, *A Terrible Night*, *A Duel in the Snow* and many more – but left the boast of 'the greatest of ape delineators' far behind him.

Paul Martinetti worked for some four years after Lauri's death, retiring around 1907 but still took a passionate interest in his profession – he had helped to found the Variety Artistes Federation in 1906. Mr & Mrs Martinetti were good friends of Belle Elmore, a music hall performer married to an American doctor called Crippen, and were present at an evening party given at Crippen's house. Shortly after, they were told by Crippen that his wife had run off to America with her paramour. Suspicions were aroused when, at a Benevolent Fund dinner, Dr Crippen arrived with his typist, and Mrs Martinetti noticed she was wearing a brooch that belonged to Belle Elmore. The Martinettis and other friends ensured that enquiries were instituted rousing the police to action. It was suggested at Crippen's trial that Mrs Crippen was poisoned by her husband immediately after the dinner at which Mr and Mrs Martinetti were present.

After 15 years of retirement Paul Martinetti's health was no longer good. He went to Algiers hoping to improve his condition, staying some months at the Mustapha Hotel. Suffering a deterioration, he was taken to the British Nursing Home in Algiers where he laid indisposed for ten days before dying on 26 December 1924. In accordance with local custom, he was buried on the following day at 4 pm. The chief mourner was Mrs Clara Martinetti, accompanied by the local doctor and nurse, the proprietor of the Mustapha Hotel, and two other friends. He left £11,408 9s 1d – £622,286 in today's money, a far different end from the many previous man-monkeys who died in poverty, often at an early age.

ARTHUR AND FRED CONQUEST

With the death of Lauri and the retirement of Martinetti, the man-monkey as a star turn rested with the sons of George Conquest – Arthur and Fred – who followed in their father's footsteps as specialists in animal impersonation, being especially in demand for pantomime.

ARTHUR CONQUEST appeared in every Drury Lane pantomime for 20 years, except for three years when he was away fighting for king and country. At various times in the pantomimes he not only played Cat, Goose, Cow and Dog, but also a parrot and a penguin. Occasionally he even appeared as a human being, playing dame roles. He was particularly associated with the Cat in *Dick Whittington* in which he ran along the padded front of the dress circle, suffering the patting and stroking of children who invariably pushed sweets into his mouth.

When not in pantomime Arthur toured the halls with sketches full of spine-chilling thrills. On a tour of America he played the Demon of Misrule, a Satanic red figure that sprang from star traps, bounding ten feet into the air in a bewildering display of trap and wire work obviously built on the Phantom Fight of father George. He also plundered his father's back catalogue by devising a sensation sketch called *Zacky* based on George's character in *For Ever*.

Then, as noted previously, Arthur acquired Charles Lauri's elaborate sketch *The Sioux* which he performed for some years. He was hailed as the legitimate successor to Lauri with some critics thinking he even surpassed the originator:

> The renown enjoyed by the late Charles Lauri as an animal impersonator now belongs in a great measure to Mr Arthur Conquest, who has taken up the role of Chadi the ape, in *The Sioux*. Mr Conquest has in many ways improved upon his famous predecessor in the part, which benefits by the artistic methods inherited from a parent who made a reputation in similar studies of animal life. Mr Arthur Conquest's portrayal of the gorilla who saves his master's little child from the clutches of the bloodthirsty Red Indians is startling in its realism, the monkey-like antics, leaps, and bounds being so cleverly executed that it is hard to believe that a human being is concealed beneath the hairy covering. Roars of laughter accompany every fantastic trick and every merry prank until the end, when the pathos of Chadi's death-scene becomes very acute.[19]

> The Sioux ... is notable for the impersonation of an ape given by Mr Arthur Conquest. Early training and constant practise have combined to make Mr Conquest's animal impersonations of surpassing excellence, and his performance of the faithful Chadi is perhaps his most finished essay. Every characteristic of the species is copied with unswerving fidelity, and it is little wonder that at the end of the eloquent death-scene the house, which has been moved alternately to laughter and tears, should display its admiration in long-sustained cheers.[20]

It appears as though two further simian dramas were in Arthur's repertoire *The Monkey Hero* (1902) and *Saved by an Ape* (1910) but as both these feature the heroine tied to railway lines being rescued in the nick of time – also the climax of *Zacky* – it looks suspiciously like the same piece masquerading under three different titles.

ARTHUR CONQUEST as Daphne

Arthur, while still playing pantomime animals, eschewed the dramatic sketches, replacing them with farces such as *Harnessing a Horse* and *The Lost Umbrella* both by comedian Will Evans with whom Arthur made a film in 1914 called *Whitewashing the Ceiling* which, like many early silent films, was a short slapstick stage routine filmed with a static camera.

But in 1926, returning to the man-monkey costume, he toured in a musical comedy called *King Rags* which starred Wee Georgie Wood, a diminutive man who passed as a boy in this rags-to-riches Ruritanian spoof. Arthur doubled as Colonel Blah and the palace ape. It was during this tour that he was inspired to come up with another ape character, and in 1927 he started the variety act 'Daphne the Chimpanzee' in Leeds. With this short turn he subsequently toured the UK and Europe for years. At first, billed under Arthur's name, it was soon realised that the impact was greater if the act was presented as a performing chimp called Daphne, leaving the audience to wonder if she be animal or human – the same ploy that man-monkeys were using 100 years previously. The act was presented by his daughter Betty, the revelation of the man inside the skin at the end when he removed his mask being a real applause puller.

Arthur retired in 1939 and died in December 1945.

FRED CONQUEST was four years older than brother Arthur and his career followed a very similar path of annual pantomimes, and travels with a sketch company on the halls the rest of the year. At the Surrey theatre – managed by his father George – Fred was in every pantomime from 1889 to 1900 playing an assortment of animal, comedy and character roles. Each year there was a trap scene which involved Fred and Arthur under George's direction.

After the sons gave up the Surrey following George's death in 1901, Fred was not a fixture at one theatre for his pantomimes, becoming a feature in most principal cities of the land playing chiefly the Goose in *Mother Goose* but also dog and parrot. In 1904, Fred assumed his father's role as Zacky in a revival of *For Ever*:

FRED CONQUEST

> *For Ever*, that typical Conquest melodrama, created some sensation when produced many years ago at the Old Surrey Theatre. It has now been revived, and last night the stock company at the Grand, Islington, presented it to a large and delighted audience. Mr Fred Conquest, in that terribly weird role, "the Man-Monkey," did not lack success, although Miss Helen Bancroft appeared to have quite failed to grasp the spirit of her part.[21]

In 1906, in partnership with Tom Craven, Fred wrote 'a New and Original Sketch of Human Interest, acknowledged by all to be the most Original and Sensational Sketch now before the public.' The catch-penny title of this opus was *The Freak's Revenge*.

The plot is melodramatic to say the least and introduces a gorilla as well as the freakish man-monkey: Arrivals at a country inn comprise Captain Vulcan with his wife and adopted daughter Netta. The landlord informs them of a travelling menagerie that has just arrived in the locality. One of the attractions is a freak known as a man-monkey who has an ape-like appearance but the intelligence of a human being. Vulcan is alarmed by this news as the creature appears to be Esau, whose wife he ran away with some years previously. The runaway wife died leaving her daughter in the care of Vulcan. The captain, making haste to leave, meets the man-monkey who recognises him as the destroyer of his domestic happiness. Esau's chance of revenge is at hand. The freak has a companion gorilla that shows wonderful intelligence and obedience to the man-monkey.

Esau plies the gorilla with whisky and, when suitably savage with drink, sends him up the side of the inn to where he believes Mrs Vulcan is lodged. Then to his horror Esau learns that the female in the room is not Mrs Vulcan but his own daughter Netta. Esau immediately follows the gorilla and is only just in time to stop the animal murdering the girl, whereupon the gorilla turns on the man-monkey and a fight to the death ensues. The gorilla is killed but Esau himself is fatally wounded in the fierce struggle and dies in the presence of Vulcan who begs forgiveness for the wrong he did all those years ago. Esau dies after giving his forgiveness.

They don't write them like that anymore! The cast of seven mainly comprised ex-members of the Surrey stock company, with Fred as the man-monkey, and Leon Dubois as the gorilla. The sketch toured a total of fifty weeks in 1906 and 1907.

FRED CONQUEST in The Freak's Revenge *the sensation play of 1906.*

In 1913 and 1916, Fred took his company to South Africa for several months. On arrival Fred needed an operation after an accident – ironically he injured himself playing a deck game on the voyage! On the first visit the troupe played a 'screamingly funny sketch' called *What a Dog* with Fred as Fido the dog. On the next visit the same piece was described as a 'farcical absurdity'. Together with one or two more farcical sketches including *Something for Nothing* Fred continued his career with this limited repertoire and does not appear to have played a man-monkey ever again.

Fred retired to his long-held home at Bembridge on the Isle of Wight, where he died on 24 March 1941 at the age of seventy.

Chapter Fifteen
20th CENTURY MAN-MONKEYS

WITH THE ARRIVAL of the 20th century the magic of the Pongo name had waned; Pongos rapidly disappearing as a plethora of man-monkeys traded under their own names or adopted stage names, leaving the field clear for James Dubois who stuck with his bill matter of 'the Original Pongo'.

Riding high above all his competitors, his jokey adverts long behind him, James Dubois was rarely unemployed. Should he have a vacant week ahead, it seems a mere mention of that in his regular card was sufficient to turn something up at the last minute. He was well regarded though it must have been very difficult for managements to decide who the superior artistes were, and no doubt many mediocre man-monkeys gained work mainly by being cheap. From the *Brighton Examiner* we have a brief but good description of the Dubois act as performed in 1889:

> By far the most important engagement at this popular place of entertainment this week is the celebrated Mr James Dubois, known as the original Man Monkey, Pongo. This clever artiste is attired in a hairy covering which gives him the natural appearance of the animal he represents, and is first introduced to the audience in a cage, which he presently breaks down, and leaping out, climbs up a rope which he ascends with marvellous rapidity nearly to the roof of the hall; he then swings himself on to the perch suspended from the ceiling in a perpendicular position, and there amuses his audience with several extraordinary feats of gymnastic display that prove as popular as they are daring.[1]

From this it is evident that Dubois copied the format of Kotaky the Pongo Redivivus, but eschewing the arty stuff of the Japanese, concentrating on the gymnastics. This was an early appearance and over his twenty-year career he no doubt streamlined his act.

James Dubois was born Alfonso Mallaird in Lambeth in 1869. It is likely that his parents were theatrical performers and placed him as an apprentice with Gingero of the Royal Tycoon Troupe to learn the business of gymnastics. He married Emily Thomas, the youngest daughter of a joiner, around 1890 when he was 21 and his wife a year older. Although his work took him all over the country and abroad, he stayed true to Oldham in Lancashire as his home base. Three children were born to the couple – Jack in 1892, Doris in 1900 and Ernest in 1905. James Dubois died on 20 February 1907 at the age of only 37. Little more than a year later, further sorrow came to his widow with her eldest son Jack dying on 30 March 1908 in his seventeenth year.

MAN-GORILLA was a performer who wore the old conventional close body-suit which was not at all gorilla-like.
The long-haired monsters had not yet taken over completely.
Illustrated coloured poster 1913

A quick trawl through *The Era* and *The Stage* gives a good look at flourishing man-monkeys for the first decade of the 20th century. Like James Dubois, other man-monkeys established in the 1880s and 1890s carried on into the next century, but new names arose too. All the following artistes are new names taken from January 1900 to December 1910. Any Pongos have been omitted as there is no way to tell them apart:

Marko, Haygo, Munko, Jacko, Peto, Pulo, Volto, Fred E Dando,

20th CENTURY MAN-MONKEYS

Lomar, Linkus, Pongorilla, Darwin, Richard Lomas, Aldro Lukos, Leon Dubois, Mons Almero, Archie Herbert, Trixo, Sabarko.

Presumably the Lomas Brothers (aka Jacko & Jocko) had split up, one remaining as Jacko and the other using his real name.

A particular oddity who seems to have been inordinately popular was the versatile multi-instrumentalist known as 'Cambo the musical monkey'. A man in a monkey outfit climbing ropes and swinging on a trapeze – ok, but playing musical instruments?

It was always difficult identifying the performer behind the mask but once long-haired gorilla suits became the norm all the existing man-monkeys tended to look the same.

MENKENGES the new modern man-monkey. Photograph of unknown date but probably turn of the century.

Of all the above performers, Aldro Lukos seems to have taken the place of James Dubois as the pre-eminent man-monkey speciality act in this country, being as busy as all the rest put together. He flourished the longest, his final date being as the cat in *Dick Whittington* in 1920, but he was man-monkeying until the end. He died in 1924 'after great suffering, leaving wife and two little children totally unprovided for'. Leon Dubois (the gorilla in *The Freak's Revenge)* first performing solo in 1907 was still in action in 1919. He does not appear to be related to James Dubois, but I could well be as ignorant of the fact as the author of *Comic Coolie* was about

E J Parsloe!

Man-Monkeys were falling from fashion which may account for the Conquests turning to all-human farces. The only new names gleaned from the following years are

1911 – Alfred Arno, and Jarko
1912 – Chinio, Jules Gavrillet Trio
1913 – Pete Almonte, who may be the same man as Peto,
1914 – Esau (stealing his name from *The Freak's Revenge*)
1916 – Jim Rallis (who was still popping up as late as 1939)
1922 – Fitzroy
1925 – Kerchak
1927 – Tarzan
1928 – Paul Frisco (also known as Poso or Paoso)
1930 – The Great Tongo
1934 – Jacko (presumably not the same artiste of that name from decades before!)
1935 – Blondin (Alberto – not the famous star, he died in 1897)
1942 – A Pongo appeared in Don Ross's stage circuses

From circa 1911 very few new names were replacing the artistes who had retired since the beginning of the century, and few of these had a lasting shelf life. One of the last sightings of any man-monkey act on the variety stage took place in a 1949 Pete Collins touring revue *Jungle Fantasy* which had a Pongo 'whose determination to come to closer terms with his audience leads to an exciting chase among the Empire's high galleries and balconies.'[2] This may have been the same artiste who went under the name King Kong Jr on a 1951 variety bill organised by and starring Harry Lester and his Hayseeds. Another performer playing as King Kong was Fritz Roth who appeared at Blackpool Tower circus in 1956.

FRITZ ROTH who performed under the name King Kong. By the 1950s the man-monkey was rarely seen onstage and his locale was almost exclusively the circus ring.

As at this period the variety theatres throughout Britain were closing wholesale because of the new entertainment medium of commercial television, opportunities for the few man-monkeys still working were restricted to circuses which, as older readers will remember, had now become an entertainment of separate acts with human performers, horses and wild animals. The circus of old that presented plays as in the theatre had long gone.

On the continent, there was more work available for speciality acts including man-monkeys, as variety and cabaret venues still flourished along with far more circus activity. Some of these acts came to Britain to work in our large travelling circuses and winter venues.

One name that had some longevity is that of Nathal. I have found the name as La Palma & Nathal in 1906, the Nathal Trio in 1914 and 1920, and Nathal the Mysterious Monkey in 1932.[3] A man-monkey prominent in the 1950s and 1960s who ascended on a vertical rope high into the roof of the big top was called Natal. I do not know if he could be of the same family. A photograph of 1947 is especially interesting as this particular man-monkey is the only one I have ever seen that has a tail!

LA PALMA & NATHAL
Poster 1906

MAN-MONKEYS

A popular man-monkey of the circus world in the mid-20th century was NATAL (left) *who appeared throughout Europe and America. Note the long tail!*

I do not know if he is any kin of NATHAL THE MYSTERIOUS MONKEY (below) *on a poster of 1932.*

Invariably the man-monkey of the 20th century was a black hairy gorilla so they all looked pretty much alike, indeed often the artiste was not even named but billed with something on the lines of *The gorilla's loose!* Major man-monkey acrobatic acts of the mid-century include that of the German troupe the Gutis who were a popular circus act in the 1950s appearing extensively throughout Europe with their *Jungle*

Land Fantasy. The personnel of the act no doubt varied over the years but in its heyday there were five in the troupe, two playing in ape skins. As well as apes they had a pantomime-type bull and a comical kangaroo. The act ended with the handbag and skirt trope as described in the preface, but whether the Gutis were the originators of that routine is impossible to say.

The Guti family went to the USA – like many of the man-monkeys of old – with an act that included Norbert Kreisch the aerialist in the personnel. He left the Gutis and joined the Wallenda troupe while devising and rehearsing his own man-monkey act which he launched under the name Norbu. He soon became a regular favourite at Circus-Circus in Las Vegas and chiefly worked in the USA though appearing in Europe with Circus Scott, and at the Deutschlandhalle in Berlin during the 1960s. The last sighting of an act under the Guti name I have located is a double act of 1976 in the USA.

The public had had 'a wilderness of monkeys' to choose from for 150 years. The novelty was bound to flag eventually, and probably the last major man-monkey performer was Natal.

NATAL makes friends in the audience!

Small family circuses certainly prolonged the 'escaped gorilla routine' as a fill-in act for some years after, but the concept was really dead and buried.

The man-monkey originated as a character in a straight play *La Perouse* followed by *Jocko the Brazilian Ape* and other dramas owing much to the original. As the man-monkey role was usurped by the gymnast in place of the actor, the plays disappeared over the latter half of the 19th century. However, as we have seen, occasional new works featuring a man-monkey character did appear, including the notorious *For Ever* of 1882.

In 1925, exactly 100 years after Mazurier startled London and set the man-monkey ball rolling, a character actor called Jacques Lerner became the talk of Paris in *Le Singe qui Parle* by Rene Fauchois. He repeated his success in Berlin and came to London to appear in an English version by Rowland Leigh called *The Monkey Talks*. In this case, however, it was not a ballet-pantomime but a straight play with dialogue.

The plot concerned a wealthy young man who falls in love with a circus artiste. He is spurned by her but stays with the circus, donning a costume to pass himself off as a genuine ape. Another circus girl does not realise he is really a man who has conceived a passion for her. Critics described the play as a fantasy and sentimental – supporting roles include broken-hearted clowns – but all agreed that M Lerner was exceptionally brilliant in the dual role of monkey in the first act and man in the second.[4]

The show transferred from the Little theatre to the larger Duke of York's, and thereafter on an extended provincial tour with D Hay Petrie taking over the man-monkey role, while Lerner went to the USA to play the role in New York and Hollywood.

In the UK, as well as the touring production of *The Monkey Talks*, there was an import from America of a comedy-thriller called *The Gorilla* which played at the New Oxford theatre in London's West End. This featured detectives, much shooting of revolvers, and a complicated plot that did not much hang together. The part of the gorilla was played by Edward Sillward who at that time was known as the man inside Nana the dog in *Peter Pan*.

Also that year the popular silent film clown Fred Evans known as Pimple toured with a revue show called *Lucky 13* in which he played in sketches including the eponymous part in one called *The Gorilla's Revenge*.

The last play to feature a man-monkey as a character was presented in the West End in 1950, in a production by H M Tennent, designed by Oliver Messel and directed by no less a person than the distinguished Peter Brook. This was *The Little Hut* by Andre Roussin, adapted by Nancy Mitford, and starred Robert Morley and David Tomlinson with

Joan Tetzel providing featherbrained promiscuity. Why all these eminent persons of the day chose to associate themselves with what must have been the flimsiest of light comedies is a mystery, but the play, considered risqué in its day, had a three-year run in the West End and was made into a film. The plot concerns three people washed up on a desert island from a wrecked cruise ship, they comprise a married couple and the husband's best friend who is secretly the wife's lover. There is a large hut and a little hut on the island and, the truth coming out, a *ménage a trois* arrangement is proposed. Then an apparent savage arrives who turns out to be the ship's cook in disguise and disappears with the wife into the little hut where the pair have a merry time (innocently) to the consternation of the two men.

In its day the piece was considered saucy and amusing with the three upper-class persons dressed in the remnants of evening dress having to rough it on the island. Nobody suggested at the time, that the piece in some respects leans heavily on *La Perouse*, especially as the play has a final flourish with the appearance of William Chappell in the role of a monkey. He was surely the last actor ever to play such a role on the legitimate stage?

Chapter Sixteen
CINEMA MAN-MONKEYS

UP TO THE BEGINNING of the 20th century all entertainment was live, and our man-monkeys appeared on stages and in circuses. After 100 years, staleness had set into the man-monkey genre but with the advent of cinema film new opportunities arose. No longer were performers tied to the wooden stage, and man-monkeys appeared in early silent films. The first mention I have found for a possible man-monkey on film dates from 1907 when a hunt in India shows a monster man-monkey stealing a British officer's child. 'The chase is an exciting one through beautiful country, and results in the capture of the brute.'[1] As early as 1913, a 24-minute film called *Balaoo the Man-Monkey* 'a thrilling drama from the famous work of Gaston Laroux the celebrated French novelist' was a principal attraction with Lucien Bataille as Balaoo.

The 1920 film *The Great London Mystery*, starring David Devant the leading stage magician of the time, featured among the cast 'a repulsive man monkey equally well portrayed by Lester Gard.'

American films, however, took to man-monkeys with greater enthusiasm, as in *The Gorilla*, a silent film of 1927, based on a man-monkey character who donned the simian disguise to murder people. The ape suit was made by a special effects and scenery builder Charles Gemora, and worn by an un-credited actor.[2] This was the progenitor for a spate of 'gorilla movies'.

The stage play *The Monkey Talks* was made into a film also in 1927 by Raoul Walsh for Fox Studio. It seems ironic that a play about a talking ape had to be a silent film as talkies were only a few months in the future, becoming standard by 1929. Lerner, of course, repeated his stage performance for the cameras, but the screenplay, and the American stage play, used a different version from the London one of Leigh. An exceedingly poor quality copy of the film may be found on You Tube.

However, rather than a man imitating a monkey, early silent films leaned towards having monkeys (ie chimpanzees) dressed up as men. Recording performing animals in short clips, the ability to do retakes, and the splicing together of separate action sequences to form a coherent story enabled chimpanzees to appear smarter – and funnier – than they really were.

Snooky the Man Monkey was the title of a serial, and another film with Snooky called *Four Times Foiled* featured 'the cleverest man-monkey in the world'. This was not a man-monkey at all but a chimpanzee dressed up in human clothes. The term man-monkey – used loosely for 100 years – was now carried forward into the film industry with a vengeance. Consul III, described as 'the GENUINE man monkey of Bostock's fame' in publicity for a film of 1917 was an actual chimpanzee from the variety theatres billed as the 'Man Chimp', and 'Almost Human'. In his act Consul would eat with a knife and fork, drink wine and whiskey, smoke cigars and a pipe, dress and undress, and ride a bicycle. Bostock actually had several Consuls, enabling him to accept simultaneous engagements.

We see the misuse of the term man-monkey even when discussing the famous Tarzan character: 'In the next "Tarzan" film, you will find that the man-monkey's famous mate will die. . . . He will have to carry on as an ape-widower, for Johnny Weissmuller has signed to make three more monkey films.' (1939).³

Tarzan is neither a man-monkey nor missing link. He is presumably meant to be a feral human being, and in the persona of the toned hairless body of the ex-Olympic swimmer he is a human action man who just happens to like progressing through the jungle swinging on convenient creepers without disturbing his brylcreemed hair.

The medium of motion film would seem an ideal opportunity to develop the concept of the man-monkey. In fact, initially the character of Tarzan had the screen to himself. Like earlier man-monkey characters, Tarzan originated as a novel or rather, strictly speaking, in a magazine. *Tarzan of the Apes* by Edgar Rice Burroughs first appeared in 1912, the book following two years later.

Tarzan, left as an orphan in the

JOHNNY WEISSMULLER

jungle, was brought up by a fictional species of ape, but he did not turn into an ape himself. Burroughs describes him as white, athletic, tall, tanned and handsome, the only hair being on his head, long, black and luxuriant. In the books – 25 further adventures appeared up to 1947 – he is more cultured than in the many films where he speaks in broken English. He is well-read, being literate in English before being able to speak the language, which he immediately does on meeting English-speaking people. He learns new languages in days, ultimately speaking many tongues, including Greek and Latin, plus that of the great apes.

Tarzan has abilities far beyond those of ordinary humans, including outdoing the great apes in their natural skills. His physical attributes are prodigious, exceeding the strongest and speediest of normal athletes, and his jungle lore is superior to the animal species that dwell there. In other words, Burroughs created a superman figure who, although actually a scion of nobility, prefers to dwell in a back-to-nature fashion.

The films starring Johnny Weissmuller gave the world a somewhat different concept from the books, so much so that Burroughs disliked them enough to produce his own version with a different actor. As Weissmuller made 12 Tarzan films between 1932 and 1948 he is the actor most associated with the role. In the first one, a stunt man called Ray 'Crash' Corrigan made his ape debut wearing a particularly ferocious skin.[4] As a result, he became a specialist in gorilla roles.

Donning a safari suit, Weissmuller went on to make 13 Jungle Jim films in six years, leaving other actors to strip off to play Tarzan. In all, 23 of them with nary a hairy chest between them. The screen Tarzan was a well-developed body-builder with a hair style usually appropriate to the period when the film was made.

So Tarzan may be 'of the Apes' but was not a man-monkey in our sense of the term. Fortunately, further confusion was avoided in the USA by the fact that the men in Hollywood favoured gorilla costumes, and films with simians were invariably gorillas. Several actors specialised in the gorilla role and from the 1930s to 1950s there was a plethora of low budget movies churned out with posters depicting various scantily-dressed (for the time) fainting females being carried away by a fierce monstrous gorilla. Britain was spared most of these.

Charles Gemora the prop man we met earlier, liking the idea of appearing as a genuine ape, made a suit for himself and, as he was a small man of 5ft 4ins, by extending the arms on his suit he made a convincing simian. By study, rehearsal and constantly improving his outfit he became the pioneer ape-man of US films appearing in some 30 movies up to 1958 including *The Leopard Lady* (1928), *Ingagi* (1930) and *Murders in the Rue Morgue* with Bela Lugosi (1932). Like many of these once horror-film actors, in the latter end of their careers both Lugosi and Gemora descended to appearing in slapstick comedies.

Once Gemora had led the way, gorillas became rather overdone in the low-budget B-films that were pumped out of third-rate studios in minimal time spans. Emil Van Horn played a gorilla exclusively during the 1940s appearing in nine films, including one with Bela Lugosi, and two serials featuring Nyoka the Jungle Girl which older readers may recall from the children's Saturday matinees of their youth. Like most film gorillas Van Horn was rarely credited, and turned to the vaudeville circuit with an act *Beauty and the Beast* in which a girl cavorted in a leopard skin costume menaced by the gorilla. Falling on hard times and unable to pay his rent, his gorilla outfit was amongst his goods and chattels retained in lieu by his landlady. He died penniless in 1967.

Another gorilla of the 1940s was the previously mentioned Ray 'Crash' Corrigan who played in several films including *The Ape* in which he was teamed with another specialist horror actor Boris Karloff. Corrigan's summit was *The White Gorilla* in which he played a man, a gorilla and the narrator. If you want a taste of these gorilla films, this one is a fine example. It is pretty dire, especially for as late as 1945, with a hero and heroine wearing make-up of which Rudolf Valentino and Theda Bara would have been proud. The reason for this is that the film utilises a great deal of footage taken from a 1927 silent serial, *Perils of the Jungle*, starring Frank Merrill the fifth screen Tarzan. These shots provide all the action in the film and are clumsily incorporated by a voiceover narration and clips of one of the modern day cast secretly observing the activity. It can still be seen on You Tube. It's awful.

On retiring, Corrigan passed on his skin and know-how to Steve Calvert who played a gorilla in Weissmuller's first Jungle Jim adventure (1948). After appearing in *Bride of the Gorilla* (1951), Calvert worked throughout the 1950s in many poor quality B-pictures mainly of the schlock-horror and corny comedy types with Bela Lugosi, Lon Chaney Jr and others. He retired through lack of work in 1960.

With even the most weak-witted cinema-goers eventually tiring of these underfunded crass horror-comedy films, gorilla actors turned to the new world of television. That type of work was taken up by George Barrows, Bob Burns, Don McCleod, and Janos Prohaska who guarded his skills carefully and was opposed to any competition from rival gorilla-men. Working mainly in television, he also appeared in feature films including *The Planet of the Apes* before dying in a plane crash.

The man-monkey of old wore what was basically a skin-tight body suit covered in short fur and relied on contorting his body to reproduce the animal image. The acrobatic variety and circus apes were clearly men wearing a monkey mask and carried on their acts as humans in a woolly costume. The acrobat was more interested in showing off his skills rather than trying to convince as a simian.

The reader will have gathered that there were no acrobatic skills nor much else involved in the filmic gorilla men who, clad in all-enveloping long hairy suits, did little more than lumber about. The fights between the white and black gorillas in *The White Gorilla* are risible. Most of the man-monkey plots in B-films were based either on mad scientists, murdering people right, left and centre, or females fainting and being carried away by the gorilla threatening rape or death. In more enlightened years we were offered the heavy-handed comedy films of Abbott and Costello, Bowery Boys, and the Three Stooges genre where former horror actors sent themselves up and a gorilla was often introduced with little or no excuse.

In the present day, dressing up in a gorilla suit has become part of the USA psyche. It seems that many people in America like to dress in gorilla suits for fun runs, conventions of enthusiasts, and surprise jokes. There is even the Gorillagram to compete with the Strippergram. Suits can be bought ready-made, though many fans prefer to build their own costumes. There are even two separate annual days – International Monkey Day (14 December) and National Gorilla Suit Day – when costume parties are held and bananas consumed.

Thus we pass on to the most famous gorilla of all time – King Kong. Whether or not they have seen the 1933 film, or any of the spin-offs, everybody has heard of King Kong – one of the few fictional names like Romeo, Shylock and Sherlock Holmes, somehow known to all as if absorbed with mother's milk. No doubt this great film gave an impetus to everything recorded in the previous paragraphs. But if the gorilla men thought they were aping (ho! ho! ho!) King Kong, they were very much mistaken.

Looking at stills from the original *King Kong* film, and the film itself, surely they are using a gymnast in an ape skin for many of the shots, it seems the obvious thing to do? Apparently not. Though some people still think there was an actor in a skin – and several stuntmen have claimed to be that man – the gorilla was actually created by stop-action models. The man responsible for these was Willis O'Brien, and several new techniques were developed for the film, such as miniature rear projections to create special effects sequences. Footage of the actors – one frame at a time – was projected on a small screen behind the models as they were animated. The film also was one of the first to use a newly created optical printer to matte together shots of the animated models and live actors.

Large models of Kong's head and hand were created, the whole film being a compilation of special effects. Spectacularly successful it led on to many further films and spin-offs. But it did not use a man-monkey! *King Kong* was re-released in 1938, 1942, and 1946. The continuing success of the film encouraged the same team plus Ray Harryhausen to make *Mighty Joe Young*, another giant gorilla film, in 1949. Although in the cast list an actor is credited as a stand-in for the ape, the stop-motion technique was again the basis of the film but, even with superior effects and a more natural *mise-en-scene*, it was not highly rated.

A later 1962 Japanese film *Godzilla v King Kong*, the third in the Godzilla franchise, did use actors in monster suits. King Kong, played by Shoichi Hirose, and the actor playing Godzilla were left to work out their own moves and choreography which they based on American Wrestling techniques. The creation of the King Kong skin was troublesome, the first suit being rejected as too fat with long legs giving Kong an 'almost cute look'. Other designs were tried before the final skin used in the film. The suit was given two separate masks, and two separate pairs of arms, one with extensions. This King Kong suit 'has widely been considered to be one of the least appealing and most insipid gorilla suits in film history.'[5]

King Kong Escapes – another Japanese film – came along in 1967 again using an actor in a body suit, this time Haruo Nakajima, who had to fight a robot King Kong called Mechani-Kong. The plot of this film is so ludicrous it makes *The Freak's Revenge* look like classic drama.

The 1976 *King Kong* was a remake of the original 1933 film, now with more modern technology available, but once again relying on an actor in a gorilla suit for the title role. In this case it was Rick Baker, a make-up and special effects expert who, with Carlo Rambaldi, designed the suit he was to wear. Baker was extremely disappointed in the final result, considering it unconvincing. The mechanical Kong masks were more successful. Seven in number created by Rambaldi, and moulded by Baker, they were fitted with cable work giving a wide range of expressions to convey various emotions. Baker wore contact lenses so his eyes would resemble those of a gorilla.

In 1986, a sequel *King Kong Lives* was produced by the same film company with effects again by Rambaldi, and actor Peter Elliott donning the ape suit. Other be-suited actors played Lady Kong and Baby Kong. The film was universally damned by one and all, taking under $5 million at the box office from a film costing $18 million to make.

In 2005, Peter Jackson, who directed *The Lord of the Rings* series, produced yet another version of the original film, setting it in 1933. The budget for this was colossal and the technical effects were now based on computer programs without an ape suit in sight.

Motion-capture acting, also called performance-capture acting, involves the actor wearing markers or sensors on a skin-tight bodysuit, or directly on the skin. The actor performs his movements in front of a blank screen. Computer sampling is done many times each second, creating a three dimensional database of points. This allows a filmmaker to create an original digital character and to place it in any desired setting using the database to provide natural movement. A refinement of the technique has the actor's face covered with many such sensors so the various facial movements and expressions of the actor are recorded. This enables natural facial movements to be transferred on to, for example, an ape so that the ape's face is not just a mask but a living image depicting all the hopes, fears and responses of the ape in a natural manner appropriate to the action that surrounds it in the film.

Jackson did not want his King Kong to act like a human being, and his team studied hours of film of genuine gorillas. Kong was Andy Serkis who was to act the role using motion capture. Serkis had already shown the effectiveness of this system as Gollum in *The Lord of the Rings*. After long sessions at London Zoo, Serkis observed gorillas in the wild in Rwanda. All this preliminary work culminated in the actor having two hours of motion capture makeup every day, with a host of tiny markers attached to different spots on his face. Then followed two months on the motion-capture stage miming all Kong's movements to be transferred by digital animation into the extremely lifelike King Kong. This film was a huge success both critically and financially.

In 2011, Andy Serkis said 'Performance-capture technology is really the only way that we could bring these characters to life. It's the way that Gollum was brought to life, and King Kong, and it's really another way of capturing an actor's performance. That's all it is, digital make-up.'

Like so many big budget adventure films of today, a multi-million dollar 'franchise' developed and, whilst preparing this book for the press, the latest King Kong film *Kong: Skull Island* was released in March 2017.

While the man-monkeys of old would be astonished at the wonders of computer-generated imagery, they would feel much more comfortable with the series of films called *The Planet of the Apes*. Just as we saw back in 1825 when the whole monkey craze was ignited by a French novel, so too Pierre Boulle's 1963 novel *La Planète des Singes* was the foundation for the 1968 film. Though the film relied on the old man-monkey trope of the actor in a hairy suit, there were two fundamental differences. Up to this period the man-monkey was portrayed as a peculiar individual, whether depicted as a feral man, missing link or authentic ape he was a unique oddity in the fictional world he inhabited. In *The Planet of the Apes* most of the characters are apes, as the plot concerns a 20th century astronaut landing on a strange planet where intelligent apes rule over primitive human beings. In this reversal the human being is the oddity.

The other fundamental difference with the man-monkey of old is the effect that the actor must create. As long as man-monkeys have performed, the actor has laboured to imitate the simian as accurately as possible, the most dedicated spending hours watching the antics and movements of actual animals. The actor in *The Planet of the Apes* has, in effect, to play an ape imitating a man. Whilst looking like simians, the apes on this planet act, talk and behave like human beings. In 1968, the main challenge was for the actors make-up to appear sufficiently ape-like, especially with the constrained budget for the film. Basically the actors, clothed like humans whilst wearing ape masks, behaved pretty much as normal.

The film was a huge hit with both critics and audiences, and immediately a sequel was demanded. This was a disappointment and, while taking almost as much money at the box office as the original, is considered to be the next worst of *The Planet of the Apes* franchise which grew thereafter. The following films with progressively tighter budgets had plot lines developing the battle between humans and apes as racial conflict became the main theme of the series.

The original series ran to five films between 1968 and 1973, the last *Battle for the Planet of the Apes* being considered the weakest. By then the production budget had been reduced from the $5.8 million of the first film to £1.7 million for the last. Then in 2001 Tim Burton directed a remake of the original *The Planet of the Apes* with a budget of $100 million.[6]

After several years lying fallow, the series was regenerated in 2011 with *Rise of the Planet of the Apes*. *Dawn of the Planet of the Apes* followed in 2014, again with Serkis in the lead, and at the time of writing, a new film is in production and we shall see *War of the Planet of the Apes* in July 2017.

As with the new *King Kong*, computer-generated imagery is now the process used to create the apes. The doyen of motion capture, Andy Serkis, playing the leading ape character can perform the tiniest moves, and convey the subtlest emotions in the motion capture studio in the closest of close-ups, all of which are transformed by digital technology into the body of a seemingly genuine animal. Now the apes are authentic animals without clothes and only a few quasi-human attributes. A host of stunt men, each wired up for CGI, can rampage as the director requires, to be enhanced and multiplied by sophisticated computer programmes.

The early Planet of the Apes *relied on prosthetic make-up for the actors which gave a mask-like appearance (left). Tim Burton's remake again used – much improved – prosthetics (right)*

The difference in the early films with the prosthetic make-up actors compared with the recent versions in which the actors are 'made-up' by CGI magic is as huge as that between a cartoon and live actors. We no longer wonder at the accuracy of the actor's portrayal of an ape, but completely accept the screen simian as a real living animal.

Face 'make up' is now done by having sensors attached to the face (above left) which transfer all the expressions and facial movements of the actor to a computer. These movements are then used to animate the facial expressions of a computer generated ape. The picture (above right) shows Andy Serkis as he appears on screen in the role of Caesar.

The gymnast in the hairy ape costume is finally no more. Although Andy Serkis is doing all his acting in the studio wired up to computers attended by scores of technical crew, like Parsloe, Wieland, Mazurier, Kotaky, Lauri and the rest of the man-monkeys discussed in this book, he deserves praise for the 'accuracy of the imitation of the appearance, movements, and habits of the animal which is so complete as to create as perfect an illusion as can be supposed upon the stage.'[7]

It is all a long way from the days of that previous doyen of man-monkeys Monsieur Gouffe. The actor in the hairy skin reached his apotheosis in the 2001 *Planet of the Apes*, and is unlikely ever to be seen again.

But perhaps later in 2017, a small travelling circus will visit your town and one of the acts will be a gymnast dressed as an escaped gorilla from *Battle for the Planet of the Apes*, who will climb up a rope to do tricks high in the big top, then descend to scramble through the audience, grabbing children's sweets, and looking for a lady's handbag to steal.

APPENDIX

NAMES MENTIONED IN THE TEXT

GLOSSARY

NOTES

BIBLIOGRAPHY

NAMES MENTIONED IN THE TEXT

James BARNES (1788–1838) Born in Enfield. Before the age of twenty been a cobbler twice, served in the forces and spent some time at sea. Took to the stage with Richardson's Travelling Theatre. Joined Drury Lane in 1809, played Sadler's Wells, went with Grimaldi to Covent Garden as Pantaloon. Partnered the famous Clown until he retired, then worked in several pantomimes with a variety of partners. Died in dire poverty in 1838.

William BARRYMORE (?–1845) Son of the more famous actor of the same name (1759–1830). 'Director of the Spectacle and Pantomime Department' at Drury Lane. Emigrated to America.

Jack BOLOGNA (1775–1846) Son of an Italian clown, making his debut at the age of 11. Came with his family to England in 1787 and was befriended by the boy Grimaldi. First played Harlequin at Covent Garden at the age of 21. Becoming Grimaldi's regular Harlequin, Bologna partnered him in the famous *Mother Goose* of 1806 which ran for 92 nights selling 300,000 tickets. Retired from regular performing in 1820. Lived in Glasgow working as a choreographer and designer of mechanical pantomime props. In 1840, briefly succumbed to the workhouse. In 1841 joined Anderson 'The Wizard of the North' as a blackface assistant named Ebony. Died in harness but penniless at the age of 71.

Alfred BUNN (1796–1860) Stage manager of Drury Lane 1823. Manager of Birmingham theatre 1826. Lessee of Covent Garden and Drury Lane simultaneously. Manager of Drury Lane 1834–1839. Bankrupt 1840 having lost £23,000. Manager of Surrey 1847–48.

Samuel W BUTLER (1803–1845) Son of the Butler who built the theatre in Richmond, Yorkshire. After the death of his father took on management of the circuit at the age of 18. Circuit collapsed in 1830. Freelance tragedian with powerful voice and great height 6ft 4in. Went to USA. Died Manchester 1845.

Lon CHANEY JR (1906–1973) Son of Lon Chaney the silent film star known as the Man of a Thousand Faces for his talent at grotesque make-ups in many horror films. Lon Jr only went into the film business after his father died but was inevitably cast in the same genre of film.

Captain CLIAS (Peter Heinrich Clias) was the author of a treatise called *An Elementary Course of Gymnastic Exercises* published about 1824. This included a *New and Complete Treatise on the Art of Swimming*. The author was Superintendent of Gymnastics at Sandhurst and other military colleges. His manual had several editions but many of his assertions were grossly exaggerated.

Robert COURTNEIDGE (1859–1939) British theatrical manager-producer and playwright. Co-author of the light opera *Tom Jones* (1907). Producer of *The Arcadians* (1909). Father of the actress Cicely Courtneidge.

T P COOKE (Thomas Potter Cooke) (1786–1864) English actor known for playing nautical roles. He played Long Tom Coffin in *The Pilot* 562 times,

William in *Black Eyed Susan* for 783 performances, and *Le Monstre* 365 times including 80 successive nights in Paris.

Charles Isaac Mungo DIBDIN (1768–1833), known as **Charles Dibdin the younger**. English dramatist, composer, writer and theatre proprietor. Apprentice and shopman 14 years to a pawnbroker. 1797 first theatre work writing a prodigious number of plays, pantomimes, songs etc at Astley's for 30/- a week. Manager Sadler's Wells 1800–1819. Installed water tanks to make an Aquatic Theatre 1803–04. Declared bankrupt in 1819. 1824–1826 manager of the Surrey where he discovered the man who became Gouffe. Later years in obscurity writing poetry and other works.

Andrew DUCROW (1793–1842) Circus equestrian. Owner of Astley's Amphitheatre. Creator of the Classic Statues act in which, wearing a white body stocking he posed as various Greek statues standing upon the rump of a white horse which circled the ring.

Tom ELLAR (1780–1842) Started as a walk-on, graduated to dancer. Principal dancer at Dublin. In 1813 junior Harlequin at Covent Garden, performing jumps for the injured Bologna. Regular Harlequin with Grimaldi and Barnes. Hailed as quicksilver in his prime, prematurely aged through mercury poison. By 1839 out of work and begging in bars. Died in 1842 shortly after assisting his bosom pal Barnes.

Robert William ELLISTON (1774–1831) Noted actor and manager. First appeared at Bath as a youth of seventeen then joined Tate Wilkinson's York circuit for two years. Returned to Bath to become the favourite actor of many including Jane Austen and George III. Moved to London where his reputation grew. At Drury Lane as leading actor from 1804 to 1809, and again from 1812. Manager of the Royal Circus from 1806 transforming it into the Surrey Theatre. Bought the Olympic Theatre in 1813 and also leased the Birmingham theatre. Gave up the Surrey in 1814, from 1819 the lessee of Drury Lane, along with provincial interests. Often drunk, lost all through ill health and bankruptcy in 1826. Recovered to lease the Surrey again from 1827 and act there until his death in 1831.

Joseph GRIMALDI (1778–1837) Son of Giuseppe Grimaldi an Italian ballet master of wayward morals. Became the most popular English entertainer of the Regency era primarily in the role of Clown in the traditional pantomime Harlequinade. Employed at Sadler's Wells during the summer season from 1780 to 1820, and at Drury Lane in winter from 1780 to 1806. Moved to Covent Garden where he flourished until 1823 when he was compelled to retire due to ill health. Outliving two wives and his son J S Grimaldi, died at his Islington home aged 58. In spite of his claiming poverty in old age, he left investments of £450 (£35,000 today).

Joseph Samuel GRIMALDI (1802–1832) Son of the famous Regency Clown. Made his debut at the age of thirteen, showing some talent which he never fostered. Worked with his father, taking over the role of Clown at Covent Garden in 1823 through his influence. Revelled in bad company, chiefly Henry Kemble, nephew of John Philip. Addicted to drink and debauchery becoming increasingly unreliable. Died in a distressed state at the age of 30.

MAN-MONKEYS

John Pritt HARLEY (1786–1858) English actor known for his comic acting and counter-tenor singing. After a long apprenticeship in provincial country theatres, first appeared at Drury Lane in 1815. Spending 20 years at the theatre, succeeded to all John Bannister's roles when that eminent actor retired. Noted for the Shakespearean clown roles. In 1858, while playing Lancelot Gobbo, he was struck with paralysis, dying two days later. Died penniless but left a collection of three hundred walking sticks.

Thomas Henry HUXLEY (1825–1895) English biologist known as 'Darwin's Bulldog' for his advocacy of Darwin's theory of evolution. Fellow of the Royal Society at 25 (1851). Royal Society Medal 1852. Served on eight Royal Commisions 1862–1884. Secretary of the Royal Society 1871–1880; President 1883–1885. President of the Geological Society 1868–1870. Many other elections and appointments to eminent scientific bodies. Many honorary memberships of foreign societies, academic awards and honorary doctorates from Britain and Germany. Appointed Privy Coucillor 1892.

Boris KARLOFF (1887–1969) Widely known for his role as Frankenstein's monster in the film *Frankenstein* (1931), and subsequent horror films. Often teamed with Bela Lugosi.

Edmund KEAN (1787–1833) Leading tragedian of the Regency Era bestriding the theatre world like a Colossus. As a boy acted in Richardson's Travelling Theatre. Leading actor and Harlequin in modest provincial companies until 26 January 1814 when he appeared at Drury Lane as Shylock and became a star overnight. Lived a tumultuous life of hard work, constant travelling and dissipation. Made and lost a fortune. Died at Richmond, Surrey at the age of 45. Still regarded as one of England's greatest actors.

Charles KEMBLE (1775–1854) Noted actor and manager, brother of John Philip Kemble and Mrs Sarah Siddons. A versatile and much loved actor. Aroused great enthusiasm when touring America with his daughter Fanny in 1832 and 1834. Beset by typical managerial money problems he retired in 1836, making a brief comeback in 1840 to take a formal farewell of his devoted public.

Bela LUGOSI (1882–1956), Hungarian-American actor, famous for portraying Dracula in the 1931 film and for subsequent roles in other horror films.

Lord MONBODDO (James Burnett) (1714–1799) Scottish judge, scholar and philosopher. Developed an early concept of evolution, some crediting him with anticipating in principle the idea of Charles Darwin's natural selection.

Stephen PRICE (1783–1840) American 'of coarse manners, repulsive conduct and vulgar conversation'. Manager of the New York Park Theatre. Obtained lease of Drury Lane 1826–1830. Bankrupt 1830. Became impresario importing English actors to tour American cities.

Tom RIDGWAY: (flourished 1830s and 1840s) The Ridgways were three brothers from a pantomime family headed by father Charles Ridgway. John played Harlequin, George was Pantaloon and Tom was Clown. George died at the early age of 22 from tuberculosis.

Isaac VAN AMBURGH (1811–1865) American lion trainer known as the 'Brute Tamer of Pompeii' and 'The Lion King'. First man to place his head in a lion's mouth. Much admired by Queen Victoria who saw him perform six times in as many months. Commanded huge salaries – rumoured to be £300 a week – and died in his bed at the age of fifty-four.

William Frederick WALLETT (1806–1892) Popular circus clown in Victorian England. After performing before Queen Victoria dubbed himself 'The Queen's Jester'. Regular performer in Pablo Fanque's circus.

Frederick Henry YATES (1797–1842) English actor and theatre manager. London debut in 1818 at Covent Garden where he remained until 1825. Bought the Adelphi theatre with his friend fellow actor Daniel Terry at a price of £30,000. Opened in October 1825, managed until retirement in 1842.

GLOSSARY

Afterpiece: A shorter work usually of a farcical nature or a dance/ballet that followed the main play in an evening at the theatre. Sometimes the afterpiece was a bigger attraction than the main feature as in the case of pantomimes and plays with man-monkeys.

At Liberty: Available for work.

'Bartlemy Fair', correctly Bartholomew Fair. A London feature from 1133 to 1855. Originally for the sale of cloth and other goods, the Fair attracted a host of acrobats, puppet men and other sideshows. Lasting as long as two weeks at its peak, by 1855 it was suppressed on the grounds of encouraging vice and disorder.

Benefit: A system of payment hallowed by time. For a particular performance, after the expenses of the house had been deducted, the chosen actor received all the takings for that one performance. The player himself had to sell the advance tickets, not the theatre. Lesser players may be granted a part-benefit meaning that two or more would share a benefit night.

Big Time: Colloquial term often used for the Number 1 variety circuit in the days when there distinct No 1, No 2 and No 3 circuits. Hence, used as a derogatory term when a performer is speaking boastfully of himself.

Bill matter: The text used to accompany the name of an artiste on playbills. In later variety days reduced to a simple slogan eg Alma Cogan – 'The Girl with a Laugh in her Voice', Sophie Tucker – 'The Last of the Red-Hot Mommas'.

Breeches role: When an actress played a part dressed as a man. A forerunner of the pantomime principal boy played by a curvaceous female slapping her thigh.

Bumper: Unusually large or abundant benefit.

Card: In showbusiness trade papers artistes could pay monthly, quarterly or yearly for a regular series of advertisements known as cards. These were of standard size and type with unchanging text. In other forms these would also carry where the performer was working that week and the next.

Exeter Change: The familiar name of Exeter Exchange which housed a menagerie from 1773 to 1829 when it was demolished to be replaced by Exeter Hall which lasted until 1909. The Strand Palace Hotel now occupies the site.

Greenroom or Green Room: A communal room backstage where actors may socialise and fill in time between scenes. In the Regency era the major theatres had more than one, restricted to players according to their financial status in the company.

Guesting: An actor engaged as a special attraction was a 'guest artiste', thus such a performer would say he was 'guesting at . . .'

Half Price: It was the custom to allow people to enter part-way through the show at half price. This concession was withdrawn for outstanding attractions.

Minor Theatre: Prior to 1843 – in London, all theatres that were not Drury Lane, Covent Garden or the Haymarket, the three major or patent theatres. In the provinces, in a town that had a Theatre Royal, any other theatre in that town.

Patent theatres: Drury Lane and Covent Garden that were the only theatres licensed by royal patent to perform 'spoken drama' after the Restoration of Charles II in 1660. As they closed for a summer recess, a third theatre the Haymarket was granted a summer patent in 1766. Only these three London theatres were permitted to be called Theatre Royal. Patents were later granted to several provincial theatres.

Pantomimist: A performer who specialises in silent roles, usually as an animal, grotesque or in a Harlequinade

Playbill: An advertisement issued daily giving details of a theatre's show and cast list posted up in public places. Extra copies were also sold at the venue. Modern programme formats did not appear until mid-19th century. Predecessor of the poster.

Post-chaise: A fast carriage for travelling post in the 18th and early 19th centuries. Usually had a closed body seating two to four persons, four wheels and was drawn by two or four horses.

Sadler's Wells Theatre: Opened in 1683 by Richard Sadler to entertain visitors to his medicinal wells. 1765 replaced with a theatre that ran a season from Easter to October. Flourished in Regency times with pantomimes starring Grimaldi. 1844–1862 occupied by Shakespearean actor Samuel Phelps. Condemned 1878. New theatre built 1879 as a Music Hall. Became cinema before closing in 1915. A total of six theatre buildings existed in succession from 1883 to the present time, the current theatre being the home of dance.

Second Spot: Speciality acts often have a different back-up act. This is known as a second spot. Thus a performer can offer a management two different acts for the price of one to enhance their booking opportunities. Now commonplace in modern circuses. Not to be confused with 'You go on second spot' which means the performer is to do his act after the opening turn.

Sinbad: A popular pantomime, often spelled as **Sindbad**. The text uses both according to how the particular production was billed.

Spot: Synonym for 'act'. Often in a pantomime, a speciality act will play a part. At a certain place in the story they will perform their 'act as known'. eg 'You do your spot in the ballroom scene.'

Top Banana: The leading or featured comedian in a burlesque show; the chief comic. (USA)

Transpontine: Situated on the south side of Blackfriars Bridge (built 1769) and Westminster Bridge (1750). Location of three popular theatres: Royal Amphitheatre known as Astley's (1773–1893), Royal Circus (1782–1806) renamed the Surrey Theatre (1806–1901) Royal Coburg (1818) renamed Royal Victoria 1833, extant as the Old Vic.

Traps: Short for trapdoors. Old time stages were festooned with different kinds of traps, often devised especially for a particular play. The Grave Trap is simply an opening in the stage floor, mainly used for *Hamlet* nowadays. Vampire Trap (1820) comprises two hinged flaps, Corsican Trap, invented for *The Corsican Brothers* (1852), enables an actor to slowly glide across the stage rising upwards. Very effective if used with a layer of dry-ice 'smoke'. The most used in Harlequinades etc was the Star Trap. This was circular with hinged flaps like a cut cake. The artiste was shot rapidly from under stage to a height enabling pirouettes or even a somersault to be accomplished before landing.

Turn: Synonym for 'act' eg 'What time do you do your turn?' *Also see* **Spot.**

Week(s) Out: Used by variety artistes to describe a period without work. More grandly known as 'At Liberty'.

NOTES

Chapter One LA PEROUSE
1 Ipswich Journal 1802_11_20
2 Hereford Journal 1811_09_04 and others

Chapter Two THE PARSLOE FAMILY
1 *The History of the English Puppet Theatre* Pg172
2 *What's the Play and Where's the Stage?* Pg 296
3 Bell's Life in London 1825_04_10
4 Bath Chronicle 1825_04_14
5 Theatrical Observer 1825_08_13
6 Public Ledger & Daily Advertiser 1825_08_16
7 Morning Post 1825_12_12

Chapter Three MAZURIER
1 Berkshire Chronicle 1825_06_18
2 Wikimedia
3 Bristol Mirror 1825_11_19
4 Worcester Journal 1825_11_03
5 London Literary Gazette
6 Evening Mail 1825_11_09
7 Morning Post 1825_11_09
8 *Prima La Danza*

Chapter Four E J PARSLOE
1 Evening Mail 1825_12_28
2 Daily Advertiser 1825_12_27
3 The Examiner 1826_01_01
4 Bells Weekly Messenger 1826_01_01
5 Daily Advertiser 1825_12_28
6 Daily Advertiser 1825_12_28
7 *What's the Play and Where's the Stage?* Page 94
8 Evening Post 1827_01_01
9 Advertiser 1827_04_17
10 Chronicle 1827_04_17
11 Playbill Birmingham 1827_7_27
12 Public Ledger & Daily Advertiser 1827_08_14
13 Evening Standard 1827_12_27
14 Taunton Courier 1828_01_02
15 Evening Mail 1827_12_28
16 Public Ledger & Daily Advertiser 1828_12_27
17 Weekly Messenger 1828_12_28
18 Ladies Magazine January 1829
19 Public Ledger & Daily Advertiser 1829_08_24
20 Morning Post 1830_06_02
21 Evening Standard 1830_12_28
22 Windsor and Eton Express 1831_01_01

NOTES

23 *History of the American Stage*
24 *Comic Coolie* Footnote
25 Evening Standard 1832_01_25
26 Belfast Advertiser 1832_01_25
27 Morning Advertiser 1847_08_09

Chapter Five C T PARSLOE
1 *Theatrical Rambles of Mr & Mrs Greene*
2 *Comic Coolie*
3 Exeter Flying Post 1828_06_26

Chapter Six GEORGE WIELAND
1 Kentish Weekly Post 1824_04_23
2 Evening Mail 1825_11_09
3 Public Ledger and Daily Advertiser 1825_11_08
4 Morning Post 1828_04_08
5 Dublin Evening Packet 1828_04_12
6 London Evening Standard 1832_12_27
7 Morning Chronicle 1832_12_27
8 London Courier 1834_04_01
9 Evening Chronicle 1834_12_27
10 Morning Post 1834_12_29
11 Public Ledger and Daily Advertiser 1835_09_07
12 Kentish Mercury 1835_10_03
13 London Courier 1835_12_28
14 Morning Advertiser 1836_12_02
15 Morning Post 1837_07_06
16 The Examiner 1837_12_03
17 The Examiner 1837_12_17
18 London Courier 1838_08_14
19 Evening Standard 1838_11_09
20 The Operative 1838_12_30
21 The Operative 1839_01_13
22 Evening Standard 1838_12_27
23 Brighton Patriot 1839_03_19
24 Manchester Times 1840_06_20
25 The Examiner 1840_10_11
26 *Joe Grimaldi His Life & Theatre* pg 244
27 Morning Post 1844_05_28
28 Lloyds Weekly 1845_11_09
29 The Times 1846_04_14
30 London Daily News 1846_12_28

Chapter Seven MONSIEUR GOUFFE
1 Morning Advertiser 1825_07_04
2 Cumberland Pacquet 1825_09_06
3 Kentish Weekly Post 1825_12_30
4 Dublin Morning Register 1826_03_28
5 Aris's Birmingham Gazette 1826_07_24

NOTES

6 Stamford Mercury 1827_03_02
7 Brighton Gazette 1827_10_25
8 Bury & Norwich Post 1828_11_05
9 Sussex Advertiser 1836_03_28
10 Exeter & Plymouth Gazette 1830_01_23
11 Taunton Courier and Western Advertiser 1838_09_12
12 Liverpool Mail 1842_08_25
13 Westmorland Gazette 1843_02_04
14 Leeds Intelligencer 1843_10_28
15 Leeds Times 1843_11_04
16 Lincolnshire Chronicle 1843_11_10
17 The Era 1844_09_08

Chapter Eight KLISCHNIGG

1 Evening Standard 1829_12_28
2 Morning Post 1829_12_28
3 Saunders Newsletter 1835_12_28
4 Dublin Observer 1836_01_16
5 Dublin Morning Register 1838_04_28
6 Morning Advertiser 1838_06_05
7 Austrian Biographical Encyclopaedia
8 The Era 1865_12_10
9 The form in Austria is Eduard von Klischnig

Chapter Nine HERVIO NANO

1 Birmingham Journal 1838_06_23
2 London Courier 1838_02_01
3 Birmingham Journal 1838_06_23
4 Playbill Leeds 11 July 1838_07_11
5 Manchester Courier 1838_08_11
6 Staffordshire Advertiser 1838_09_01
7 Leamington Spa Courier 1838_10_20
8 Leamington Spa Courier 1838_10_20
9 Morning Chronicle 1839_01_03
10 Bells Life in London 1839_01_20
11 Leamington Spa Courier 1839_04_06
12 The Era 1839_06_16
13 *A History of the New York Stage*
14 Morning Advertiser 1842_11_12
15 The Era 1843_08_27
16 The Era 1843_10_29
17 Morning Advertiser 1845_05_16
18 Poster, Evanion Collection, British Library
19 Morning Post 1847_03_18

Chapter Ten MARTINI

1 Edinburgh Evening Courant 1832_10_25
2 Aberdeen Journal 1832_11_07
3 Windsor & Eton Express 1842_04_02
4 The Era 1842_08_05

NOTES

5 Morning Advertiser 1844_03_18
6 The Era 1845_08_17
7 Playbill (silk) V & A collection
8 Cork Examiner 1846_05_27
9 Morning Post 1846_11_03
10 The Era 1847_02_14
11 The Era 1847_12_26
12 The Era 1849_04_22
13 The Era 1850_03_03
14 The Era 1851_06_01
15 *Recollections of an Equestrian Manager*

Chapter Eleven HARVEY TEASDALE
1 Derbyshire Courier 1849_12_08
2 The Era 1855_12_30
3 *Old Wild's*
4 The Era 1858_01_31
5 The Era 1859_09_04
6 Huddersfield Chronicle 1860_05_05
7 Freeman's Journal 1860_12_13
8 Sheffield Independent 1861_04_06
9 Cardiff Times 1862_01_03
10 Sheffield Daily Telegraph August 1862
11 Sheffield Independent 1862_08_13
12 Sheffield Independent 1865_01_26
13 Sheffield Independent 1904_06_06

Chapter Twelve A WILDERNESS OF MONKEYS
1 Frankfurter Conversationsblatt. No 167, 1838
2 South Bucks Free Press 1862_01_17
3 Bury Times 1862_01_18
4 Norfolk News 1861_12_21
5 Buckingham Advertiser 1863_06_06
6 Oxford Times 1863_07_04

Chapter Thirteen MR PONGO
1 The Era 1878_02_03
2 London & Provincial Entracte 1879_01_11
3 London & Provincial Entr'acte 1878_02_09
4 See inside front cover Illustrated poster from www.circusmusem.nl
5 See inside front cover Illustrated poster from www.circusmusem.nl
6 See inside back cover Illustrated poster from www.circusmusem.nl

Chapter Fourteen MAN MONKEYS IN PANTOMIME & PANTOMIMIC SKETCHES
1 Unknown

NOTES

2   Clerkenwell News 1867_12_27
3   The Era 1868_01_19
4   London and Provincial Entracte 1876_12_30
5   Illustrated Sporting and Dramatic News 1882_10_07, Aldershot Military Gazette 1882_10_07, Lichfield Mercury 1882_10_27
6   The Era 1873_03_16
7   The Era 1877_12_30
8   The Era 1879_12_28
10 The Era 1880_02_01
11 London & Provincial Entracte 1881_01_01
12 London & Provincial Entracte 1881_03_19
13 The Era 1892_04_30
14 The Amusing Journal 1894_09_22
15 Dundee Evening Telegraph 1903_02_21
16 The Era 1876_12_31
17 The Era 1879_04_20
18 Pall Mall Gazette 1886_12_28
19 The Era 1905_09_23
20 The Era 1906_09_22
21 St James's Gazette 1904_10_11

Chapter Fifteen JAMES DUBOIS AND 20TH CENTURY MAN-MONKEYS

1   Brighton Examiner 1889_11_05
2   The Stage 1949_12_15
3   Illustrated posters on www.circusmusem.nl
4   A photograph of the production with Lerner can be found in *Illustrated Sporting and Dramatic News* 1925_09_26

Chapter Sixteen FILMS

1   Entr'acte 1907_01_30
2   Article by Bill Adcock on www.bloodsprayer.com
3   Liverpool Evening Telegraph 1939_01_28
4   Article by Bill Adcock on www.bloodsprayer.com
5   The paragraphs on B-picture man-monkeys is a digest of information from www.bloodsprayer.com, www.hollywoodgorillamen.com, www.horrorpedia.com and www.mentalfloss.com. Information on 'King Kong' mainly from Wikipedia
6   Information on 'Planet of the Apes' mainly from Wikipedia
7   Morning Post 1825_11_09

BIBLIOGRAPHY

There is very little in print about man-monkeys and their work. I have scoured many likely and unlikely places for information but very few books have yielded anything further than the odd sentence of value. Hence here is no mighty list, but just a few that have provided mainly clues to be followed, and background material.

A History of the American Theatre from Its Origins William Dunlap 1832
A History of the New York Stage T Allston Brown 1903
A Major London 'Minor' The Surrey Theatre 1805-1865 W G Knight 1997
Actors by Daylight 1838
Amphitheatres and Circuses T Allston Brown 1861
Blondin: His Life and Performance G L Banks 1862
Cambridge Guide to Theatre 1995
Conquest: The Story of a Theatre Family Frances Fleetwood 1953
Jay's Journal of Anomalies Ricky Jay 2001
Joe Grimaldi: His Life and Theatre Richard Findlater 1978
Memoirs of Charles Dibdin the Younger George Speaight 1956
Memoirs of Grimaldi 'Boz' 1838
Microcosm of London Rudolph Ackerman 1810
Old and New London Edward Walford 1843, 1892
Old Drury Lane Edward Stirling 1881
Old Wild's William Broadley Megson (ed) 1888
Some Account of the English Stage John Genest 1832
Survey of London Vol 35 2008
The Prince of Wales's Theatre London, 1771-1903 R L Lorenzen 2014
The Thrillmakers Jacob Smith 2012
Voyage de La Pérouse Autour du Monde 1797

NEWSPAPER CUTTINGS were the major source of my research, and the British Newspaper Archive online has proved invaluable as little would have been accomplished without it.
PLAYBILLS have also been essential to my task and the most successful sources here have been:
The John Johnson Collection of Printed Ephemera
The Online Theatre Histories Archive
www.circusmuseum.nl   www.europeana.eu   www.leodis.net

ACKNOWLEDGEMENT

My thanks go to the helpful staff at the British Newspaper Archive, the libraries that have given free access to use their illustrations, Don Stacey and Ernest Albrecht for modern circus information, and my wife Brenda for all her invaluable assistance as editor, proof reader and grammarian. Any mistakes are my own.

INDEX

Aberdeen, 41, 113, 213
America & American, 38, 39, 42, 46, 53, 56, 81, 84, 107, 110, 137, 173, 174, 175, 176, 192, 197, 207, 208, 213
Ashton-under-Lyne, 116

Barnes, James, 11, 12, 27, 28, 31, 34, 35, 54, 55, 58, 59, 203
Barrymore, William, 45, 46, 47, 49, 50
Bernaschina (mm) 137
Birmingham, 30, 33, 77, 85, 91, 100, 103, 104, 107, 113, 151, 166, 204, 206
Blackburn, 124
Blanchard, Tom (clown) 31, 33, 34, 82
Blondin, 138, 139, 140, 141, 142, 186
Bologna, Jack (harlequin) 3, 5, 11, 204, 205
Brighton, 11, 103, 131, 160, 212, 213,
Brussels, 171, 177
Bunn, Alfred (manager) 61, 63
Bury St Edmunds, 78

Calvert, Steve (mm) 195
Canterbury, 8, 117
Carlisle, 121, 131, 132
Cheltenham, 41, 49, 104
Chikini (pantomimist) 47, 49
Clown, 8, 9, 10, 11, 12, 14, 25, 28, 30, 31, 34, 35, 36, 37, 39, 41, 44, 50, 56, 57, 58, 59, 61, 63, 66, 67, 96, 122, 123, 125, 126, 127, 128, 129, 165, 166, 204, 206, 208
Columbine, 10, 12, 28, 31, 35, 37, 126
Como Tarro (mm) 153
Conquest, Arthur (mm) 179
Conquest, Fred (mm) 179, 180
Conquest, George (mm) 149, 157, 158, 159, 164, 178
Cooke, T P (actor) 18, 27, 34
Cork, 88, 117, 131,
Corrigan, Ray 'Crash' (mm) 194, 195
Crippen, Dr, 178
Dando, Walter (inventor) 161
Darwin, Charles, 143, 150, 207, 208

Darwin (mm) 185
Davidge, G B (manager) 79, 82, 91
Deptford, 116
Dibdin, Charles, 44, 64, 65, 66, 67, 68, 71, 76, 77, 87, 90, 205, 217
Dover, 117
Driffield, 122
Dublin, 42, 58, 77, 86, 94, 95, 108, 127, 131, 205, 213
Dubois, James (mm) 135, 151, 153, 183, 184, 185
Dubois, Leon (mm) 182, 185

Edinburgh, 41, 47, 113
Egyptian Hall, 109, 110
Ellar, Tom, 11, 27, 28, 31, 35, 55, 57, 59, 60, 113, 121
Elliston, Robert, 4, 18, 32, 39, 45, 46

France, 1, 2, 21, 67, 92, 93, 96, 110, 138, 148, 158, 160, 174

Gainsborough, 88
Gemora, Charles (mm) 192, 194, 195
George Barnwell, 31
Gilbert, Mr (pantomimist) 56
gorilla, 3, 144, 160, 176, 179, 181, 182, 185, 188, 189, 190, 192, 194, 195, 196, 197, 201
Gouffe (mm) 21, 46, 62, 64, 65, 68, 69, 70, 74, 75, 76, 77, 78, 79, 80, 81, 82, 84, 85, 86, 87, 88, 89, 90, 91, 95, 98, 99, 112, 113, 116, 117, 119, 121, 130, 134, 135, 148, 155, 161, 163, 201, 205
Grantham, 77
Gravesend, 52, 88
Grimaldi, Joseph (clown) 3, 4, 7, 9, 10, 11, 12, 15, 21, 25, 26, 28, 31, 33, 34, 35, 38, 42, 47, 49, 50, 55, 57, 58, 61, 62, 63, 66, 79, 157, 165, 204, 207, 210, 214,
Grimaldi, J S (clown) 11, 25, 27, 206
Grimsby, 122
Gulliver's Travels, 28
Gutis, The (mm) 188, 189

Halifax, 123, 125, 131

INDEX

Harlequin, 5, 10, 11, 12, 28, 30, 31, 37, 49, 50, 55, 56, 57, 60, 61, 63, 67, 113, 123, 133, 159, 167, 204, 205, 207, 208

Harlequinade, 11, 27, 36, 50, 58, 61, 92, 157, 165, 169, 171, 177, 206, 210

Harris, Sir Augustus, 157, 168, 169, 174, 177

Haydon, Benjamin Robert 109

Hervio Nano (see Leach, Harvey) 98, 99, 100, 104, 105, 106, 108, 109, 110

Hewett, Henry (landlord) 127

Hone, Mr (magistrate) 78, 80

Hornshaw, John (see Gouffe) 67, 68, 81, 85, 89, 90, 91

Howell, Mr (harlequin) 4, 30, 35, 36, 49, 50, 56, 61, 63

Huddersfield, 123, 125, 131, 132, 214

Hull, 86, 98, 124

Inverness, 86

Jocko (character) 14, 15, 17, 18, 20, 21, 22, 23, 26, 28, 30, 33, 65, 67, 68, 76, 78, 79, 82, 84, 85, 86, 87, 88, 93, 95, 96, 98, 113, 116, 118, 121, 130, 139, 143, 150, 151, 168, 170, 172, 175, 177, 189

Johnson, Fred (mm) 145

Kean, Edmund (actor) 5, 29, 79, 81, 86, 88, 95

Kemble, Charles (manager) 4, 18, 206, 207

King Kong, (character) 3, 186, 196, 197, 198, 199, 200

King's Lynn, 84

Kirby, John (clown) 66

Klischnigg, Edward (mm) 25, 49, 64, 92, 93, 94, 95, 96, 97, 99, 106, 137

Kotaky (mm) 145, 148, 149, 150, 151, 183, 201

Lauri, Edward (clown) 129,

Lauri, Charles (clown) 165,

Lauri, Charles Jr (mm) 166, 167, 168, 169, 170, 171, 172, 173, 174, 175, 176, 177, 178, 179, 201

Lauro, Ching Lau (mm) 30, 131, 133

Leach, Harvey (see Hervio Nano) 64, 96, 98, 103, 104, 105, 106, 107, 108, 109, 110, 111

Leeds, 5, 88, 101, 103, 113, 126, 127, 129, 131, 132, 135, 151, 180, 214,

Leicester, 77, 131, 135

Leno, Dan (mm) 150, 169

Lerner, Jacques (mm) 190

Littlehampton, 116

Liverpool, 4, 6, 42, 84, 86, 118, 122, 123, 124, 127, 131, 132, 214

London, 1, 4, 5, 15, 23, 25, 37, 38, 39, 46, 52, 55, 58, 59, 60, 64, 65, 66, 67, 68, 69, 75, 79, 81, 82, 85, 87, 88, 89, 92, 95, 96, 99, 107, 109, 110, 116, 120, 122, 131, 132, 138, 144, 145, 156, 157, 158, 159, 161, 168, 169, 170, 171, 190, 192, 206, 207, 208, 209, 210, 211, 212, 213, 214, 215, 216

Mamok the Monkey, (character) 95

Manchester, 41, 58, 103, 113, 121, 125, 127, 131, 173, 204, 213, 214

Man-Monkey Plays:

Albo, the Monkey from Malicolo, 96

Balaoo the Man-Monkey, (film) 192

Child of the Wreck, The 138

Crom-a-boo, 25

For Ever, 163, 164, 179, 181, 190

Gnome Fly, The, 85, 96, 99, 100, 101, 105, 106, 160

Hexen am Rhein, 60

Jack Robinson and his Monkey, 32, 33, 41, 42, 46, 81, 88, 118, 121

Jocko, or the Monkey of Brazil, 94

Jocko, or The Ourang Outang of Brazil, 76

Jocko, the Brazilian Monkey, 11, 23

Jungle Land Fantasy, 188

La Perouse, 1, 2, 3, 4, 5, 6, 10, 11, 15, 20, 22, 30, 33, 42, 44, 45, 49, 54, 62, 79, 95, 105, 108, 127, 130, 135, 143, 189, 191

Life in the Indies, 125

Monkey of Arragon, The, 79

Monkey That Has Seen the World, 37

Monkeymania, 155

INDEX

Peter Wilkins, 28, 30, 31, 33, 35, 39, 42, 43, 118, 124, 158, 160
Philip Quarl, 6, 44, 45, 53, 76, 118
Pitcairn's Island, 81, 84
Pulverino Pongo, 122
Scenes at the Zoo, 155
Baboon of Paraguay, The, 79
Cabin Boy and His Monkey, The, 43
Dumb Savoyard and his Monkey, The, 37, 46, 47, 48, 49, 52, 60, 63, 116, 118, 121, 130
Freak's Revenge, The, 181, 185, 186, 197
Gorilla, The, 190,
Gorilla, The, (film)192
Great London Mystery, The, (film) 192
Island Ape, The, 68, 69, 74, 76, 77, 79, 81, 112, 155
King of the Hills, The, 95
Knight and his Page, The 76
Mandrill, The, 80
Mayor and the Monkey, The, 100
Monkey and the Bridegroom, The, 95, 96
Monkey and the Gypsy, The, 96
Monkey Lover, The, 52
Monkey Servant, The, 95
Monkey Talks, The, 190, 192
Musical Monkey, The, 53
Nondescript of the East, The, 88
Planet of the Apes, The, (film) 3, 4, 195, 199, 200
Runaway Brazilian Ape, The, 86
Sailor and the Monkey, The, 155
Sioux, The, 170, 172, 174, 179
Spider & the Fly, The,158
Troubles in Monkeyland, 154
Two Monkeys, The, 84
Wanderow of Malabar, The, 80
Web of Fate, The, 85
Wild Man, The, 9, 29
Wild Man of Hütteldorf, The, 97

Marmazette (character) 46, 52, 63, 116
Martinetti, Paul (mm) 82, 149, 168, 174, 175, 176, 177, 178

Martini, Frederick (mm) 64, 95, 113, 115, 116, 117, 118, 119, 121
Marzetti (mm) 43
Matthews, Tom (clown) 61
Mazurier, Charles-François (mm) 12, 14, 15, 17, 18, 19, 20, 21, 22, 23, 24, 25, 26, 27, 30, 31, 32, 33, 34, 37, 39, 41, 43, 44, 45, 46, 49, 51, 52, 54, 57, 61, 62, 63, 64, 65, 75, 76, 77, 79, 92, 93, 95, 98, 99, 116, 131, 148, 150, 168, 175, 190, 201
Menage, Master (mm) 3, 62
Moncrieff, William Thomas, 37
Mongo (character) 175, 176
Martine, Mons (mm) 113
Morelli, Master (mm) 4, 5, 6, 9
Mortini (mm) 112, 113
Moss, Dick (mm) 153
Motion-capture, 198
Monroe, Mr (manager) 103, 104
Mushapug (character) 33, 34, 35, 41, 42, 46, 49, 81, 113, 118, 119, 124
Natal (mm) 187, 189
Nathal (mm) 187
New York, 37, 38, 39, 42, 43, 50, 81, 96, 98, 106, 108, 110, 161, 165, 173, 190, 208, 213
Nondescript (character) 29, 42, 88, 118, 158
Norbu (mm) 189

Orang-utan, 20, 66, 79, 130, 143, 144

Pantaloon, 6, 10, 11, 12, 28, 34, 35, 37, 42, 54, 55, 61, 63, 67, 123, 204, 208

Pantomimes:
Astrologer, The 8
Bang Up, or Harlequin Prime, 9
Daughter of the Danube, The, 53, 57, 61
Davy Jones, 49
Demon Dwarf, The, 103
Devil on Two Sticks, The, 53, 57, 160
Don Juan, 30, 34, 123, 127
Flip Flap Footman, The, 59
Forty Thieves, 167
Grim Goblin, 161
Harlequin & Golden Eyes, 25

INDEX

Harlequin and Cock Robin, 35
Harlequin and Fortunato, 11
Harlequin and Little Red Riding Hood, 33
Harlequin and Mother Malkin, 42
Harlequin and Mother Shipton, 28
Harlequin and Number Nip of the Giant Mountain, 31
Harlequin and Peeping Tom, 58
Harlequin and the Enchanted Fish, 59
Harlequin and the Magic Rose, 25
Harlequin in the Flower World, 96
Harlequin Magic Lantern, 53
Harlequin Ogre, 125
Harlequin Traveller: or the World Upside Down, 50
King Arthur and the Knights of the Round Table, 51
Le Diable de l'Eglise, 165
Little Hunchback, The, 57
Mother Goose, 10, 27, 28, 30, 38, 57, 156, 181, 204
Nix the Demon Dwarf, 160
Old Mother Hubbard and her Dog, 50
Robinson Crusoe, 20, 28, 41, 42, 44, 61, 68, 159, 168, 171, 173
Shipwreck of Policinello, 17, 23
Sleeping Beauty in the Wood, 126
Spirit of the Air, The, 56
Sprite of the Snow-Drift, The, 61
Whittington and His Cat, 52

Paris, 4, 14, 17, 18, 21, 23, 24, 27, 43, 46, 49, 52, 93, 110, 165, 167, 168, 170, 171, 190, 205
Parsloe, Mr, 14, 32
Parsloe, C T (mm) 11, 26, 43, 82
Parsloe, E J, (mm) 5, 9, 11, 12, 25, 26, 27, 29, 32, 34, 35, 36, 37, 38, 39, 41, 43, 44, 46, 49, 51, 63, 64, 69, 81, 82, 85, 113, 118, 123, 124, 133, 158, 186, 212
Parsloe, James, (prompter) 12, 36, 39, 54, 60, 176
Parsloe, Masters, 8, 9
Patterson, William (mm) 132, 136
Paulo (clown) 27, 35
Payne, Harry (clown) 166, 169
Petworth, 113, 115

Plimmeri (mm) 95, 131, 135
Pongo (character) 142, 144, 145, 148, 149, 150, 151, 152, 153, 154, 155, 166, 167, 183, 184
Pongo Redivivus (mm) 145, 147, 148, 149
Portsmouth, 118, 132
Price, Stephen (manager) 46, 81
Punch (character) 15, 17, 19, 30, 37, 52, 53, 54, 92

Ravel Family, 43, 82, 138, 174
Ravel, Gabriel (mm) 43, 82
Rich, John (manager) 28
Ridgway, Tom (clown) 12, 67, 68, 208
Rook, Constable, 106, 107
Roth, Fritz (mm) 185
Royal Tycoon Troupe (mm) 152, 183

Sapajou (character) 18, 79, 95, 96
Serkis, Andy (actor) 198, 200, 201
Sheffield, 41, 84, 105, 108, 120, 121, 122, 123, 127, 128, 129, 132, 168
Shentini (mm) 121, 131, 134, 135, 136
Sherborne, 112, 113
Simon, M (mm) 66
Simpson, Mr (stage manager) 103, 104, 105, 106, 107
Southby, Mr (clown) 36
Spanish Pongo (mm) 110, 151, 152, 153
St Helen's, 127, 128
Sterling, Pedro (mm) 148, 150
Stirling, Edward (actor) 67

Tarzan, (film character) 186, 193, 194
Taunton, 85, 210, 214
Teasdale, Harvey (mm) 120, 121, 122, 123, 124, 125, 126, 127, 128, 129, 151
Tenterden, 117

Theatres, Music Halls etc (London):
Adelphi, 15, 58, 59, 60, 61, 99, 100, 103, 104, 118, 122, 208
Alexander Palace, 149
Alhambra, 169, 170
Aquatic (Sadler's Wells), 8, 9, 205

INDEX

Astley's, 12, 15, 25, 53, 65, 108, 205, 211
Borough, 171
Bowery Theatre (USA) 37, 38, 81, 96, 106, 108, 109
Britannia, 122
Coburg, 11, 12, 44, 51, 65, 79, 81, 92, 94, 211
Covent Garden, 2, 3, 4, 5, 7, 8, 9, 11, 12, 15, 18, 19, 21, 22, 23, 25, 26, 28, 30, 31, 33, 34, 35, 36, 37, 39, 41, 42, 45, 50, 54, 59, 62, 75, 81, 93, 124, 166, 167, 168, 175, 204, 205, 206, 208, 210
Crystal Palace, 138, 145, 161, 171
Drury Lane, 4, 5, 7, 15, 18, 23, 27, 30, 32, 34, 35, 36, 39, 45, 46, 47, 48, 49, 50, 51, 52, 53, 54, 56, 58, 59, 61, 62, 65, 78, 81, 92, 93, 112, 116, 133, 156, 165, 166, 167, 168, 169, 170, 171, 174, 177, 179, 204, 206, 207, 208, 210
English Opera House, 54
Garrick, 85, 171
Grecian, 158, 159, 161, 163, 167
Haymarket, 3, 210
Lyceum, 171
New City, 37, 39
Oxford, 63, 142, 145, 190
Pavilion, 34, 49, 80, 88, 97, 105, 119, 133
Queen's, 51, 103, 118
Royal Albert Saloon, 116
Royal Olympic, 108
Sadler's Wells, 7, 8, 9, 15, 25, 34, 50, 52, 60, 66, 81, 86, 107, 204, 205, 206, 210
Surrey, 12, 15, 22, 25, 32, 33, 34, 37, 39, 41, 46, 49, 61, 65, 66, 67, 69, 75, 76, 77, 79, 82, 85, 91, 94, 95, 129, 163, 164, 180, 181, 182, 204, 205, 206, 207, 211, 217
Vauxhall Gardens, 30, 133, 166
Victoria, 86, 94, 105, 211
Westminster Aquarium, 144

The Era, (newspaper) 126, 127, 128, 130, 132, 148, 151, 152, 153, 174, 176, 177, 184, 214, 215
Thompson, C Pelham (author) 46, 49
Tom Thumb, General, 109
Tunbridge Wells, 108

Ulverston, 87
USA, 66, 81, 82, 84, 106, 120, 138, 162, 165, 174, 189, 190, 194, 196, 204, 211

Valerio, Carlos (wire walker) 141, 142
Van Amburgh, (lion trainer) 56
Van Horn, Emil (mm) 195
Victoria, Queen, 165, 208
Vienna, 94, 96, 97, 149

Wallett, William (clown) 78
Warwick, 104, 106, 131
Wieland, George (mm) 15, 44, 45, 46, 47, 48, 49, 50, 51, 52, 53, 54, 55, 56, 57, 58, 59, 60, 61, 62, 63, 64, 69, 85, 93, 95, 99, 158, 201
Wild, Sam (manager) 124, 135, 215,
Williams, Mr (victim) 105

Yates, Frederick (manager) 60, 99, 100, 103
York, 5, 37, 81, 103, 124, 126, 128, 190, 206
Young, Selena (aerialist) 142

Zanfretta, Enrico (pantomimist) 170
Zanfretta, Mdlle (dancer) 168, 169, 171

NB: (mm) signifies a Man-Monkey,

Theatrical Fund, 34, 54, 57, 60, 63

ILLUSTRATIONS

Intro *Memoirs of Grimaldi 1838*
Page 1 *Voyage de La Pérouse Autour du Monde 1797*
Pages 3 & 8 *Microcosm of London 1810*
Pages 9, 29, 101, & 107 Harvard Theatre Collection, Houghton Library, Harvard University
Page 10 19th century scrap figures
Pages 14, 32, 44 & 62 *Old and New London 1843 & 1878*
Page 16 Rijksmuseum, Netherlands
Pages 17, 19, 24, 40, 55, 59, 66, 81, 76, & 95 New York Public Library
Page 20 Corson Collection, University of Edinburgh
Pages 54, 60, 158, 175, 182, 202, & 211 ©V & A Museum
Page 75 Print 1828
Pages 80, 154, 156 National Library of France
Page 82 Folger Shakespeare Library
Page 83 State Library of New South Wales
Page 92 Austrian Biographical Encyclopedia
Pages 94 & 96 Stadtgeschichtliches Museum Leipzig
Pages 102, 114 by kind permission of Leeds Library and Information Services - www.leodis.net. All rights reserved.
Page 136 Mediatheque de Chaumont
Page 139 *Blondin: His Life and Performances 1862*
Pages 140, 144, 162, 164, & 166, Newspaper Images ©The British Library Board. All rights reserved. With thanks to The British Newspaper Archive
Page 169 Van Bosch, Paris c.1894
Page 172 *Strand Magazine 3 October 1894*
Page 180 Publicity Postcard
Pages 142, 156, 184, 185, 186, 187, 188 www.circusmuseum.nl
Pages 188 & 189 Private collection, by kind permission of Don Stacey
Page 193 Trailer screenshot (MGM)
Page 200 & 201 Ares Rio/www.flickr.com
Page 201 www.mounirzok.com

Front cover based on an illustration from New York Public Library.

What's the Play and Where's the Stage?
A Theatrical Family of the Regency Era

Alan Stockwell

420 pages   Hardback
ISBN 978-0-9565013-6-3

The lives of eminent London actors of the Regency period – Kean, Mrs Siddons, Kemble, Cooke, Macready, Grimaldi *et al* are more than amply recorded. This book ploughs a more unusual, rarer, furrow. It reveals the theatrical lives of a family of provincial players who tramped the highways and byways bringing the latest London hits and classic plays to unsophisticated audiences in tiny country theatres and large manufacturing towns. The author offers not a specialist tome for theatre historians but a beguiling story of a family of three thespian siblings, their spouses and their children. This is a Regency world far removed from the novels of Jane Austen, the marked difference being that for the Jonas and Penley Company of Comedians this was real life.

'. . . hugely entertaining . . .' (*Jane Austen's Regency World* magazine)

'. . . a detailed 'eye-opening' story of the young women in the family . .'
(*The Irvingite* Newsletter of the Irving Society)

'. . . the content is entertaining and the writing style engaging . . . he is able to bring his subject alive and establish a clear narrative.'
(*Theatre Notebook* Journal of the Society for Theatre Research)

For full reviews see www.vesperhawk.com

www.ingramcontent.com/pod-product-compliance
Lightning Source LLC
Chambersburg PA
CBHW060511100426
42743CB00009B/1282